D0787446

SHADOWBOXING

SHADOWBOXING

Representations of
Black Feminist Politics

JOY JAMES

WITHDRAWN FROM COLLECTION V2

St. Martin's Press
New York

SHADOWBOXING: REPRESENTATIONS OF BLACK FEMINIST POLITICS
Copyright © Joy James, 1999. All rights reserved. Printed in the United
States of America. No part of this book may be used or reproduced in any
manner whatsoever without written permission except in the case of brief
quotations embodied in critical articles or reviews. For information, address
St. Martin's Press, 175 Fifth Avenue, New York, N.Y. 10010.

ISBN 0-312-22070-7

Library of Congress Cataloging-in-Publication Data

James, Joy
    Shadowboxing : representations of black feminist politics / by Joy
James.
        p. cm.
    Includes bibliographical references and index.
    ISBN 0-312-22070-7 (cloth)
    1. Afro-American women—Political activity. 2. Radicalism—United
States. 3. Feminism—United States. 4. Stereotype (Psychology)-
-United States. 5. Racism—United States. 6. United States—Race
relations. I. Title.
E185.86.J35 1999
305.48'896073—dc21   99-17389
                                                            CIP

Design by Acme Art, Inc.

First edition: September, 1999
10 9 8 7 6 5 4 3 2 1

DEDICATION

Sending her children to chapel and Sunday School on army posts and air force bases, my mother raised me in the state orthodoxy. Following tradition, I dutifully pursued instruction first in Catholic universities, then in seminary, only to find a spiritual home on the fringes of the South Bronx, in the religious house of Madrina. Aware of the rivalries between canonical and heretical views, I eventually sheltered in the camp of the latter, despite my early upbringing. Reminding that suppressed knowledge inevitably resurfaces, radicalism reconnected me with the spiritual and political heresies that make American life meaningful and its betrayals bearable.

Forewarned by the Gospel of Thomas: "If you bring forth what is within you, what is within you will save you. If you do not bring forth what is within you, what is within you will destroy you."[1] Prodded by 1 Corinthians 13: "If I speak in the tongues of [wo]men and of angels but have not love, I am a noisy gong or a clanging cymbal." Pressed by 1 Corinthians 14: "And if the bugle gives an indistinct sound, who will get ready for battle?" Challenged by dual conflicting realities. Inspired by committed youths and the spirit of struggle continuously reborn. This work is dedicated to the mothers, Minnie James, Mattie Bailey, and Beatrice Adderley; the truth-telling kin; my partner, WJM; and, to the memory of Ingrid Washinawatok (1957-1999), whose courage and loving spirit outlive the executioners' act and corporate-state destruction of indigenous lands and peoples.

MAY 17 2000

CONTENTS

ACKNOWLEDGMENTS

I began this work at the suggestion of Lewis Gordon. AfraShe Asungi, T. Denean Sharpley-Whiting, K. Kim Holder, Nell Painter, Michiko Hase, Dylan Rodriguez, Robin D. G. Kelly, Emily Blumenfeld, Julia Sudbury, as well as St. Martin's editor Maura Burnett and its anonymous reader all provided important editorial reviews.

Special thanks to critic-supporters and kin Beatrice Adderley, AfraShe Asungi, Tracey Sharpley-Whiting, Kim Holder, and Elizabeth Hadley for their lengthy midday and late-night conversations, which sustained my efforts to articulate questions and our collective insights about politics, race, gender, community, and revolutionary desire. Each in unique ways strengthened this manuscript.

In the house of academia, research assistants Heather Larrabee, Leviticus Ra-Za'mien, and Sabrina Hodges contributed essential technical support for this book.

Shadowboxing is one of many works refracting "official" or state politics. Although its author is represented as an individual writer, its insights come from many political and cultural workers. To these intellectual and spiritual warriors, my thanks.

Unlock the silence and let us speak to the world.
—Ingrid Washinawatok

People of color have always theorized . . . our theorizing (and I intentionally use the verb rather than the noun) is often in narrative forms, in the stories we create . . . [in] dynamic rather than fixed ideas. . . . How else have we managed to survive with such spiritedness the assault on our bodies, social institutions, countries, our very humanity? And women, at least the women I grew up around, continuously speculated about the nature of life through pithy language that unmasked the power relations of their world.
—Barbara Christian

Get used to being outrageous.
—The Urban Bush Women

PREFACE

Beyond conventional politics, conditioned under marginality and censure, black feminist power emerges to display a radical singularity, one that has yet to be fully theorized. This political theorizing of radical black feminism begins in reflection with the "Introduction: Warrior Tropes," chapter 1, which provides an autobiographical snapshot of a youth grappling with antiracist feminism evolving amidst black fighters.

Emphasizing revolutionary tendencies in women's resistance politics entails looking at both historical legacies and contemporary practices. Chapter 2, "Forging Community: From Segregation to Transcendence," examines new forms of racial and class stratification resulting from opposition to affirmative action and advocacy for a racialized incarceration. Resurgent neoconservatism hostile to "racial preferences" for education and employment acquiesces to racial bias in imprisonment and state execution. Emergent segregated communities stemming from neoconservatism coexist with political communities shaped by antiracist and feminist and African sensibilities. Collective identity that crosses spatial and temporal borders to establish high standards for political accountability creates the context for transcendent community. A review of African worldviews and African American political ideologies highlights intergenerational responsibilities that counter the new segregation and also provide a context for studying the liberation limbos of both ancestral and contemporary black female radicals. (Such worldviews and politics are not particular to African Americans given that the diaspora has "Africanized" many national cultures and, as some scholars argue, the Genome Project marks all people as of African descent.[1])

The search for antiracist community can be measured by the heroic efforts of activist or ancestral African American women. Most Americans are unfamiliar with the history of militant black female fighters, yet their stories are readily available. Memoirs such as *Crusade for Justice: The Autobiography of Ida B. Wells; Angela Davis: An Autobiography;* and *Assata: An Autobiography* touch a raw nerve among those who become politically stressed or polarized when facing radical and revolutionary social justice battles.[2] (Paradoxically, political autobiographies expand an intellectual base for progressive struggles while simultaneously providing a comfort zone that validates images of revolutionaries marketed as commodities through publications for consumers.) Reading such autobiographies reveals rebellions that democratized American politics. Tens of thousands were and are inspired by Ida B. Wells's crusade against lynching, Ella Baker's organizing for civil rights, Angela Davis's support for prisoners (beginning with the Soledad Brothers in the late 1960s), and Assata Shakur's revolutionary battles in the black liberation movement (a movement eventually destroyed by the Federal Bureau of Investigation [FBI]'s illegal counterrevolutionary program, COINTEL-PRO). The works of the four women highlighted here—Wells, Baker, Davis, and Shakur—are not uniformly "radical" or "revolutionary"; nor are they without their contradictions. Nevertheless, seeking liberation, each pushed beyond conventional politics. Agitating for economic and social justice, each offered models for shadowboxing as black female resistance to political and social or state dominance.

In twentieth-century movements, African Americans fought in marginal sites and forward movements—limbos—to build radical communities that challenged political and social exclusion. "Protofeminists and Liberation Limbos," chapter 3, focuses on antilynching crusader Ida B. Wells at the turn of the century and civil rights activist Ella Baker during the depression decades. It discusses both the gray areas of indeterminate place and the limber flexibility surrounding black women's organizing. Chapter 3 also observes how black women's legacies can be appropriated; for instance, in the 1987 Tawana Brawley case African American spokesmen accused white state officials of abducting and raping Brawley, using "symbolic rage," the historical victimization of black females, and the memory of antilynching crusades to imitate the prosecutorial performances of white lynch mobs (allegedly protecting the virtue of "their" females).[3]

Following the unique limbos, or political maneuvers, executed by Wells and Baker, black women continuously organized and shaped liberation leadership, leaving significant, although scarcely noted in conventional politics, imprints on the movements of the 1960s and 1970s.

Chapter 4, "Radicalizing Feminisms from 'The Movement' Era," reviews the emergence and conflicts of feminism in the 1960s and 1970s. It offers working definitions of "radicalism" and "revolutionary" politics for contemporary struggles. Building on these definitions, "Revolutionary Icons and 'Neoslave Narratives,'" chapter 5, examines several leaders in those movements, focusing on the radical Angela Davis, now public intellectual-academic, and the revolutionary Assata Shakur, currently in political exile in Cuba. In the 1970s, targeted for political activities but imprisoned on criminal charges, each woman mirrored archetypes shaped by Wells and Baker. At a time of mass, militant unrest, through bold confrontations with state authority, Davis and Shakur forged prototypes for late-twentieth-century black female radicalism. Rising public recognition for their contributions has led to a celebrity status—one that can transform the radical iconoclast into a deradicalized icon. (The destruction or co-optation of radical movements was furthered by commodification and performative politics that simplistically reduced the revolutionary Malcolm X to an "X" insignia on apparel; the radicalism of the women's movement to bra-burning; and liberation politics to the slogans of stage personas.) Since the 1970s, conservatism increasingly mainstreamed countermovements that challenged or dismantled feminist and antiracist gains—ones modified and institutionalized by liberals—generated from the social upheavals engineered by militants. The rise of a commodified black female radicalism in popular iconography coexists with new forms of racial and economic containment. As iconography deflects from contemporary repression and radical opposition, it promotes the disappearance of black female agency in political struggles.

Depoliticizing representations promote a restricted, dysfunctional democracy with cultural images that obscure black women's contributions to democratic politics. Where commercial and stereotypical portrayals of black females center not on political agency but on fetish and animalized sexual imagery, blacks, females, and politics become effaced or distorted. "Depoliticizing Representations: Sexual-Racial Stereo-types," chapter 6, details racial and sexual caricatures corseting the black female body. These stereotypes have a strong historical legacy. Intellec-tuals and activists have both satirized and critiqued denigrating stereo-types; yet "progressive" political cinema promotes black female visibility to recycle vilifying images. For instance, American filmmaker Warren Beatty's *Bulworth* circulates images of black females as tragic mulattas, tricksters, and femmes fatales. Heralded for its liberal race politics, this film's commercial attraction partly relied on the image of the white antihero protagonist aided by the eroticized black femme fatale. Its commercial and liberal appeal is fixed on the black female body.

Sexual-racial stereotypes circulating from a dominant culture clash with representations disseminated by black male feminists. Beyond the limiting roles of patriarchal protectors or oppressors, black males func-tion as both racial and gender allies to black females. Male theorists are playing increasingly promising roles in black feminisms (for instance, "Depoliticizing Representations" cites the literary contributions of gay African Americans to black male feminism or profeminism). In some of their analyses, however, these contributions suggest new forms of erasure for black female radicalism. Chapter 7, "Fostering Alliances: Black Male Profeminisms," examines the engagements of influential black and Latino academic writers with feminist theory. Recognizing the dominant role that these writers have in representing male antiracist feminisms, it focuses on Michael Awkward, Lewis Gordon, Devon Carbado, and Richard Delgado to examine male literary interventions in and inven-tions of feminisms. As is the case for black feminisms, there are a multiplicity of black male profeminisms. Literature significantly and disproportionately shapes representations for black feminisms and pro-feminisms; for instance, writings by nonactivists interpreting the 1995 Million Man March largely overshadowed the profeminist analyses of African American male *activists* who were critical of the event's patriar-chal politics.[4] Although better known than their activist counterparts, the works of male feminist writers, particularly black writers, have received insufficient critical attention. This literature, which forms an emergent ("black") profeminist canon while influencing male profemi-nist activists, at times reveals contradictory tendencies. On one hand, it refutes the stereotype of black males as more sexist or antifeminist than white males; on the other hand, it can introduce images of black male agency that deflect from black radical women, as progressive men repoliticize and frame feminism to include male agency.

Finally, "Conclusion: Black Shadow Boxers," chapter 8, draws on the history of black pugilists in a so-called white culture to illustrate the symbiotic relationship between African American women and men "boxing" as Others in American society. Varied depictions or erasures of black women shape and frame feminism. The Conclusion reviews mainstream portraits depicting feminism as bourgeois and white; it also examines contemporary antiracist and feminist castigations that frame black feminisms for their alleged neglect of—in effect, independence from—some of the interests of either black males or white females.

Warrior Tropes

(For Jesse)

Our revenge will be the laughter of our children.
—Bobby Sands

It perhaps takes less heart to pick up the gun than to face the task of creating a new identity, a self perhaps an androgynous self, via commitment to the struggle.

—Toni Cade Bambara

Antiracist feminisms emerge from and are shaped by the conflicts and compassion guiding lifelong battles. Political ideologies frame these battles that separate the moderate from the militant. Conventional discussions of class or gender or race rarely reflect the struggles of radicalized racialized females. Although antiracist discourse at times seems to express more strongly the felt impact of the oppression of black females, it often fails to reflect their realities. On any given day, mirror reflections become shadows, as images fluctuate between those of soldiers routinized by obeying orders and warriors scarred and skilled from battle.

Both soldiery and shadow-warriors shape the family and social histories that brought me to a radical black feminism, one keenly aware of the conflicts between soldiers as state employees and warriors as rebel liberators. This awareness recognizes that hired fighters or soldiers routinely fall from the grace of self-directed dissidents; yet they manage to grasp at a benediction that eludes most revolutionaries—respite from interminable, soul-penetrating political battles—while sharing the internal and intergenerational turmoil of freedom-seeking rebels.

In the book's photograph, my mother, younger sister, and I stand in and throw Kurosawa-like shadows that project traces of our other selves and relations, shaped in love and conflict. We collectively cast the self-assurance, timidity, and wariness of warriors-in-training. I display my mother's "mop-up" after my older brother "did" my hair with cutting shears. Part of her dissatisfaction stemmed from her frustration that I consistently refracted rather than reflected Euro-American iconography for beauty, departing even from the standards for "colored beauty" embodied in the "mulatta." Dark-skinned, I held the dubious distinction of being the first preschool (perhaps the only) female with an Afro on our southern military post during the early 1960s. The photograph also shows that my face reflects a skeptical stance toward my father, the visitor-parent taking the picture. Later that distance and distrust would be extended to his employer.

Today what unsettles me most about the picture is *where* it was likely taken, not who took it. During the early 1960s, my father was stationed at Fort Benning, the military post in Georgia where the Bay of Pigs was planned. There I first encountered dogwood and learned to associate its showy flower clusters with the preference for cool forest shade behind our houses. Decades later I would learn to associate Fort Benning with the School of the Americas (SOA), known among human rights advocates as the "School of the Assassins."[1]

This fifty-year-old training site was relocated from Panama to Fort Benning and expanded in the 1980s under the Reagan administration. SOA teaches counterinsurgency and "population pacification" techniques to torturers and executioners compliant with U.S. foreign policy. SOA, as part of U.S. foreign policy, has predictably increased "low intensity" conflict in Guatemala, Nicaragua, El Salvador, and Haiti and supported recent military-paramilitary death squad activities against indigenous peoples in Chiapas, Mexico. In my mind, the photo from my childhood couples the image that extends from the collective body of my mother, sister, and self with my adult awareness of the ignominy of soldiers, states, and shadow governments.[2]

A child-detective, growing up among shadow boxers, I would myself shadow the cocktail parties my parents threw for fellow black officers and military wives. Getting up repeatedly for water during late nights, I took mental notes on highballs, honey-colored Scotch, silk and satin cocktail dresses, cigarette and cigar smoke, blues and jazz, ice and laughter. I don't remember the exact words of the fragments of adult conversations that I heard; but I do recall the routinized sounds of mockery for their employer, notes that echo for me as an employee of state universities.

In cocktail conversations, voices spoke of tours of duty, racial indignities, institutionalized racism, and the policing of "nonwhite" Korea, Dominican Republic, and Vietnam. Having aligned themselves with a desegregated subculture that would rank as America's first and foremost integrated sector, my parents' narratives never seemed to discuss their own domestic alienation from the civil rights movement that dogged their purchased patriotism in the 1960s. I recall no mention of the use of the 101st Airborne (of which my father was once a member) in the 1967 occupation of Detroit to quell the urban rebellion. Nor of the United States being haunted by political memories of wars that revealed its unprincipled and destructive policies. Nor the mutiny of black troops' alleged grenade "fragging" of racist white officers that led my father to "Nam," where Vietnamese referred to Americans as "long shadows" and U.S. commandos in the war, with no rules of engagement, worked as assassins.[3]

With so much unspoken, my parents and their friends seemed to be battling in their silence and even in their laughter. They ridiculed their dependency—despite college, my father could find work only as a cook, so like other formally educated blacks he reenlisted—and performed hazardous duties with a false obsequiousness. Their conversations jeered at jobs they paid heavily for in order to acquire the mercurial respect of ritualistic deference and the material solidity of comprehensive medical care, pseudo private schools, and subsidized housing. They masked the convergence of shame (from an inability to rebel when refused service in a segregated South) and sacrifice (in active duty). At the same time, their sense of pride in belonging with the victor seemed constantly disturbed by their interminable battles to become comfortable within a degraded democracy.

I never recalled my parents (or their friends) discussing violence, either foreign or "domestic" (in the nation and the home). Perhaps, having seen so much terror themselves—my father in combat, my mother in a childhood tour of duty in the 1930s and 1940s in rural Mississippi, both parents in daily living "black" in white America—they wanted their silence to shield their children, and themselves, from their own memories.

It was a false protection largely because fighting and violence are too familiar in American culture and in my own family story. Born in Frankfurt, Germany, I was soon returned to the United States to be raised and schooled on army posts in the North- and Southeast. While the United States waged a foreign military and a domestic police campaign to destroy revolutionary movements, I remained pre- or apolitical, at least until the family "settled" in San Antonio, the home of my patriarch and photographer.

In Texas, I became desensitized toward America's comfort with weapons and sensitized to political struggle. Apolitically participating in mainstream America's preadolescent fascination with weapons while in middle school,[4] I located my unimaginative parents' handguns about the same time that twenty-year-old Black Panther leader and decorated Vietnam veteran Geronimo ji Jaga (Elmer Pratt)—after being forced underground by the FBI's illegal and deadly counterintelligence pro- gram—established a military camp for black revolutionaries in Texas.[5] Four years earlier, in 1966, national discomfort with displays of weaponry predictably flared with the rising specter of the Black Panther Party for Self-Defense. Predictably, a home where no one discussed the civil rights or black liberation movements offered no words or language to evaluate militant, non-nonviolent fighters who advocated armed self-defense against state repression. For the next decade, though, I would be too young and politically isolated for the heated debates about armed struggle in antiracist or revolutionary battles to register in my consciousness.

Firing rifles first in high school Junior Reserve Officer Training Corps (JROTC), I later repeated the drill in a Catholic university. These experiences granted me a skeptical view of women warriors employed by the state, somewhat akin to the cynicism I had inherited from my parents concerning black fighters. This perspective distanced me from liberal feminist advocacy for the largely white body of young female cadets, destined for the officer corps who were attempting to integrate elite military schools. It also increased my empathy with the majority of enlisted women: young, working-class black and brown females who— seeking the economic resources that my parents had provided me— survived basic training and passed weapons instruction only to fail to attain middle-class status and security.

The long process of politicization began at home. Being raised by skeptical African American women discouraged me from a career as a state soldier or hired fighter. My mother and aunt, "the twins," were apolitical political exiles from rural Mississippi who reconstructed themselves while employed as suburban officers' wives. I studied as they—all the while demanding respect—inadvertently satirized the pretensions that they acquired. In their household, I read E. Franklin Frazier's *The Black Bourgeoisie*.[6] At thirteen, as an alienated suburbanite, I began asking questions about the conflicting sentiments and antiradical or antirevolutionary tendencies of the black middle class.

At fifteen, as a subscriber to *Ms.* magazine—considered "radical" reading then in Texas—I had encountered the works of prominent white feminists Kate Millet, Erica Jong, and Betty Friedan. I began leaving the books of bourgeois white feminists in the home of Sue, the affluent white woman whose children I baby-sat. Sue's boredom, depression, and leisure—her "help" included a Chicana maid and first myself and later my younger sister to watch her three young sons— suggested that the literature might be of interest, if not useful. The books went untouched. Weeks later after I walked them back up the street, I found that my now-divorced mother—laboring for low-paying wages outside the home to meet family expenses—had no time and little inclination to read this feminism.

At seventeen, I asked a liberal professor at my Catholic school to help me locate communists in San Antonio. He warned me against doing so but gave the phone number for an elderly white Communist Party USA (CPUSA) leader who sold from his garage-bookstore works by Karl Marx, V. I. Lenin, and Frantz Fanon along with pamphlets on labor history and revolutionary struggles. (Attempts to synthesize African and women's liberation through these texts marked my emergent antiracist feminist consciousness.) Local reactionaries had burned down the home-based CPUSA store more than once by the time I met him. Each time he rebuilt. At a political party in his backyard, I was introduced to one of the town's few Black Panthers, who in turn introduced me to the works of Amilcar Cabral. These encounters set me to thinking about social and political repression, militant ideas, and political courage. It would be several years, though, before my political actions began to more closely and consistently reflect my evolving critiques.

An early lackluster conformity to discipline and an ideologically vague progressivism were gradually supplanted by radical critiques obtained from meeting activists while I was in graduate school in New York, working to counter police brutality, violence against women, South African apartheid, the embargo against Cuba, and the Central Intelligence Agency (CIA) or "contra" wars in Nicaragua, El Salvador, and southern Africa. In the 1980s, known as the ultra-conservative or reactionary "Reagan years," African American women hosting book readings in Africana art galleries in the East Village and the Harlem State Office Building introduced me to *Assata Shakur: An Autobiography*.[7] Shakur in turn introduced me to the Black Panther Party, the Black Liberation Army, and revolutionary black feminism. By then my preadolescent fascination with guns had been transformed into an adult focus on my father's employer's use of repressive sanctions and political violence against insurrections. In dual focus, I saw radical organizing for community development and political autonomy and the sometimes sophisticated, sometimes brutal police and military destabilization of perceived threats to state dominance. As I became increasingly absorbed by the latter, I began to shadow or follow the state with an emergent perspective that demystified and de-demonized (at least in theory) revolutionaries' deployment of military strategies against police and state violence.

Conflictual communities prodded me to think critically about "my" military, black petit bourgeois caste engulfed by a dominant, more privileged white bourgeoisie. Serving as a progressive professor, I studied parallels to the dichotomized world and "war" stories of my youth. With a respite from the skirmishes of my first academic job, and in filial duty, in the early 1990s I vacationed with my disintegrating father who had been in self-exile for decades. At his request, on what would be his last Christmas, I accompanied him to a firing range to try his Magnum. At fifty-eight, this retired career officer prematurely and permanently self-destructed. (Reportedly, more Vietnam vets have killed themselves in suicide than died in the war.) With flag-draped coffin, to the sounds of a nineteen-gun salute and bugles playing Taps, he was ceremonially interred in a military burial. Then, living with a phantom soldier and the funeral decorum of grief, I worked to make distinct political sounds. In the hope that these sounds would be underscored by and projected with some compassion mixed with outrage, I focused on social bias and repressive state practices.

As I learned to confront militarism, state co-optation and repression, and resistance (in the form of radical antiracist feminism evolving on U.S. battlefields), I encountered my own dark reflections—and those of Others—as African shadow boxers in American culture.

BLACK FEMINIST POLITICS

> [W]e find our origins in the historical reality of Afro-American women's continuous life-and-death struggle for survival and liberation. Black women's extremely negative relationship to the American political system (a system of white male rule) has always been determined by our membership in two oppressed racial and sexual castes. . . . Black women have always embodied, if only in their physical manifestation, an adversary stance to white male rule and have actively resisted its inroads upon them and their communities in both dramatic and subtle ways.
>
> —The Combahee River Collective

Of the many branches of black feminisms extending from battles for a liberated African and female existence in "America," the following discussion takes root in black female radicalism.[8] Rather than attempt to offer a comprehensive survey of the ideological diversity or plurality of black feminisms—or the more subtle differences found even within radical black feminism (the feminism of choice here)—I examine the relationship of select black female militants to feminist and antiracist politics and participatory democracy, while reviewing images that detract from black women's contributions to democratic culture. Consequently, *Shadowboxing* stands as something of an anomaly in mainstream social and political thought, as well as in black feminist thought. Its discussions seek to unmask political dominance and the limits of liberalism or civil rights advocacy. The book highlights black women's challenges to state power and antiradicalism within conventional politics and within feminist and antiracist politics, as well as describes how cultural stereotypes obscure political agency. In a sense, this writing mirrors the historical role of blacks, females, and black females as petitioners and agitators in— or appendages and shadows of—American society and politics.

Although they have been marginalized, studies of black female radicalism nevertheless offer an important service in that they map shared and contested political terrain. Such studies contradict conservative or neoliberal claims that elite or institutional opposition to racial and gender equality is merely a fiction promoted by "victim" rhetoric or studies. Despite exclusionary practices set by racism, sexism, and class bias, African American women have made gains in the "public realm" of electoral politics and appointed office; these are the political victories most often seen and celebrated in antiracist feminist politics. The 1992 election of Carol Mosely Braun as the United States's first black woman Senator, and the reelections of Democratic leaders Maxine Waters, Cynthia McKenny, Corrine Brown, Carrie Meeks, and Eleanor Holmes Norton to the U.S. House of Representatives stand as key examples of black female progress in electoral political power. Outside of congressional halls, black women also have mobilized the "private realm" of local and religious communities, neighborhood schools, and cultural centers. Directly or indirectly opposing institutional control, and social and state neglect or violence, they have informed American political culture by leaving indelible marks in anti-violence campaigns, resource redistribution for underresourced communities, youth and women's groups, and labor and civil rights activism. Both the highly visible Congresswomen and the nearly invisible community activists shape models of political progressivism.

Yet black women and feminists are not uniformly progressive, although they all invariably face marginalization and opposition fueled by white supremacy, corporate capitalism, patriarchy, and homophobia. Radical or revolutionary black feminisms also face resistance from liberal and conservative feminisms and antiracisms. *Shadowboxing* explores how black feminists have to negotiate the "internal" opposition of antiradicalism among feminists and antiracists and the counterfeminism evident among radicals.

Battling with state power, official culture, as well as anti-radicalism and counterfeminism among progressives, subordinate women have forged a feminist politics through militant antiracist movements whose contributions set the context for this text. This emphasis on political militancy and radicalism differs somewhat from the emphases of contemporary black feminisms that focus on cultural politics as isolated from state power and middle-class sensibilities. Deconstructing representations of black females as sexual deviants—images that promote antiblack and antifemale contempt and violence—has been a primary concern of black women writers and activists in the United States for centuries. I examine such concerns only in relation to their critical opposition to representations that detract from black women's political militancy. For instance, commercial images of the sexualized allure to or aversion for black females eclipse images of black female political agency in conventional culture: As the political outlaw is transformed into the sexual outlaw, the activist becomes a commodity consumed in the hunt, imprisonment, or rehabilitation.

Given the centrality of cultural criticism in black feminist discourse, it is important to note the contributions of cultural black feminisms deconstructing fetish. In visual culture, fetish has been associated with blackness as primitivism and sexual license. The fetishized are seen as interlopers, imitating or contaminating a "civilized" citizenry. Critiquing or accommodating fetish with the ingenuity of subordinate cultures grappling with bad press, black women have produced diverse representations of black females and feminisms.

Following the black, brown, and red and women's liberation movements of the preceding decades, in the 1980s there was an explosion of black feminist culture and writings to challenge caricatures or one-dimensional representations of black females. As a consequence of these contributions, black feminisms became best known, and taught, through memoir, fiction, and film that examined gender conflict and community relations, but often in abstraction to political radicalism that confronted state or corporate systems. Popularized through Hollywood and television, key works include Alice Walker's *The Color Purple*, Gloria Naylor's *Women of Brewster Place*, and Terry McMillan's *Waiting to Exhale*. That liberal black feminisms are filtered through the cultural commodities market warrants a critical response. As author bell hooks notes: "Our creative work is shaped by a market that reflects white supremacist values and concerns. . . . novels highlighting black male oppression of black females while downplaying white racist oppression of black people would be more marketable than the reverse."[9] Some contemporary feminist and race discourse plays to the market, which provides steady incentives to present black feminisms in "acceptable," conventional forms.

Despite the drives of the market, and criticisms that black feminist productions promote "antiblack male stereotypes," such works have proven indispensable in highlighting the issues of alienation, abuse, and resistance in the lives of black females. They also illustrate the idea and practice of black female independence from both black males and white males and females. To some extent, though, racial-sexual fetish in a mass market undercuts the progressive politics of the works, an inevitable result in a market economy. Marketed as exotica, black feminist sensibilities and literature often appear as a source of emotive stories of feminine colored pain and ethnic eccentricities for consumers. The discomfort that arises from the telling of black women's stories may have more to do with a reluctance to hear the abuse and struggle, pain and anger embedded in the tale; this may be particularly so if the narratives are encountered through commercial culture. Inadvertently, as black women manage images auctioned in a market they do not control, black feminisms function as spectacle and black feminists as storytellers for a society nursed on the colonized frame.

Although fiction has the greatest currency in black feminism, currently the most prominent delineators of black feminist politics are its academics and social theorists. For instance, sociologist Patricia Hill Collins describes a cross-gender (but not transracial) Afrocentric feminism as "a process of self-conscious struggle that empowers women and men to actualize a humanist vision" and "develop a theory that is emancipatory and reflective" for black female struggles.[10] Citing an undifferentiated, monolithic black feminism, she notes its limbo status in respect to both white and black women: The "term *Black feminist* both highlights the contradictions underlying the assumed Whiteness of feminism and reminds White women that they are neither the only nor the normative 'feminists'. Because it challenges Black women to confront their own views on sexism and women's oppression, the term *Black feminism* also makes many African American women uncomfortable."[11] Exploring a type of feminism unique to black females or women of color, Alice Walker, who has achieved prominence as both progressive theorist and novelist, contrasts black feminism with white or Eurocentric feminism to introduce the term "womanist." Walker renders the adjective "black" superfluous for feminist or gender-progressive women of African descent and "women of color" in order to posit a culturally specific womanism, noting that white women feel no need to preface "feminist" with "white," understanding the term as stemming from their racial/ethnic culture.[12] bell hooks' expansion on Collins's humanist-Afrocentric vision and Walker's cultural critique, (which has been embraced by "womanist theology"), repoliticizes feminism as "a struggle to eradicate the ideology of domination that permeates Western culture on various levels as well as a commitment to reorganizing society so that the self-development of people can take precedence over imperialism, economic expansion, and material desires."[13]

All three writers identify a feminism/womanism with a unique cultural worldview that shapes gender consciousness. To some degree, then, we can distinguish between a conventional feminism embraceable by all progressive women, including those who happen to be black, and a *black* feminism or womanism, one particular to women of African descent. Yet there is a third form of feminism applicable only to those black women who are left of liberal or stand outside conventional politics. For example, hooks's comprehensive definition of feminism as opposition to white supremacist-capitalist-patriarchy goes beyond the negative impact of gender, race, and culture to highlight an antiracist, socialist feminism applicable to all like-minded women. Her analysis is more explicitly about state practices and institutions; it encompasses progressive, anticapitalist women to emphasize exploitation tied to corporate capitalism and racial imperialism. Therefore, it also provides a bridge to this discussion of black radical feminism.

Unlike many cultural feminists, this noted cultural critic describes being politicized by black or "third world" male revolutionary intellectuals. hooks writes: "I am often asked to chart a critical genealogy of my intellectual development. In the years before I became deeply engaged with the feminist movement and with the writing of feminist theorists, all the progressive critical thinkers who nurtured my emergent radical subjectivity were men: [Frantz] Fanon, [Albert] Memmi, [Amilcar] Cabral, [Paulo] Freire, Malcolm X."[14] The interest of black women such as hooks in radical subjectivity tied to political movements shapes this text's focus. Like hooks, a number of black women have been radicalized by the insurgent speech and struggles of black males (men who at times are credited as the only significant leaders of movements co-organized and led by black women).

The focus here is on women who uniformly considered themselves "antiracists" but not necessarily "feminists" yet who nevertheless expanded antiracist women's politics, community development, democratic power, and radical leadership. Given the primacy of movements in the formation and articulation of black female militancy, history plays a central role in contemporary analyses. In the 1960s, black women participated in the Southern Christian Leadership Council (SCLC), the Student Nonviolent Coordinating Committee (SNCC), the Congress on Racial Equality (CORE), the Organization of Afro-American Unity (OAAU), and the Black Panther Party (BPP). Emerging from the black liberation and antiracist movements that helped to redefine radical action, in the 1970s black women's organizations such as the Combahee River Collective issued cogent manifestoes that articulated a revolutionary black feminism.[15]

Historically, the strongest motivation in the development of black feminist politics in twentieth-century America stemmed from rebellions against racism or U.S. apartheid and segregation, specifically antiblack racism, revolts against racialized sexism and sexual violence, and wars against poverty.[16] Conventional political discourse—whether conservative, liberal, or radical—that obscures these battles and their emergent feminisms raises the leviathan of patriarchy, white supremacy, and capitalism to overshadow the work of black and female struggles (especially working-class or poor black female ones). African American women shadow both a subordinate race and gender—a fact noted in the black feminist adage: "All the women are white, all the blacks are men, but some of us are brave."[17]

Seeking to frame some aspects of that courage, I sketch a political trajectory in black feminisms to explore key intersections along the American cultural curve. The intersections include community, black women's political practices, revolutionary iconography, state punishment, fetishistic representations of sexuality and victimization, and black male patriarchy and profeminism. The discussions center on black women's quests for economic resources, social and racial justice, cultural autonomy, and sexual safety. Also discussed are the abolition of racist policing and executions as well as advocacy for political dissent and self-defense amid state repression.[18] Balancing historical and political critiques with cultural criticism, these observations contradict the grand narrative or "official story" of U.S. democracy as benignly impartial or just in respect to black or "colored," gay/lesbian or bi/transsexual, female, poor, and working-class life.

In a culture that greets antiblack and antifemale violence, and the vilification and abuse of black females and their kin, with considerable equanimity, many shadowbox. Those women who do so with distinct political intent to revolutionize rather than reform shape the concerns of this work. Battles to expand democratic freedoms amid a culture of dominance reveal fears and desires. *Shadowboxing* struggles with primal drives and the status of African American women as companion-challengers to a dysfunctional democracy. Rather than showcase black feminism-as-spectacle, it attempts to unlock the glass case of the American shadow box that restricts, but has never shielded, the African female resistance displayed.

TWO

Forging Community: From Segregation to Transcendence

I had seen their tears and sighs, and I had heard
their groans, and I would give every drop of
blood in my veins to free them.

—Harriet Tubman

Racial, racist, and antiracist communities are social communities; they are spiritual communities as well, embodying both the political and the transcendent. "Community" shapes political rhetoric, concepts, and practices in late-twentieth-century U.S. society. Yet racial and class or economic segregation have become normative. During the current U.S. "economic boom," which reflects the expansion of concentrated wealth and corporate financing of electoral politics, with the curtailment of social services and mass political rights, civic and grass-roots organizations have heightened their calls for term and campaign contribution limits.

Advocates for electoral reform have noted that material resources and wealth increasingly remain the possession of elites: From 1980 to 1990, the U.S. House Ways and Means Committee reported that pretax income for the poorest first decile fell from $5,128 to $4,695; for the richest sector it mushroomed from $312,816 to $548,969. While class and social divisions are magnified, bold visions for economic redistributive justice to underresourced sectors are largely absent from corporate and state-funded media and education. Consequently, the nation seems to be suffering a severe national deficit both in funds for redistribution to nonelites and in radical thinking for racial parity in economic resources. This illusion of scarcity of resources for redistribution coexists with a rhetoric of abundance for the population in general and the corporate-managed economy specifically. Conventional political discourse pays little attention to advocacy for redirecting material resources and the dissemination of transformative ideologies, partly because a form of American race rhetoric masks the stratification of economic wealth and the emergent activism and theories that challenge impoverishment in this "age of abundance." Conventional race rhetoric is able to foster a sense of "community," one predicated on segregation and the denial of its resurgence as both a racial and economic phenomenon. It also functions as a form of policing, multifaceted in its scope and intent and capable of setting borders for those "worthy" and "unworthy" of participating fully in the political economy of a bourgeois democracy.

Conventional race rhetoric is compatible with conservative and reactionary racial rhetoric. Far-right rhetoric increasingly rejects the overt race hatred of white supremacist demagoguery to make the allegedly race-blind argument that neither blacks nor whites should succumb to race mixing because both groups must preserve and take pride in their respective racial heritages. This stance legitimizes rightist racial policing. It is counterpoised with the centrist race rhetoric emanating from the President's Race Initiative, or PRI, for race civility within a neoliberal paradigm. Yet President Bill Clinton's PRI did not challenge economic stratification as a form of racial division. Therefore, although distinct entities, the new segregationist—conservative—and new integrationist—neoliberal—race discourses both stem from the same conventional approaches to solving the "race problem" within the dominant political and economic systems. Unconventional or radical race rhetoric for community, emanating from activists and political prisoners, maintains that racialized U.S. domestic and foreign policies have created such severe conditions of repression and illusion that reasonable responses embody radical and revolutionary theory and struggle for systemic changes.[1] Such changes include full and meaningful employment, comprehensive medical and educational services, and the abolition of prisons and the death penalty as racialized sites for repression and exploitation. Predictably such discourse and activism send alarm signals throughout corporate and middle America, which respectively seek and acquiesce to greater state police powers.

Policing is justified because it offers protection: protection from rhetorical excess, criminality, and political extremism. Race rhetoric in the marketing of scarcity functions to sell the consumer "protection." Most discourse on affirmative action and racial containment (and resegregation) through prisons focuses on the selling and buying of protection or insurance—moral, physical, psychological, and political. The arenas for racial discourse on affirmative action and incarceration mark the parameters of left liberalism in black feminist politics. These arenas are explored later. Another distinct form of community, one that emphasizes a black cultural context in confrontation with racist exclusionary practices and politically repressive measures, is also examined as an alternative to a regenerating segregation.

SEGREGATED COMMUNITY:
FROM AFFIRMATIVE ACTION TO INCARCERATION

Affirmative action has a dual impact on segregation for racialized communities. Many speak of affirmative action disparagingly as "racial" or "group preferences," only within the areas of employment and education, not in the areas of incarceration and execution. Even those who believe that affirmative action is the key antiracist measure and litmus test for racial progressivism often do not analyze its deployment in incarceration as the method of resegregation for the racially privileged and disenfranchised. Increased competition for jobs and educational slots and a countercultural movement to the civil rights gains of previous decades have all fostered advocacy for the resurgence of segregation. Despite economic and educational abundance in the United States, economic and educational access has proven elusive for many black

Americans. Race rhetoric that obscures the relationship between racial-sexual disenfranchisement and corporate capitalism has reduced the demand for egalitarian economic and educational access. Consequently, political manipulation of racial and economic fears continues to reify and fuel racialized communities.

Much has been said about affirmative action, particularly within academe, where it has become the dominant discourse on racial inequality and a standard for determining racist or antiracist attitudes.[2] Affirmative action is embraced as the promise of moral protection against racism (specifically, white supremacy); conversely, anti–affirmative action advocates claim they seek protection from "reverse racism," marketing "fairness" in a popularized vision of a visually impaired or color-blind American society. Both proponents and opponents of affirmative action engage in advocacy, advocacy made problematic by the fact that often it takes little account of the conservative origins of affirmative action and its liberal intent. Given the origins of affirmative action, simplistic characterizations citing those who advocate it as "antiracist" are untenable. For, as Berkeley sociologist Troy Duster notes, former President Richard Nixon supported affirmative action.[3]

Following the 1963 assassination of John F. Kennedy, Lyndon B. Johnson maneuvered through Congress the 1964 civil rights legislation mandating selected forms of affirmative action in the workplace. While the Democratic president engineered the passage of legislation, Nixon institutionalized affirmative action, mandating that in select work sites corporations implement affirmative action programs. In his review of the memoirs of the Republican president's senior domestic aide, John Ehrlichman, his chief of staff, H. R. Haldeman, and historian Kenneth O'Reilly's work entitled *Nixon's Piano*, Duster notes that Nixon's support for affirmative action in employment was based on a shrewd cynicism and insight that it would be the wedge issue in the Democratic Party, splintering its coalitions of (white) labor, African Americans and Jews.[4] "Surely," writes Duster, "Nixon is wearing, even now, that familiar taut smile. . . . "[5] However, even Nixon, as prescient as he was, could not foresee that although "group interests were central to the fate of affirmative action . . . those group interests would reincarnate themselves in the disguise of claims to individual fairness."[6] According to Duster, the former president's racially contentious vision allowed him to see that economic or class aspirations are racialized in the United States and so manifest themselves in a racial-collective formation; therefore, the majority of whites would assert themselves as a group, with collective interests. And, in fact, this is what they did in the 1970s, in opposition to affirmative action and other civil rights initiatives and in the largely white male flight from the Democratic to the Republican Party.

Although the Republican Party would undermine the economic interests of middle- and working-class whites, its use of economic fears and racial indignation, coded in the rhetoric of white innocence and victimization (traceable at least to the postbellum era and the rise of lynching, the convict prison lease system, and Jim Crow segregation) solidified group interests racialized as "white." Consequently, in the 1980s key Republican strategist Lee Atwater informed the Republican National Committee (RNC) that "class struggle in the South continues with the [white] populists serving as the trump card." The populists, according to Atwater, lean toward economic liberalism but social conservatism. "When Republicans are successful in getting certain social issues to the forefront, the populist vote is ours," he wrote.[7] Best known (along with Roger Ailes, currently a news pundit for the Fox Network) as one of the architects for the Willie Horton campaign to elect George Bush as president, Atwater understood that using economic and education redress mechanisms such as affirmative action could turn them into social issues that most white (especially southern) workers would vote to oppose. In fact, most whites voted against their own class interests during the 1980s by electing pro-corporate Republican administrations that cut social services: from 1980 to 1989, U.S. average hourly wages decreased from $19.84 to $19.66 per hour, while from 1989 to 1993, average U.S. household annual income fell 7 percent. Anti–affirmative action race rhetoric obscures white group interests by positing the notion of competing deserving and "undeserving" *individuals,* when in fact the battle is about racialized *groups* juxtaposed with the subordinate status of blacks.[8]

Conservative and neoliberal antiracist discourse works to counter race-baiting and scapegoating often without appealing to the political context and the co-optation of the radical antiracist struggle. For instance, offering his own vision of fairness, morality, and good business, in 1997 Houston mayor Bob Lanier worked vigorously against an anti–affirmative action initiative so that it was eventually defeated by a vote of 55 to 45 percent. As a wealthy white real estate mogul, Lanier stumped against the initiative with the adage "Let's not go back to the time when all of the people who did business with the city looked like me."

At the time, only 20 percent of Houston's contracts went to women and people of color. Through the media, Lanier asserted a set of moral claims about fairness ("whites shouldn't have everything") and placed those claims squarely before voters with the reworded initiative that altered the initial 1964 Civil Rights Act wording. Originally, anti–affirmative action advocates crafted language that stated that the initiative *prohibited discrimination* based on race or gender or religion; Lanier's political crew changed the language so that the initiative's consequences were explicit and unambiguous; altered, it stated that a pro vote would oppose affirmative action for women and minorities. Yet this pro–affirmative action stance is abstracted from the larger political context of antiracist and antisexist struggles. To the degree that the struggle around affirmative action in education and employment has become synonymous with antiracist struggle in the United States, it has obscured the program's political intent, and serves as a surrogate for black and feminist struggles.

Some intellectuals seek to dispense with explicit antiracist strategies such as affirmative action. Their race rhetoric becomes an advocacy to struggle against discrimination and economic disenfranchisement that people of color face by dealing with class issues. Black neoliberal class discourse attempts to revitalize affirmative action as a class-based remedy, and, as such, as an alternative to a race-based strategy. Maintaining that affirmative action has "failed" because it is politically unpopular in a counter–civil rights era, Harvard sociologist William Julius Wilson argues that massive intervention to expand urban housing desegregation and affirmative action is impractical because most Americans resist "race-specific policies." The *Chronicle of Higher Education* reports that at the August 1997 American Sociological Association meeting in Toronto, Wilson proposed a program modeled on the Works Progress Administration (WPA) of Franklin Delano Roosevelt's New Deal. Wilson's stated aim was to "inspire progressives of all ethnicities with a race-blind vision of social justice."[9] Failing to note the racial bias of the New Deal programs (the 1934 National Housing Act and the 1935 Wagner Act for labor inscribed and exacerbated racism),[10] Wilson conveniently ignores the political reality that if mainstream America is hostile to affirmative action, it likely would not support a WPA work program, particularly now, when the poor have been racialized as culturally or inherently undisciplined and opportunistic (if not parasitic) and therefore socially and economically criminal. The selling of scarcity also has convinced many Americans of the viability and moral necessity of coerced, subsistence-wage labor through the workfare and prison industries. Both sectors are being privatized, a move that promotes superexploitation in the search for profits. Wilson attempts to counter the demand for racial or group preferences as white rights and entitlements by banning all rhetoric that refers to race and racism in affirmative action and by opening all such programs to whites—that is, white *males,* because the programs are currently open to white females.

In fact, the Clinton administration uses the same tactic in attempting to expand support for affirmative action by promoting the visibility of white women as its beneficiaries. In September 1997 the administration modified federal affirmative action policies to comply with the 1995 Supreme Court ruling restricting the use of race as a consideration in awarding federal contracts.[11] Under the program known as "8a," through the Small Business Administration (SBA), 3,000 companies became eligible to apply for federal contracts. In fiscal year 1996, 6,115 companies were awarded federal contracts totaling $6.4 billion according to the *New York Times.* Of these, all but 27 were owned by ethnic minorities.[12] Through the SBA, Asians' participation in the federal program grew from 10.5 percent of contracts in 1986 to 23.7 percent in 1996; African Americans dropped by more than a quarter, from 50.5 percent in 1986 to 36.7 percent in 1996; Latinos stayed at 30 percent.[13]

The fact that affirmative action gains are overwhelmingly attributed to blacks in national racial rhetoric and imagery, although quantitatively the greatest beneficiaries have been white women and increasingly other people of color, attests to the endurance of the black/white binary in the American mind and the racialization of the deserving industrious sector as "white" and the parasitic sector as "black."

But the concept of group or collective white victimization and the need for group white racial redress appears even when there is no mention of race. Consider the anti–affirmative action rhetoric of Louisiana governor Mike Foster, who in 1997 labeled law students at Tulane University's law clinic "vigilantes" for litigating on behalf of a local black neighborhood that, having suffered from toxic waste dumping in the past, opposed a chemical company locating a plant in its community. Foster threatened to revoke the university's tax breaks and revenues, while leaders of the Chemical Consortium of Corporations vowed not to provide financial gifts to the school, because its students were, in effect, biting the hand that fed them.

In a 1997 letter to Tulane's president, Louisiana's Secretary of Economic Development, Kevin P. Reilly, Sr. suggested that the reason only 54 percent of Tulane Law School graduates pass the bar exam the first time might be linked to their clinic's advocacy/activism. Although none of this overtly appears as policing race rhetoric, it is coded by its speakers as such. For aligning themselves with impoverished blacks, largely white affluent students are accused of political extremism, ingratitude toward parental authority, and being afflicted by the bell curve's decline in intelligence. The Tulane episode suggests that class issues are racialized in the United States, despite Wilson's attempt to use class to bypass the issue of racism and social dilemmas about how to deploy responsible race rhetoric in public discourse.

In their rhetoric, the U.S. President, Houston's former mayor, and Harvard's sociologist do not address the ways in which affirmative action is tied to black performance to undermine its value as an antiracist project. Black performance in relation to affirmative action or "racial preferences" has an economic role; consequently it enhances the market value of the institutions or corporate entities within which people of color function. These corporate sites are not inherently vested in the development of African American, Latino, Asian, or Native American communities as a value in themselves; rather, state and corporate consumers are the greatest beneficiaries from the appearance and performance of people of color in state-corporate institutions.

For example, as a result of affirmative action, we encounter the phenomenon of black students performing as athletes to generate wealth in public schools such as the University of Texas, the University of Massachusetts, and the University of Colorado (whose football coach's 1997 annual salary exceeded $400,000). As such, black youths function as commodities or producers of commodities.

In 1996 the Fifth U.S. Circuit Court of Appeals ruled in favor of Cheryl Hopwood and three other white students who sued the University of Texas law school for racial discrimination after they were denied admission.[14] In retaliation to the Hopwood case, Texas State Representative Don Wilson (D-Houston) introduced a bill in March 1997 to eliminate athletic scholarships at state universities unless the athletes meet the same academic requirements as nonathletes, with the rationale that if affirmative action is bad for nonathletes, it should be bad for athletes. The Texas legislature did not pass that bill. Its members considered keeping revenues from sports more essential than establishing a logical coherence to the stance on affirmative action, particularly given the selling of the idea of economic scarcity to Americans through state budgets, which increasingly spend more on prisons than universities and schools.

In addition to functioning as athletic entertainers and employees, students perform as "diversity investments." In the wake of the Hopwood decision and California's anti–affirmative action proposition 209, fewer gifted black and Latino students have enrolled in both Texas and California state schools, which they view as racially hostile. (Mexican-American or Chicano/a students have renamed UT Austin the University of Tejaztlan at Austin). Private institutions have "raided" what are now considered "scarce commodities." The selling of scarcity is fueled by rather limited notions of what constitutes a stellar student of color.

"People of color" can be seen as multicultural units for private wealthy institutions or corporations. Investments in multiculturalism give schools the appearance of being academically enriched in "diversity," where colored students (like those faculty members who are raided or recruited) share their narratives and appearance to become part of the unpaid educational performers in service of diversification; this service is unlike that which ethnic *majority* faculty, staff, and students perform. Fragile coalitions between "people of color" (that euphemistic homogenizing phrase) are sometimes frayed by contests over which group is most valued as Other in the white corporation.

In the new segregation, universities are becoming increasingly white while prisons are becoming increasingly black or brown as "racial preferences" follow the imagined desires of ethnic majorities. Students are not the only racialized performers under affirmative action. Nonstudents function as performers in the penal economy. Racial group preferences, although denounced in education and employment, are not equally condemned by conservatives and liberals. In regards to policing and incarceration, their political stances seem fairly similar.

In 1998 members of the Congressional Black Caucus satirized police patrol pullovers of motorists targeting African Americans as an infraction known as DWB—Driving While Black. The racist bias reflected in sentencing has created a society in which a black person is eight times more likely to be sentenced to prison for committing (or being convicted of) a similar offense as a white person. Defendants receive the same sentencing for the sale or possession of one unit of crack—considered a black or latino urban drug—as for one hundred units of powder cocaine—considered a white suburban indulgence. Although the majority of cocaine and crack offenders are whites, most of those sentenced to prison for drug use and sale are African American and Latino. Affirmative action for prisons does not seem to stir up the national American conscience, or inspire as much debate in media, academic, or political circles, as does affirmative action in education and employment.

The proliferation of prisons, described as the "prison industrial complex" by some human rights advocates, is enmeshed in both educational and racial policies. For instance, in 1997, California had the largest prison population (housing approximately 135,000 people); more of the state's general fund goes to prisons (9.4 percent) than to higher education (8.7 percent). California prisons house twice the number of African Americans than do its four-year universities as increasingly educational programs are banned for incarcerated peoples.[15]

In the postbellum era, racist rhetoric fueled the rise of lynchings and the convict lease system, both of which targeted African Americans. Following the Civil War, the Thirteenth Amendment to the Constitution codified slavery. While ostensibly abolishing it, that amendment in fact legalizes and demarcates prisons as the areas in which slavery, or "involuntary servitude," is permissible: Those duly convicted of a crime in a court of law can be forced into involuntary labor. One of America's great intellectuals, W. E. B. Du Bois, notes in *Black Reconstruction* that, after the Civil War, southern planters who earlier had used slave labor began to rely solely on convict labor because of the profit margins, as African Americans were imprisoned for minor infractions of the law or for simply being "in the wrong place at the wrong time."[16] In the late nineteenth century, black women and men often labored yoked together in stockades, as labor exploitation and brutality that had existed under slavery created new gender parity within growing prison populations.

Today the economic incentives and profiteering around involuntary servitude or prison slavery rarely enter mainstream race rhetoric. Yet there are now nearly 2 million people behind bars in U.S. prisons, jails, and detention centers, three times the number documented for 1980. In 1995 African Americans comprised 12.5 percent of the U.S. general population and 50 percent of the U.S. prison population, according to the Washington, D.C.-based Sentencing Project. According to the Bureau of Justice Statistics, "during the 12 months that ended June 1995, the number of prison inmates grew 89,707, to that date, the largest annual increase in U.S. history."[17] In 1995 the imprisoned population in the United States equaled or exceeded the populations of thirteen states and many major U.S. cities. Nearly one in every twenty-five adults in the country goes to jail each year.

Wackenhut Corrections Corporation and the Corrections Corporation of America (CCA) are under contract to run ninety-three minimum- and medium-security facilities with more than 60,000 beds. In 1995 *Forbes* magazine cited Wackenhut as one of the "200 Best Small Companies" given its decade of growth. Currently, over one hundred private prisons exist. Common in the United States from the mid-nineteenth to the early twentieth century, private prisons were largely abolished in 1925, when newspaper exposés brought public attention to brutal beatings, malnourishment, and labor exploitation, coupled with complaints from labor and business about unfair competition. They reemerged decades later in 1984, when the federal government hired the Corrections Corporation of America, which also operates prisons in Britain and Australia, to run a detention center for immigrants in Houston, Texas.[18]

Since 1990, thirty states have made it legal to contract prison labor out to private companies. Sales from prison industries rose from $393 million in 1980 to $1.81 billion in 1995, according to a spokesperson at the Justice Department. U.S. Census Bureau data reported that nearly 600,000 full-time employees worked in corrections in 1995; the only Fortune 500 company with a larger workforce is General Motors. Ironically the estimated annual cost of corporate crime is between $174 and $231 billion, while the economic cost of "street crimes" (burglary and robbery) is estimated at $3 to $4 billion. States enforce laws that penalize poor and working-class people while virtually ignoring white-collar crimes.[19]

Prisons are self-perpetuating because reform campaigns assume that the prisons are the only effective strategy for countering crime. Consequently, prisons are proposed as remedies for reform's own failure according to human rights activist Angela Davis, who contends that "the failure of the prison combined with the inability to conceptualize penal strategies that [serve as an alternative] reflect the assumption that as brutal as prisons may appear, public order will always depend upon the existence of prisons, whether they are represented as places of rehabilitation, deterrence, or retribution."[20]

In October 1997 the state of Colorado held its first execution in thirty years. This became an opportunity for people statewide to reflect on the role of rehabilitation and deterrence in state punishment and killings. However, most public reflections and conversations did not adequately address the racist nature of U.S. policing. According to the Death Penalty Information Center, about 50 percent of those now on death row are people of color, from minority groups representing only 20 percent of the U.S. population. Nearly 40 percent of those executed since 1976 have been black; from 1977 to 1986, 90 percent of prisoners executed were convicted of killing whites, although the number of black victims was approximately equal.

In nearly every death penalty case, the race of the victim is white; in fact, a person is four times more likely to be sentenced to death for being convicted of killing a white person than for killing a black person. Of the 229 executions in the United States since the reinstatement of the death penalty, only 1 involved a white defendant for the murder of a black person. The American Bar Association has called for a moratorium on executions given the racial bias in death sentences.[21] However, nationwide, from Colorado to Texas to Missouri, state-sanctioned killings are increasing. Perhaps the most eloquent spokesman on incarceration and state executions is Pennsylvania's death-row inmate and black political prisoner Mumia Abu-Jamal. Abu-Jamal writes in *Live from Death Row:*

> Mix in solitary confinement, around-the-clock lock-in, no-contact visits, no prison jobs, no educational programs by which to grow, psychiatric treatment facilities designed only to drug you into a coma; ladle in hostile, overtly racist prison guards and staff; add the weight of the falling away of family ties, and you have all the fixings for a stressful psychic stew designed to deteriorate, to erode one's humanity—designed, that is, by the state, with full knowledge of its effects.[22]

In the racialized democratic state, visceral forms of contemporary violence are exposed by "prison intellectuals" and prisoner rights advocates. The brilliance of Abu-Jamal's book is its dissection of the most violent places in U.S. society—prisons, which coincidentally are also administered by the state. In his foreword to Abu-Jamal's second book, *Death Blossoms,* and his Pacifica radio introductions to Abu-Jamal's commentaries taped at Pennsylvania's SCI Green and available on the CD, "All Things Censored," Cornel West notes that state-corporate policies are destroying poor/working-class and black communities and that exploited or unemployed people are being incarcerated in ever greater numbers.[23] Political leaders are aware that the death penalty is applied in a class- and race-biased manner: Most of those on death row are poor people and people of color.

Recent legislation in some seven states, including Pennsylvania and California, prohibits prisoners from granting interviews. Consequently, it is increasingly difficult for prisoners' voices to be heard. This is particularly true for the more than one hundred political prisoners that Amnesty International documents in the United States (a significant number of whom are incarcerated for militant organizing for black liberation). Consequently, some of the most controversial and incisive analyses of political resistance and state dominance have disappeared from conventional American culture.

Like the written word, oral literature has had an impact on the incarceration politics that surround the "new" segregation that fosters not only racial but also political and ideological containment. Political testimonies from family members, lawyers, religious leaders, and journalists with access to the incarcerated contest the increasing censorship of prison intellectuals. However, such censorship has already become institutionalized. In 1996 National Public Radio canceled Abu-Jamal's commentaries after it was intimidated by the Fraternal Order of the Police and conservatives such as former Senator Bob Dole. In 1997 the president of Temple University barred the university radio station from airing "Democracy Now," produced by journalist Amy Goodman, because it featured Abu-Jamal's radio commentary taped from his prison cell. Community Radio, not Public Radio, airs controversial commentaries as Pacifica affiliates (WBAI in New York and KGNU in Boulder) bring to their listeners (or Web browsers) critical analyses censored from mainstream and noncommercial radio.

Most of the public attention on inequities and abuses in policing and sentencing focuses on males. Class and racial inequalities have created conditions where one of every three black males is tied to the criminal justice system (and, as a convicted felon, cannot vote). The most barbaric forms of inequitable and racialized treatment include prison beatings and torture as well as the reappearance of chain gangs. After progressives successfully brought lawsuits in 1997 and 1998 to ban chain gangs as cruel-and-unusual punishment, wardens devised outdoor hitching posts, where prisoners were tied all day, even in inclement weather, for offenses such as refusing to work (at times at hazardous labor or for wages as low as twenty cents an hour). The most repressive forms of segregation evoke America's antebellum punishments of enslaved Africans.

Discussions around human rights abuses within penal systems tend to overlook the conditions of women. Traditionally women have made up a small percentage of the prison population, yet recently their incarceration rates have increased over 300 percent as compared with a 214 percent increase for men. Between 1930 and 1950 two or three prisons were built or established nationwide per decade for women; in the 1960s seven more were built; in the 1970s seventeen were created; in the 1980s thirty-four were opened to house women. In 1994 black women represented 82 percent of women sentenced for crack cocaine offenses; for drug offenses overall, they made up 50 percent.[24] Female offenders are mostly women who ran away from home; a quarter have attempted suicide; more than half have been abused physically, with 36 percent abused sexually.[25]

The Prison Activist Resource Center, based in Berkeley, California, notes significant facts about imprisoned U.S. women: The majority are incarcerated for economic, nonviolent crimes, such as check forgery or illegal credit card use. Eighty percent of women in prison report annual incomes of less than $2,000 in the year prior to their arrest; 92 percent report incomes below $10,000. Of the women incarcerated for violent crimes, most are convicted for defending themselves or their children from abuse. In 1997 California prisons incarcerated 600 women for killing their abusers in self-defense. (On average, prison terms are twice as long for killing husbands than for killing wives.)

Black women are twice as likely to be convicted of killing their abusive husbands as are white women. Fifty-four percent of women in prison are women of color. Ninety percent of incarcerated women are single mothers; there are 167,000 children in the United States who have been separated from their incarcerated mothers, and sometimes the loss of contact is permanent. The average age of women in prison is twenty-nine years old. Fifty-eight percent have not finished high school. Inequities in sentencing due to racism and economic discrimination linked to sexism are common. Black women, on average, receive longer jail time and higher fines than white women do for the same crimes.

Twenty-five percent of U.S. political prisoners are women. In 1997, approximately 138,000 women were incarcerated in U.S. jails and prisons.[26] The dramatic increase in incarceration rates is partly due to working-class and poor women's worsening economic conditions and partly due to increased arrest rates in the wars on crime and drugs. Women prisoners spend an average of seventeen hours a day in their cells, with one hour outside for exercise; male prisoners spend on average of fifteen hours a day in their cells, with one and a half hours outdoors.

In the face of the isolation, exploitation, and abuse of incarcerated women and men that strain notions of conventional community, prisoners recreate new forms and meanings of "community." For example, former political prisoner and African American revolutionary Dhoruba Bin Wahad, lecturing after over nineteen years of incarceration due to COINTELPRO malfeasance, stated that prisons were black communities. The relationships of these black (and brown, red, yellow, and antiracist white) communities in the enslaved (as constructed by the Thirteenth Amendment) world with their counterparts in the "free" world are shaped by ideologies of connection, commitment, and struggle tied to understandings of transcendence.

TRANSCENDENT COMMUNITY

Perhaps one of the most debated issues in American politics is the value of an independent African American political-cultural community. Not unique to, but nevertheless a strong characteristic of, black feminisms are expressions of responsibility and accountability that place community as a cornerstone in the lives and work of black females. Community in fact is understood as requiring and sustaining intergenerational responsibilities that foster the well-being of family, individuals, and a people, male and female. Even if the idea is discredited by the dominant culture, the knowledge that individual hope, sanity, and development come through relationship in community resonates in black politics.

Community is an American ideal and a frustrated endeavor. It is also a politically charged concept. Americans honor or disregard holidays thought to unify them as a nation with a common identity. The Fourth of July has significance for some as the "birthday" of a nation; for others, it is an opportunity to vacation and picnic. Columbus Day is a source of ethnic pride for Italian Americans who celebrate it and of consternation for Native and other Americans who condemn it. The commemoration of historical figures on President's Day has considerably less sway in the popular mind. For many Americans, holidays are apolitical. But African Americans have continuously politicized and problematized national holidays. For instance, abolitionist Frederick Douglass's Fourth of July

Oration delivered in Rochester, New York, in 1852 eloquently relates the sentiment of past *and present* radicals:

> What to the American slave is your Fourth of July? I answer: a day that reveals to him, more than all other days in the year, the gross injustice and cruelty to which he is the constant victim. To him your celebration is a sham; your boasted liberty, an unholy license; your national greatness, swelling vanity; your sounds of rejoicing are empty and heartless; your denunciation of tyrants, brass-fronted impudence; your shouts of liberty and equality, hollow mockery; your prayers and hymns, your sermons and thanksgivings, with all your religious parade and solemnity, are, to him, more bombast, fraud, deception, impiety and hypocrisy—a thin veil to cover up crimes which would disgrace a nation of savages.[27]

African Americans who resisted an uncritical acceptance of U.S. state and society not only censured American holidays and democratic pretensions, they also introduced their own memorial days to mark black political history and aspirations. For example, Kwanzaa was idealized and promoted by Maulana Karenga, former leader of Us (the cultural nationalist organization whose 1968 conflict with the Black Panther Party led to the tragic deaths of Panthers Alprentice "Bunchy" Carter and John Huggins). Juneteenth is celebrated nationwide on June 19 as the day on which, in 1865 in Texas, Union Major General Gordon Granger announced the 1863 Emancipation Proclamation.

In the spirit of Douglass, Juneteenth 1998 was honored with the first gathering of the antiracist, profeminist Black Radical Congress (BRC) in Chicago. The BRC Conference Call, for community and a congressional gathering, invokes the politicized spirit of collective struggle in African American life:

> If you believe in the politics of Black liberation, join us. . . . If you hate what capitalism has done to our community—widespread joblessness, drugs, violence and poverty—come to the Congress. If you are fed up with the corruption of the two party system and want to develop a plan for real political change, come to the Congress. If you want to

struggle against class exploitation, racism, sexism, and homophobia, come to the Congress.[28]

Stating that the Black Radical Congress exists for "everyone ready to fight back," the call urged participation by singling out its black fighters: "trade unionists and workers, youth and students, women, welfare recipients, lesbians and gays, public housing tenants and the homeless, the elderly and people on fixed incomes, veterans, cultural workers and immigrants. You!" The congress attracted nearly 2,000 participants, all seeking some form of black unity or community amid political battles.[29]

African Americans are likely more politically and historically-minded than most Americans regarding national figures and their oppositional place in contemporary culture and identity. For example, blacks who are indifferent or loath to celebrate George Washington (who owned slaves) or Abraham Lincoln (who sought to exile or "repatriate" blacks after the Civil War) will pay tribute to Frederick Douglass, Harriet Tubman, Malcolm X, and Martin Luther King, Jr.

Many Americans follow liberating traditions that acknowledge their ancestors as a spiritual-political resource. For instance, European American culture honors ancestral spirits, often ones connected to cultural and racial quests for autonomy and racial supremacy. Confederate soldiers and slaveholders appear in the iconography of statues in public parks in Memphis, Jackson, or Birmingham to instruct or inspire devoted or casual attention. The fervor of canonical reverence in the battles over reading lists belies academic disdain for ancestral worship as primitivism. Popularized Euroamerican ancestors include "founding fathers" George Washington and Thomas Jefferson and the sanctified Elvis. These icons evince complex relationships often obscured by facile representations of white American freedom and "civilization" that fail to acknowledge its dependency on enslaved or exploited African Americans. Since the civil rights movements mainstreamed black icons, national American culture has jumbled the contradictory values of ancestors who promoted oppositional worldviews: Holidays, coins, and postage stamps pay tribute to presidents who were enslavers, such as Washington and Jefferson (the white abolitionist revolutionary John Brown, who organized the insurrection at Harper's Ferry, is rarely memorialized) as well as antiracist activists Ida B. Wells, Malcolm X, and Martin Luther King, Jr.

Speech about the ancestors enables critical appraisals of historical oppression and also establishes communal ties to support and reflect political-spiritual, secular-sacred traditions and practices. Ancestors illuminate an avenue for liberation. Instructional, and often inspirational, calls to expansive community come from various sites that nevertheless point to commonalties based on shared values. In the 1980s activists fighting U.S.-funded contras in Nicaragua or death squads in El Salvador honored and resurrected their dead by calling "Presente!" after their names in roll calls for the deceased. (In November 1998, at protests at the School of the Americas in Fort Benning, several thousand largely white, middle-class and religious demonstrators responded to the names of those slain under the direction of U.S.-trained death squad leaders with the same call.)

Strongly invested in their ancestors who served as liberators, African Americans' attachments to historical figures such as Douglass, Tubman, Wells, Malcolm X, King, Fannie Lou Hamer, and Ella Baker have deep political and emotional resonance and rootedness. Although the names of females are not mentioned as often, calls to the ancestral presence appear in African American religion, politics, art, in literary and oral culture. These evocations speak to desires for the well-being of community.

A theory of African ancestors in communal development exists as a cultural coda for black feminisms. African decolonization struggles and historical women's rights and international black freedom movements influenced black women's politics. The manifesto of the black feminist Combahee River Collective reflects the sensibility of transcendent community and duty toward organizing for liberation:

> There have always been Black women activists—some known, like Sojourner Truth, Harriet Tubman, Frances E. W. Harper, Ida B. Wells Barnett and Mary Church Terrell, and thousands upon thousands unknown—who have had a shared awareness of how their sexual identity combined with their racial identity to make their whole life situation and the focus of their political struggles unique. Contempo-

rary Black feminism is the outgrowth of countless generations of personal sacrifice, militancy, and work by our mothers and sisters.[30]

Communal development rather than individualism was the marker of both nineteenth- and early twentieth-century "racial uplift," in which prominent blacks were to help elevate their less fortunate brethren. In fact, the status of the individual was tied to her or his role in race leadership and in the black community. Contemporary African American responses to black ancestral leaders, and the place of "ancestral mothers" in black women's stories, illustrate a basic philosophy guiding black feminism today. For instance, the African American women's cultural group Sweet Honey in the Rock honors the ancestors in song. Dedicated to Baker, their "Ella's Song" uses excerpts from Baker's civil rights speeches: "We who believe in freedom cannot rest, until the killing of black men, black mothers' sons, is as important as the killing of white men, white mothers' sons." Introducing the song "Fannie Lou Hamer," Sweet Honey founder Bernice Johnson Reagon, a former Student Nonviolent Coordinating Committee activist, depicts a worldview: recognizing civil rights leader Hamer as a symbol of resistance. Reagon calls her name in the African tradition of offering libation to our forebears, "those who provide the ground we stand on."[31]

Traditional worldviews rooted in and influencing American culture are theoretically and practically lived by black men, women, and children. This leads some to argue that the schisms between political ideologies, gender, sex, class, language, ethnicity, and sexuality are bridged to some extent by shared cultural practices. It is assumed that these practices, in one sense of *shadow*, shelter blacks from danger or invasive observation. In the privacy and protection of a "subculture" that has Africanized the Americas, African Americans as observers or shouters participate in a community that intellectually and emotionally transports them considerable distances from the constraints of a racist society. Worldviews, based on resistance to enslavement and disenfranchisement and on African philosophies, are often in conflict with conventional culture. Part of the conflict stems from African Americans' political and cultural ties to African beliefs and struggles and to black radical or revolutionary politics.

The militancy of the Combahee River Collective statement resonates with the spirit of Amilcar Cabral found in *Return to the Source: Selected Speeches*. Like Combahee, Cabral offers a language that transcends spatial and temporal borders. As secretary-general of the African Party of the Independence of Guinea and the Cape Verde Islands in the decolonization movement from Portugal, Cabral was considered a brilliant practitioner of liberation theories. His courage, revolutionary thought, and eloquence attracted men and women worldwide. In his "Second Address Before the United Nations," reprinted in *Return to the Source,* he states: "it is difficult to believe that responsible men exist who fundamentally oppose the legitimate aspirations of the African people to live in dignity, freedom, national independence and progress, because in the modern world, to support those who are suffering and fighting for their liberation, it is not necessary to be courageous; it is enough to be honest."[32]

A generation ago, amid "Third World" decolonization struggles, Cabral understood "African" to include blacks in the Diaspora and America. During his last visit to the United States in 1972, the Africa Information Service convened, at his request, a black political gathering in New York City, with over one hundred representatives from thirty organizations. In his presentation, "Connecting the Struggles: An Informal Talk with Black Americans," Cabral referred to those gathered as "African brothers and sisters" and asked for their assistance to the liberation movement in the following manner: "All you can do here [in the United States] to develop your own conditions in the sense of progress, in the sense of history and in the sense of the realization of your aspirations as human beings is a contribution for us. It is also a contribution for you to never forget that you are Africans."[33] Disavowing his expression of a shared "African" identity as "racist," Cabral counseled black Americans on how to fight white supremacy:

> In combating racism we don't make progress if we combat the people themselves. We have to combat the causes of racism. If a bandit comes in my house and I have a gun I cannot shoot the shadow of this bandit. I have to shoot the bandit. Many people lose energy and effort, and

make sacrifices combating shadows. We have to combat the material reality that produces the shadow. If we cannot change the light that is one cause of the shadow, we can at least change the body. It is important to avoid confusion between the shadow and the body that projects the shadow. We are encouraged by the fact that each day more of our people, here and in Africa, realize this reality. This reinforces our confidence in our final victory.[34]

The possibility of victory, even if not perceived as "feminist," was always understood as crossing gender lines. Victory was also never conceptualized outside of the political context of cultural worldviews. Assassinated by Portuguese agents on January 20, 1973, Cabral in spirit continues to appear to women and men who connect freedom and community to the legacies of slain visionaries. In some ways he remains connected by activists and "living thinkers" who realize, while expanding or detracting from, his legacies.

Congolese philosopher K. Kia Buseki Fu-Kiau writes in *The African Book Without Title*: "Mbungi a kanda va kati kwa nsi ye yulu: The Center [cavity] of the community is located between the above and the below world. The reality of the cultural heritage of a community, i.e., its knowledge, is the experience of that deepest reality found between the spiritualized ancestors and the physically living thinkers."[35] In Kongo philosophy, "living thinkers" are initiates who channel between the metaphysical and the physical. The prominence of storytelling and activism in black feminism reflects traditional African cosmology, where thinkers in service to community travel full circle to realize metaphysical ideals in the physical realm. Political and politicizing, theorizing connects spiritual and material worlds to merge ideals—freedom, beauty, justice—with political action. (Practice merges theory with physical activity beyond the exercise of thought.) Defining theorizing as activist and communal repoliticizes rather than diminishes its intellectual content to serve nonelite interests. Theorizing is done from the standpoint of the individual in relationship to community. Therefore, where a person stands to theorize determines the theory's beneficiaries. At the crossroads, the center within community, the horizon of family, friends, and people (nation) intersects with the vertical climb and descent of ethics, ancestors, and progeny. The center within community offers a unique vantage point often revealed within the life stories of revolutionary leaders. Transcendent community reflects a theory of knowledge based on experience, reflection, judgment, and action. In this epistemology, the experiences of living thinkers produce reflections that incite judgments to inspire ethical action that renews the cycle—with new experiences, self-reflections, judging, and organizing.[36]

This worldview posits the nonduality of time and space to belie socially constructed dichotomies between the sacred and secular and the spiritual and political, the individual and community. Conventional divisions and distinctions within past, present, and future time—for instance, postbellum and postmodern liberation struggles—and geographical space—such as Africa and America—go largely unrecognized. Here new "old" meanings are established so that both time and space are seen to coexist and overlap.[37]

Theologian John Mbiti's *Traditional African Religions and Philosophies* describes aspects of a cultural worldview that shadows America:

> Most peoples . . . believe that the spirits are what remains of human beings when they die physically. This then becomes the ultimate status . . . the point of change or development beyond which [one] cannot go apart from a few national heroes who might become deified. . . . [Wo]Man does not, and need not, hope to become a spirit: [s]he is inevitably to become one, just as a child will automatically grow to become an adult.[38]

Rather than essentializing Africa, Mbiti's work describes the diversity of religions throughout the continent. But he maintains that various organizing principles prevail despite ethnic and societal differences. The cosmology he documents rejects socially constructed dichotomies and resonates within American culture through people of African descent.

Recognizing the political place of African American cultural views that manifest and mutate through time and space does not construct these views as quintessential or universal to everyone of African descent. Some reject while others pursue transcendent community in order to affirm African beliefs resonating throughout American culture as a form of political resistance to culture annihilation or assimilation.

Transcendent community is thought to extend through time and space, unbound by spatial or temporal limits; therefore, its "transcendence" includes the ancestors as well as the present collective and future unborn children. All comprise "community." The content and quality of communal relations is set by practice. (Consequently, a person's ability to consider community as encompassing those who do not live in the "free" world becomes in some ways a test of the limits of transcendence.) Here, relationships are determinant and shape the pursuit and construction of transcendent community. Here the collective supersedes individualism. Although articulated by individuals, knowledge and wisdom are acquired through a collective effort. When knowledge is "the experience of that deepest reality found between the spiritualized ancestors and the physically living thinkers," it can develop only in relationship, in transcendent community.

The conventional dismissal of these values and their contextual frameworks is traceable to European colonization on several continents. Historically European racial mythology mandated that physiology and ancestry designated whether a people could create theory and philosophy or merely ape superstition. The current dismissal of "discredited knowledge" stems from the historical disparagement of the African origins of these views. Fu-Kiau notes that European invasions of Africa were justified as necessary interventions "to civilize" African peoples; for Fu-Kiau, the consequence of this "civilization" is that "African people are still known as people without logic, people without systems, people without concepts. . . ."[39] In racialized societies, people whose traditional culture is "known" to be illogical, without complex belief systems, are generally suspect as contributors to intellectual life. Spoken and unspoken debates about epistemic "subcultures" meander amid a broad ideological spectrum. A by-product of these debates is that they mask commonalties of nonmainstream, noncommercial cultures.

Beliefs in the spiritual as inseparable from the mundane or secular, as nature as essential to humanity, the feminine and masculine as complementary, are not compatible with unidimensional foci. Nor are these beliefs exclusively "African." Native American worldviews share the concept of community extending through time. In the indigenous view of "seven generations," actions are guided by concerns for future generations.[40] Lee Maracle's *Oratory: Coming to Theory* points to a Native American cosmology where theory and philosophy function as a "place of prayer, to persuade." Maracle writes:

> We regard words as coming from original being—a sacred spiritual being. The orator is coming from a place of prayer and as such attempts to be persuasive. Words are not objects to be wasted. They represent the accumulated knowledge, cultural values, the vision of an entire people or peoples. We believe the proof of a thing or idea is in the doing. Doing requires some form of social interaction and thus, story is the most persuasive and sensible way to present the accumulated thoughts and values of a people.[41]

Here the Native American "orator" functions in a manner similar to the African American "living thinker."

Living thinkers mirror worldviews that present service and community as indispensable; knowledge and responsibility as intergenerational; and community as a changing and thorny tie. Such views offer nonconventional wisdom. In black feminist politics, progressive African American women have embraced this wisdom that has been discredited by conventional knowledge. For instance, Nobel laureate Toni Morrison offers a sketch of one form of community shadowing American society that illustrates this cultural embrace.[42] As the bard of black communal life that is shared by females and males (and the dead and the living), Morrison's cultural commitments obscure her status as a "feminist" for conventional thinkers yet reveal the worlds of black women seeking or fleeing community.[43] In "Rootedness: The Ancestor as Foundation," Morrison writes:

> There must have been a time when an artist could be genuinely representative of the tribe and in it; when an artist could have a tribal or racial sensibility and an individual expression of it. There were spaces and places in which a single person could enter and behave as an individual within the context of the community. A small remnant of that you can see sometimes in Black churches where people shout.

It is a very personal grief and a personal statement done among people you trust. Done within the context of the community, therefore safe. And while the shouter is performing some rite that is extremely subjective, the other people are performing as a community in protecting that person.[44]

CONCLUSION

For some, the greatest spiritual development is tied to service to the community; through such service a person eventually evolves to become an elder and later an ancestor, always with an eye to communal responsibilities. The global immiseration of the poor, "blacks," and females and children has pushed even the privileged toward an activism that seeks the legacy of past leaders.[45] Communal needs often are contextualized within crises: Worldwide, women and children of African descent are disproportionately represented among victims of violence, the incarcerated, the malnourished, illiterate, ill, and dying.

Pragmatism and "unorthodox" spirituality reflect the needs (and demands) for vision, language, and action that further survival and freedom. Transcendent community remains more often the ideal than the reality. In segregated states and societies, black women are subordinate Others. They exist as outsiders within not only American culture but also diasporic Africana or African American cultures. Desires to control or minimize this outsider status promote censorship and marginalization of the "outsider's outsiders"—the incarcerated or those who exist outside of the "free" world. To this population may be added other overlapping groups: prostitutes, lesbians/gays, bi- and transsexuals, the poor, immigrants, the disabled, and political radicals or revolutionaries. Existing in both the free world and its negation, they remain suspect. Not all are welcomed as peers in the transcendent community embattled by and located within the larger segregated state that resists the "Beloved Community" of Martin Luther King Jr. Yet historical or ancestral models for forging this community continue to challenge restricted notions of communal democracy.

THREE

Protofeminists and Liberation Limbos

The fact that the adult American Negro female
emerges a formidable character is often met with
amazement, distaste and even belligerence. It is
seldom accepted as an inevitable outcome of the
struggle won by survivors. . . .

—Maya Angelou

Limbos entail vulnerable backbreaking postures as well as isolated states.
Rarely ladylike, limbos repudiate the gentleness of the cult of "true"
womanhood, a bourgeois construct for civility that can weigh heavily on
the outspoken and independent to censor black female militancy. Those
who advocate civility as a precondition for transcending antiblack female
stereotypes can depict the combativeness of rebels in "rude" opposition to
racism, homophobia and sexism, corporate capitalism, and environmental
pollution as a personal failing in deportment. In limbos, shadow boxers,
particularly historical women or "protofeminists," who preshadowed contemporary black feminist radicalism, provided models and strategies for
resistance that rejected strict black female adherence to middle-class norms.

Limbo has multiple meanings. In its primary usage, fraught with negativity, it refers to Christian constructs of a site neighboring hell, prison, oblivion and neglect, or suspension between two states. In its secondary usage, marked by play, struggle and pleasure, limbo refers to the black/Caribbean performance where dancers lean backward, with knees bent to pass below a bar that blocks their path. It represents determined progression despite the vulnerability of the position. Growing up in the southern United States and the Caribbean, generations of black children danced under broom handles that were successively lowered with each procession, singing "Do the limbo, limbo rock—all away around the clock;" only the very flexible and very audacious improvisers advanced more than several rounds. As dances that choreograph social change, political limbos occur among—and cast their own unique—shadows.

Black feminist conservative, liberal, or radical ideologies revolve around the varied meanings of limbo, as African American women evoke and evade its respectively positive and negative implications. They evoke the ability to move forward in emancipation projects, while they evade the relegation of black female concerns to marginal sites where issues of racial-sexual and economic oppression are distanced from the centers of social and political debate. Like unbaptized children and the "pre-Christian righteous," black feminisms often have been relegated to an outer realm where, while not exactly punished for their sins, they are ghettoized for an alleged poor timing and inability to reflect larger philosophical metaparadigms.

Similar to the feminisms of other women of racially oppressed or marginalized peoples, the feminisms of black women routinely extract females from the gray areas of political isolation. Through reflections and interventions, they interpret and dissect, describe and agitate within American society. African American feminisms display an agility and imaginative power in both building paradigms and trashing them.

A fluid flexibility allows such feminisms to bend lower and lower and with limber steps dance past a descending bar of political and intellectual dismissals. The evocative agency of their liberation limbos asserts the centrality of racial-sexual struggles and analyses often passed over in mainstream discourse. Yet in the wake of feminist antiblack racism and black antifeminism, black feminisms appear to progress only with great effort.

In their attempts to synthesize emancipation theories, various black feminisms improvise integrative analyses of race, gender, sexuality, and class that focus on commonalties in liberation struggles. The utility of black feminisms in progressive movements is largely determined by their capacity to illustrate and analyze the intersections and multidimensionality of oppression and freedom. They forgo one-dimensional liberation theories that focus on patriarchy *or* white supremacy, or transnational capitalism *or* homophobia, as isolated phenomena. Liberation workers contextualize the meanings of progress and resistance by understanding space and time in ways that reflect the intersecting realities of black women's lives.

For instance, linear arguments about oppression suggest that people prioritize, countering first classism, then perhaps racism, and, next, possibly sexism and heterosexism. Even if people reorder this sequence to rerank struggles, linearity continues as reasoning malfunctions. Every American is born into multiple experiences and struggles shaped by social caste and state policies infused with ethnocentrism or racism, classism, and (hetero)sexism. Verbal abstractions concerning linear struggles can and do prioritize "primary" over "secondary" oppressions, despite the fact that oppression is multivaried and integrated.

One of black feminism's most important contributions, then, is that it highlights the limitations of such thinking while exploring the intersections of oppression and freedom. Proceeding past lowering booms—anti–civil rights initiatives, rising sexual violence and incarceration, resurgent poverty, and elite intellectual discourses alienated from concrete struggles for survival and freedom—historically black women have formulated and formed black feminisms in national and international liberation movements. In the process, they have created a radical black feminist politics.

Limbos are ideal spaces for witnessing and generating movements to address the inadequacies of linear liberation theories that offer little resistance to the complexity of dominance that manifests over time in multiple, intersecting layers and sites. In the limbos of social movements, the past, present, and future coexist and overlap. Time is nonlinear. Space and community are expansive. In their progressive, forward movement, contemporary black feminisms often bend backward toward historical protofeminist ancestors like abolitionist Maria W. Stewart, Ida B. Wells, and Ella Baker. In so doing, these feminisms routinely retrieve from the sidelines of conventional political memory important ancestral leaders for current considerations and political struggles.

Political amnesia, the gray area surrounding political agency, partly stems from the erasure of historical figures—particularly those female ancestors who militantly fought as racial and gender outsiders for democracy, only to be marginalized later from "respectable" political community. One early black female activist caught in limbo between "respectable" white and black worlds was Maria Stewart (1803-1869). A peer of the military strategist Harriet Tubman (c1823-1913), Stewart, like her abolitionist friend David Walker, advocated the right of black self-defense or armed struggle against enslavement.

The first U.S. woman to lecture publicly on political issues and the first published African American female political writer, Stewart was a protofeminist who called for women of African descent to develop their highest intellectual abilities. Born a free African in Boston, widowed at an early age, childless, and impoverished by white swindlers, Stewart wrote for and eventually became copublisher of *The Liberator,* an abolitionist paper established by Walker. Deeply affected by Walker's assassination, presumably by pro-slavers, Stewart became noted for antislavery activism. Forged in a radical religiosity, her increasing militancy incensed white racists. It also alarmed and alienated Boston's conservative free blacks. Claiming religious authority through conversations with God, Stewart maintained that divine revelations shaped her speeches and writings as well as grounded her hope in African liberation. These assertions estranged her from the Paulist scriptures of the male-dominated church, which advocated the subservience of women and their ouster from ministry.

Assuming that the martyrdom which claimed Walker awaited her, Stewart wrote: "Many will suffer for pleading the cause of oppressed Africa, and I shall glory in being one of her martyrs. . . . [God] is able to take me to himself, as he did the most noble, fearless, and undaunted David Walker."[1] Yet unlike Walker, Stewart was not murdered. There are other forms of martyrdom.

Stewart's militant public life was cut short by African American elites. She suffered continuous criticism and censorship from Boston's African community, which determined that she offended the "proper lifestyle" of a woman of her caste by assuming public leadership. Pro-slavery voices cursed her incendiary abolitionism. Boston's blacks silenced her for violating bourgeois sensibilities. In "Farewell Address to Her Friends in the City of Boston, Delivered September 21, 1833," she castigates her own: "I find it is no use for me as an individual to try to make myself useful among my color in this city . . . my respected friends, let us no longer talk of prejudice, till prejudice becomes extinct at home. Let us no longer talk of opposition, till we cease to oppose our own."[2]

The Farewell Address was Stewart's last public speech until the close of the Civil War. Throughout the war, she worked as matron of the Freemen's Hospital in Washington, D. C., and coordinated refugee camps for African Americans. Her archetypal black female militancy would be reborn in successive generations. During the war in which Stewart served with distinction, Ida B. Wells was born into slavery. In the postwar, post-Reconstruction decades that followed, black women risked martyrdom to become leading strategists in a protracted struggle against racial terror and disenfranchisement. By the end of the century, female antilynching crusaders shaped an archetype of black female militancy that would in turn foster black feminist politics.

ANTIVIOLENCE MOVEMENTS: IDA B. WELLS

To justify their own barbarism they assume a
chivalry which they do not possess. True chivalry
respects all womanhood. . . .

—Ida B. Wells

The Memphis Diary of Ida B. Wells, edited by Miriam Decosta-Willis, reveals the private concerns of antilynching crusader Ida B. Wells (1862-1931).[3] Detailing Wells's life from age twenty-four to sixty-eight, the diaries recount the mundane distractions and preoccupations of a young, unmarried woman and, later, wife, mother, and matron. Scholar Mary

Helen Washington writes in her foreword to *The Memphis Diary:* "Every woman who has ever kept a diary knows that women write in diaries because things are not going right." According to Washington, Wells recorded intimate details of her life as "a way of clarifying and affirming her own growth" and to express her feelings about being "stuck in an unfulfilling job, struggling to make ends meet as she tries to keep up with the Black bourgeoisie in Memphis, and desperately trying to find a satisfying romantic relationship with a man."[4] These concerns may sound depressingly or humorously familiar to those who can trace their postmodern frustrations to the postbellum age.

The vulnerability expressed in *The Memphis Diary*—which Wells never intended for publication—proves to be its most striking feature because of the strong contrast it offers to the public figure of Wells as the courageous and militant "race woman" of the turn-of-the century antilynching crusades. With pistol at hand, she fearlessly castigated a society that upheld white supremacy through violence while masking white racist terror as sexual protection. The private life revealed in the diary, unlike the public life documented in her memoir *Crusade for Justice,* presents an insecure young woman who grows into a maturity as a fighter who, despite her strength, seems to be weighed down by domestic concerns and the lack of resources and public recognition that she rightly believed her due.

As a militant, Wells coupled speech with a courageous insurgency that became noteworthy for her refusal or inability to compromise. Curiously, a few contemporary feminists have depicted her as reluctant to speak about, or "indifferent" to, sexual violence against white women. Such feminists have alleged that she blamed white rape victims for the lynchings of their black assailants. These reductionist and conservative portraits of Wells's iconoclasm inaccurately reflect both her sexual politics and the historical record.[5]

Credible historical accounts depict Wells as a radical antiracist motivated by a public hostility toward lynchings rather than personal animosity toward white women. Contempt for sexual violence in their lives likely would have alienated her influential white women supporters. Wells never categorically denied that black men assaulted white women. The body of her writings and research, in which the word "many" is generally used to describe false accusations of rape, makes no assertion of universal black innocence. Her position is best revealed in a letter by Boston's Women's Era Club leader Florida Ruffin Ridley, which is reprinted in her memoir:

> All that we ask for is justice—not mercy or palliation—simply justice. Surely that is not too much for loyal citizens of a free country to demand. . . .We do not pretend to say there are no black villains. Baseness is not confined to race. We read with horror of two different colored girls who recently have been horribly assaulted by white men in the South. We should regret any lynchings of the offenders by black men but we shall not have occasion. Should these offenders receive any punishment at all, it will be a marvel.[6]

Similarly, Wells adhered to women's club leader Mary Church Terrell's 1904 rebuttal to an article in the *North American Review* that justified lynching by depicting black males as sexual predators of white females. Church Terrell decried the belief that African Americans were insensitive to rape, writing: "[I]t is a great mistake to suppose that rape is the real cause of lynching in the South. Beginning with the Ku Klux Klan the negro has been constantly subjected to some form of organized violence ever since he became free. . . . out of every 100 negroes who are lynched, from 75-85 are not even accused of this crime, and many who are accused of it are innocent. . . ."[7] The antilynching campaigns, as battles against racial-sexual terror, provided the model for twentieth-century militant antiracist feminism.

Although whites had been the majority of the lynching victims in the antebellum years, after the Civil War whites were rarely lynched. Rather, lynchings became a barbaric form of collective punishment meted out against black communities to ensure white dominance. Ritualized murders of black Americans were rationalized by the mythology of black rapists obsessed with white females. Sexual realities became convoluted by sexual politics, which inverted the interracial sexual violence of the era. The sexual politicians of lynching grossly exaggerated the likelihood of black male assaults on white females while ignoring the widespread prevalence of white male sexual assaults against black females.

By draping lynching in the cloak of antisexual violence rhetoric, and thus by legitimizing (and therefore, logically, increasing) violence against them, the lives of millions of black females were destabilized. Feeding on the racist stereotypes of black bestiality, lynch mythology masked sexual violence against black females and justified racial violence against blacks.

Nineteenth-century African Americans recognized that lynchings were part of a terrorist campaign in an undeclared racial war to destroy the newly won independence of free black communities. Racialized, antiblack atrocities became routine rituals as whites sought to remove African Americans from economic and political power. After the aborted Reconstruction, through legislation and extra legal violence as well as the rise of the convict prison lease system, most southern blacks were forced into economic subservience and dependency.[8]

Analyzing the "political economy of racism," historian Jack Bloom describes how white supremacy found its most violent expression in the Ku Klux Klan, which had widespread support among whites:

> All classes in the South appear to have been involved in [the Ku Klux Klan] and to have used it for different purposes. In the predominantly white counties, which were usually located in the hills away from the fertile plantation areas, the Klan was used to drive blacks out so as to eliminate them as competitors with white laborers. In the black belt, the upper classes sometimes opposed the Klan because its violence was disruptive to labor and investment alike. Nonetheless, the upper class used the Klan to control black labor, even to the detriment of white labor. Blacks who tried to leave the area were threatened with murder, and some of them were killed. When they did leave, they were sometimes pursued and dragged back, even across state lines.[9]

At the turn of the century, within the climate of a low-intensity race war, black women led the antilynching campaigns as an antiviolence, antiracist feminist movement. They highlighted the racial inversion of sexual violence as propaganda to justify white supremacy and obscure sexual assaults. Waging the campaigns as resistance to both racial and sexual violence, antilynching crusaders such as Wells, Ruffin Ridley, and Church Terrell established a political language to critique U.S. racial-sexual politics and challenge the "moralism" of the white-dominated press, courts, and police.

Skeptical that media, court, or mob prosecution was motivated by the desire to end sexual violence, these women conducted and publicized investigative reporting to ascertain facts distorted or denied by mainstream institutions. Their demands for justice challenged the U.S. "red record," in Wells's words, of African Americans disproportionately sentenced, brutalized, imprisoned, and murdered at the whim of whites; the low visibility of sexual assaults against black women; and pervasive social and government indifference to sexual and racial violence.

Denouncing the lynchings of African Americans for alleged and real crimes against property and whites (which included social "crimes" such as talking back), the crusader Wells argued that the charge of rape, used in only a fraction of lynchings, became the general rationalization for racist violence in that era. With this accusation, even those who considered themselves above the mob mentality acquiesced to lynchings as a preventive measure to ensure the safety of white females. At the same time, these apologists turned a blind eye to the more prevalent problem of white male sexual violence against women, particularly black women.

To demystify the belief that white men enforced written or unwritten laws for the protection of white females, Wells engaged in a radical critique of lynching apologias, exploring their basis in psychosexual mythology. She proved relentless in her critique of the sexual politics of lynching. Her demystification of "rape," controversial a century ago and remaining so today, was the cornerstone of moral and political resistance to racist violence justified as the vindication or prevention of *sexual* violence.

In her memoir she recalls her initial belief in European American assertions that lynching was to protect white women's virtue and restrain the "sexual savagery" of African American men. The 1892 Memphis lynchings of three friends and associates—Thomas Moss, Calvin McDowell, and Will Stewart for competing with white businesses by opening the People's Grocery Company—taught her otherwise.[10] According to Wells, that was the year of the greatest number of reported lynchings, most of which were committed in Tennessee, Alabama, Arkansas, Georgia, and Mississippi[11]: Of the 241 murdered, 160 were African American, including 5 women or girls.[12]

As an editor and co-owner of Memphis's African American paper, the *Free Speech,* Wells began, through her writings, to promote militant critiques and confrontations. In May 1892, after more lynchings followed the deaths of her friends, Wells wrote an editorial ridiculing the charge of "rape" as justification for racist killings. Her editorial reads in part: "Eight Negroes lynched since last issue of the *Free Speech.* Three were charged with killing white men and five with raping white women. Nobody in this section believes the old thread-bare lie that Negro men assault white women. If Southern white men are not careful they will over-reach themselves and a conclusion will be reached which will be very damaging to the moral reputation of their women."[13] In response, the city's white citizens burned the paper's offices and threatened to lynch the writer. The bounty they placed on Wells's head exiled her from the South for decades. Yet that year African American women convened in Brooklyn, the largest gathering of club women during that era, for a testimonial for Wells and raised $500 to publish an antilynching pamphlet, *Southern Horrors,* and to finance her first antilynching speaking tour.

Wells publicly exposed the fact that voluntary sexual relationships between European American females and African American males were defined by whites as "sexual assaults" in order that consensual relations could be reconstructed as rape.

> With the Southern white man, any mesalliance existing between a white woman and a colored man is a sufficient foundation for the charge of rape. The Southern white man says that it is impossible for a voluntary alliance to exist between a white woman and a colored man, and therefore, the fact of an alliance is a proof of force. In numerous instances where colored men have been lynched on the charge of rape, it was positively known at the time of lynching, and indisputably proven after the victim's death, that the relationship sustained between the man and woman was voluntary and clandestine, and that in no court of law could even the charge of assault have been successfully maintained.[14]

Such voluntary interracial associations were punishable by the death of the African American male involved. Although there were instances of white females being ostracized, institutionalized, and beaten for engaging in such alliances, a repudiation of the relationship through the rape accusation brought absolution. African American males had no such escape clause. Consequently, Wells asserted that these liaisons were often "voluntary" only on the part of the white females involved.

African American antilynching activists rejected the dominant culture's distortions concerning sex and violence. Although they had no control over how white males treated white females, black women organized, through the Negro Women's Club Movement, against their own sexual exploitation and against assault by men both white and black. These activist-writers did not separate the issues of gender and sexual violence from race politics. For decades women such as Wells urged American white women to respond to the political use of the rape charge in lynchings. Black women recognized the connections between resistance to sexual violence and resistance to racial violence: Neither for white nor especially for black women was there prosecution of sexual assault under the lynch law, where prosecution of actual sexual violence was irrelevant. Resisting racial violence and protesting white supremacist terror and sexual violence against African American women, children, and men, women in the antilynching campaigns could not realistically separate instances of racist and sexual violence, for race was "sexualized" and sex was "racialized." The dual realities of the assaults against African Americans did not permit prioritizing "race" before "sex." Consequently, black women built institutions and women's organizations that confronted sexual violence at the same time that they challenged the lynch law.

Wells methodically critiqued the white press and conducted painstaking research and investigative reporting to verify the accuracy of white newspaper articles and editorials vilifying African Americans.[15] Doing so was particularly important since the white press gave the imprimatur for society's racism. Expressing courageous commitments in political writing, Wells's exhortations in her *Free Speech* editorials led thousands of African Americans to leave Memphis for the western territories in a mass migration that caused a serious financial loss for the city's white merchants. Her editorials also inspired hundreds of African Americans to boycott the electric trolley. The efficacy of her political writing is evident in the success of the boycott and the intense hatred many whites felt toward this young black woman. She had a keen organizational sense and understood the political economy of racism.

In 1893 and 1894, when there was no response from national religious, civic or women's groups, or even the government, to counter lynching, Wells took the campaign and the story of the political economy of racism to England in speaking tours. Meeting there with prominent leaders, she worked with women's groups to help launch the first antilynching organization in the world, the London Antilynching Committee. Due to financial pressure from the English—England imported and processed southern cotton—lynchings were halted in Memphis for several decades. By coupling economic boycotts with black institution-building, Wells played a critical role in developing a number of significant political African American institutions, such as the Club Movement, the National Association for the Advancement of Colored People (NAACP), and the Afro-American press.

Although economic competition was a major factor in white violence and lynchings, Wells also noted emotional or psychological motivations: "The more I studied the situation, the more I was convinced that the Southerner had never gotten over his resentment that the Negro was no longer his plaything, his servant, and his source of income."[16] Contemporary Church Terrell was blunter: "Lynching is the aftermath of slavery. The white men who shoot negroes to death and flay them alive, and the white women who apply flaming torches to their oil-soaked bodies today, are the sons and daughters of women who had but little, if any, compassion on the race when it was enslaved."[17]

Wells's ability to depict the society that condoned lynchings was an essential aspect of her public speaking and writings. She focused on the duplicity of the legal system in lynching and sexual violence, its double standards, and the cultural taboo surrounding interracial sex.[18] Her analysis of the politics of lynching appears in her news dispatches, where she identifies three supporting pillars: The

> machinery of law and politics is in the hands of those who commit the lynching . . . it is only wealthy white men whom the law fails to reach . . . hundreds of Negroes including women and children are lynched for trivial offenses on suspicion and in many cases when known to be

guiltless of any crime . . . the law refused to punish the murderers because it is not considered a crime to kill a Negro. . . . Many of the cases of "Assault" are simply adulteries between white women and colored men.[19]

One of the first to publicly criticize state complicity in racial repression, Wells's critique led her to indict white American's "law and order" rationalizations for lynchings.[20] The first rationalization was that lynching existed to suppress African American–led "race riots," which, as Wells observes, never materialized. The second reason for white terrorism was that it prevented "Negro domination" of whites through the vote; however, by the late 1800s, African Americans had already been so persecuted as to effectively prevent their serious participation in most elections.[21]

When this second reason became acknowledged as specious, a third rationalization for the unrelenting white mob violence and an acquiescent state emerged, according to Wells:

> Brutality still continued; Negroes were whipped, scourged, exiled, shot and hung whenever and wherever it pleased the white man so to treat them, and as the civilized world with increasing persistency held the white people of the South to account for its outlawry, the murderers invented the third excuse—that Negroes had to be killed to avenge their assaults upon women. There could be framed no possible excuse more harmful to the Negro and more unanswerable if true in its sufficiency for the white man.[22]

Wells's image on a 1990s U.S. postage stamp for Black History Month belies her confrontation with the state. She refers to but never fully addresses the state's complicity in lynching in *Mob Rule in New Orleans*. The government's failure to prosecute lynchers partly explains why some lynch mobs consisted of up to 10,000 whites. Although she carried a pistol, Wells never fully analyzed the "criminalization" of African American self-defense, particularly in response to police brutality and killings. Aware of the role of the police and probably the presiding district judge in the 1892 Memphis lynchings, she never explicitly outlined the state's role in appropriating the function of the lynch mob. Historical dilemmas continue to confront African Americans today: sentence disparities, "legal lynchings" through racialized sentencing, the racist application of the death penalty, guard killings of black prisoners.[23] Despite evident abuses, Wells appealed to the state, and remained largely silent about the possibility of African American resistance strategies to the government.[24]

The antilynching crusades were an early form of radical black feminism, and the crusaders' legacies and impact are felt today. Author Joanne Braxton writes that while reading autobiographies of women such as Ida B. Wells she first met the "outraged mother" or ancestor mothers "in search of a tradition to claim them."[25] According to Braxton, a balance between the "confessional narrative and the historical memoir" allows Wells to relate both her public and private "duties" and contributions and "to demonstrate her development as a political activist and as an outraged mother." For Braxton, Wells's memoir "looks forward to the modern political autobiographies of Anne Moody, Shirley Chisholm, and Angela Davis. It represents an important link between the old and the new, part of the lost ground of Afro-American literary tradition."[26]

In spite of her remarkable achievements, Ida B. Wells had discernible flaws. She seems to have promoted self-serving mythology in her memoir when she writes, without fully crediting him for his influence on her development, that Frederick Douglass believed in African American men's proclivity toward rape; there is no known record of this as Douglass's position.[27] Also, at times Wells's single-minded pursuit of justice limited her compassion for those caught in the political fray. For example, early in her career, when her *Free Speech* editorials exposed the sexual relationships of incompetent black women teachers with corrupt white male school board members, Wells showed little pity for the woman who committed suicide when her "mesalliance" was publicized. The white school board, angered at the exposure of its corruption, fired Wells, who subsequently became a journalist.

An organizer of the Alpha Suffrage Club, Illinois's first African American Women's Suffrage Club, Wells merged gender, sexuality, and race. She also forged a link between racial and sexual violence useful to black males as well as antiracist whites and organizations such as the

NAACP and the white Association of Southern Women for the Prevention of Lynching, which formed after the height of lynching and remained marginalized among white feminists. Organizing against lynching created a unique form of feminism shaped by race, sex, gender, and class as Wells merged two activist and powerful influences, black feminism and black nationalism. For Braxton:

> The result of this fusion was the development of a race-centered, self-conscious womanhood in the form of the black women's club movement. Whereas the white woman's movement reflected her commitment to temperance and suffrage, the black woman's movement was born in the outrage of the slave mother and the struggle against lynching. Racial oppression, not sexism, was the primary issue. For an Ida B. Wells or a Frances E. W. Harper, a blow at lynching was a blow at racism and the brutally enforced sexual double standard that pervaded the South. It was a defense of the entire race."[28]

Black women, as iconoclast feminists organizing against racist violence, invariably worked for "the defense of the entire race." It does not necessarily follow that their politics served only male interests.

Varied responses to Ida B. Wells and the antilynching crusaders are found today. As noted earlier, although in previous centuries interracial rape against African American females was common (the vast majority of sexual violence against females stemmed from white males), today, the greatest number of assaults against black females are by black males. In the United States, where nine out of ten reported sexual assaults occur within the same ethnic group according to FBI statistics—the 1983 Cambridge Documentary Film *Rape Culture* places the figures in reported interracial rapes at 8 percent for white male assaults of black females and 5 percent for black male sexual assaults against white females—the most "heinous" and sensationalized assaults are the less than 10 percent that are interracial. For many African Americans, the assault of black females by white males remains the most horrific manifestation of sexual violence, just as whites had mandated (and continue to perceive) black assaults of white females to be the most heinous form of sexual abuse.

Given racism's long history in the United States, a suspicion of state authority, particularly in interracial rape cases, is common place in African American communities. Ida B. Wells wrote in *A Red Record*: "Think and act on independent lines . . . remembering that after all, it is the white man's civilization and the white man's government which are on trial. . . ."[29] Yet a singular focus on white malfeasance and sexual policing of blacks may obscure black sexual policing of black females. Logically, if a white female falsely accused a black male of rape in order to shield a white male (or herself) from retribution, a black female might choose or be coerced into the same strategy. In the perverse inversion of racial progress, blacks can now, without corroborating evidence, accuse whites of rape without the threat of death by lynching.

In contemporary organizing around interracial rape cases in which black females are victimized, black males who see themselves as the "natural" protectors of black females can appropriate the words of female antilynching crusaders. In patriarchal race crusades, male dominance of the discourse belies the protofeminist fiery oratory and fierce analyses of women such as Mary Church Terrell and Wells in their opposition to racial and sexual violence.[30] Some antiracists invoke Wells's militancy without her feminism in order to put the "white man's government" on trial. The judicial and social indifference to antiblack violence, police malfeasance and racialized violence marauding as "protection" for the "law-abiding," or for whites, encourage acquiescence to this form of counter-feminism as well as to black female dependency on black males for "protection." As contemporary black rhetorical vigilantes stake a "protective" claim on the black female body, establishing their proprietorship, they displace black female agency and silence forms of feminist resistance.

In recent memory, the most controversial example of such a claim has been the 1987 Tawana Brawley case, where in November of that year a black teenager alleged that she had been abducted and gang-raped by a group of white men that included state officials. In the Brawley case, her advocates Al Sharpton, Alton Maddox, and Vernon Mason deployed Ida B. Wells's dissection of American racial-sexual politics, using historical narratives to mobilize contemporary black public outrage against white men by portraying Brawley as the personification of black female prey hunted by white male predators.[31] Their prosecutorial performances turned a family tale of private pain and assault into a public spectacle of racial rage. In the process, black females, as exploitable and expendable, became mere backdrops to unfolding racial dramas, produced and directed by men. Three years after and thousands of miles apart from the Brawley incident, the issue of protection was raised again by black women in Oxford, Ohio.[32]

In 1990, the Ku Klux Klan, based in its national headquarters in Indiana, decided to stage a march and rally in the local campus town of Oxford. The general negative responses to the Klan's march centered on individual expressions of intimidation and anger. Little collective, organized response existed until one night when, as part of a women's film festival, a small number of students viewed William Greaves's documentary, *Ida B. Wells: A Passion for Justice*. During the discussion session that followed the video screening, an African American woman senior moderated as students shared their impressions of Wells's courage and influential activism, which began at such a young age—their own age. Later in their dorm rooms, women continued exploring their inspiration for the story of Wells's resistance in juxtaposition with their feelings of anger and fear about the upcoming Klan march. Discussions turned into strategy sessions. Within a day, young women decided to allow their admiration for Wells to lead them to organize a countereducational critique on the racism, homophobia, sexism, and anti-Semitism that was visibly increasing on campus prior to the Klan's display of power.

Leading the organizing, African American female students formed a coalition with whites, Jews, gays, and lesbians. Some of the young black women leaders at that time experienced the most violent racial-sexual assaults on the campus during their student years. At an early organizing meeting, one senior spoke of being dragged off a catwalk into bushes as her white male assailant yelled "nigger bitch" while punching her repeatedly. As she struggled away, she noticed white student spectators who made no effort to assist or intervene. Later she found the university's investigation and handling of the attack to be equally unresponsive. Unlike the model of militancy embodied by Wells, and the emergent antiracist feminism of the youths, faculty criticisms and complaints about white-dominated universities did not translate into support for the student-initiated organizing. Only a few faculty or administrators (two white female and one black female professors) publicly supported a student "speak-out" (an open-mike educational gathering, not a demonstration or rally) against racist, sexist, and homophobic violence prevalent at the university. University employees mirrored the divisions among African American students; more cautious or conservative ones dismissed student organizers as "radical" and ridiculed them for "overreacting." Rather than pull blacks together, if only in a temporary formation, the KKK march exacerbated divisions among students, faculty, and administrators.

Loyalty to the university, along with homophobia, sexism, and caste elitism, as well as fear of confrontation, allowed faculty and more conservative African American students to distance themselves from black female student activists and others who organized to counter the Klan. Faculty and administrators likely viewed their class and caste status as granting immunity from the most extreme forms of violence.[33] Youths face the greatest dangers from racial-sexual violence. Racist/anti-Semitic verbal abuse and physical violence increased on campus prior to the Klan demonstration. At the same time that most black and white faculty refused to actively support student organizing, the university administration refused to publicly and aggressively denounce and prosecute hate speech and hate crimes on campus.

The Klan marched in the university town on its designated weekend, undisrupted by the nonviolent black or multiethnic protesters who modeled the civil rights movement. However, white antiracist skinheads (a minority among skinheads), largely nonstudents and nonuniversity employees, carpooled or took buses in from Cincinnati and derailed the march, tossing Molotov cocktails at the Klan demonstrators, which forced local police to cancel the event. The following Sunday, a multiracial alliance of students held a speak-out against hatred in the campus chapel with a full-capacity gathering and an open mike, denouncing anti-Semitic, racist, and heterosexist bias and violence.

An iconoclast eventually marginalized by most of white America and the black middle class for her militancy, Wells conceivably could have recognized in such disparate responses by the youths (for some, she stood as icon) the mirrored images of her own politics. Her legacy—which included educational interventions, political writings, and unwavering advocacy for black self-defense against violent racist attacks—is met with ambivalence by contemporary Americans. For most Americans, Ida B. Wells resides in the shadows of political memory, but her legacy manifests itself in the contemporary activism of antiracists. It also resonates within the struggles of women and men in the civil rights movement of the 1930s through the 1960s. Within the praxis of Ella Baker, we see that under prolonged conditions of stress and struggle, Ida B. Wells's radical iconoclasm has become normative.

ON AND OFF
THE AUCTION BLOCK: ELLA BAKER[34]

> [W]herever there has been a struggle, black
> women have been identified with that struggle.
> —Ella Baker

Ella Josephine Baker (1903-1986) was field organizer for the National Association for the Advancement of Colored People (NAACP) in the 1930s and 1940s. In the 1950s she became the first de facto director of the Southern Christian Leadership Conference (SCLC). She convened the 1960 student conference at her alma mater, South Carolina's Shaw University, that led to the formation of the Student Nonviolent Coordinating Committee (SNCC) and later served as a key SNCC advisor. A brilliant strategist in the civil rights movements, she is usually remembered through her contributions to SCLC and especially SNCC, the radical young people's organization that ended in 1968. Yet Baker also organized for the Free Angela Y. Davis campaigns during 1971 and 1972 and the Puerto Rican Independence Movement.

Decades before Baker helped to develop progressive organizations, her labor activism made "work" central to critiques of racism, classism, and sexism and emphasized struggles against racism and sexism as key to dismantling economic oppression. Merging activism with rhetoric about black liberation, she was both political worker and intellectual, and therefore also embodied the form of "black women's work" expressed as political activism. Baker's iconoclasm stems from the fact that she became a key leader in an antiracist movement represented in American culture as driven by male charismatic figures.

Baker addressed the issue of women's rights only infrequently and only within the context of black freedom struggles. This is characteristic of her protofeminism. More men and women are becoming aware of her contributions, despite the conservative and liberal bias that privileges men, whites, and the affluent and has led some male civil rights leaders and historians to deemphasize the role of black women in this movement. For many, leadership and agency have been distorted as primarily the attributes of male political and intellectual elites. It is not surprising that the contributions of radicals—particularly black women such as Baker who spoke and organized against racism, capitalism, and imperialism—have gone largely unrecognized.

Joanne Grant's documentary, *Fundi,* and biography, *Ella Baker: Freedom Bound,* provide important historical information on Baker's political contributions to U.S. democracy.[35] Several years after Ida B. Wells's death, in 1935, civil-rights leader Ella Baker coauthored with Marvel Cooke a pioneering essay, "The Bronx Slave Markets," on the economic and sexual exploitation of black women domestics during the depression, which was published in *The Crisis,* the national publication of the NAACP, developed by its editor W. E. B. Du Bois into a major intellectual vehicle for civil rights.[36]

The article reveals Baker's antiracist feminist sensibilities and her emergence as a radical activist-intellectual highly critical of unfettered capitalism. These views later shaped her conflicts with the male petit bourgeois clergy of the Southern Christian Leadership Council headed by Martin Luther King, Jr., and the liberal elites of the civil rights establishment. Baker's political stance, shaped during the 1930s, proved to be an astute standard for black women's concerns and conflicts. In the ensuing generations, her political ideas about sex, gender, race, labor exploitation, and violence have had a profound impact on the youths of the civil rights movements and were discernible in the work of the young leaders of the 1960s.

With political instincts grounded in New York City organizing during the depression, Baker preferred to take her political directives from poor or working-class African Americans rather than civil rights elites, a preference that led some of the latter to marginalize her. Labor activism in Harlem planted her work in the political-economic conditions and collective leadership of black workers, youths, and women. With these roots, as a young black woman worker, Baker used her own caste position to deepen the relevance and efficacy of black liberation politics.

African American women labored in ways unlike the construct of the repressed bourgeois housewife popularized by Betty Friedan's *Feminist Mystique* in the late 1960s. For most of the postbellum nineteenth and twentieth century, "black women's work" generally meant field or domestic labor for whites in the South. In the North, it expanded to include factory work. For a more privileged minority of African American women, it also included teaching, which brought both status and a reprieve from dehumanizing physical labor. Still, African American women were harassed and fired from teaching positions due to their political activism.

This was the case for Ida B. Wells at the turn of the century and decades later, during the midcentury civil rights struggles, for Septima Clark and Jo Ann Robinson, and in the late 1960s for Angela Davis. A college graduate from Shaw University, Baker recognized the limitations imposed on antiracist educators by white-controlled school boards and rejected a teaching career. In 1927, joining hundreds of thousands of black women migrating in search of work and relief from Jim Crow, Baker left her home and a somewhat protected, privileged place in Littleton, South Carolina, for New York City. There she secured employment in the menial and racially/sexually exploited labor sector, considered traditional "black women's work."

Even though Baker married former Shaw University classmate T. J. Roberts in the early 1930s (she rarely referred to this brief marriage in her later life), she needed to find work. Most African American men were also segregated into low-paying subsistence wages in public "domestic work." By "1930 two types of workers symbolized the status of all black male wage earners in the urban North—the New York City apartment house janitor and the Pittsburgh steelworker who manned a blast furnace during the hottest months of the year."[37]

Racist and sexist hiring policies—the few African American businesses tended to hire men as clerical workers, with the bias that men were, and should be, the primary "breadwinners"—meant that for several years, Baker's first and only paying job was as a restaurant waitress. Rather than submit to exploitation, Baker began organizing with other African American workers for jobs and collective economic gains. In 1930, 5.5 percent of African American women were employed in industry compared to 27.1 percent of foreign-born and 19 percent of U.S.-born white women.[38] After later obtaining factory work and eventual employment as a journalist and paid political organizer, Baker gained a wide range of work and social experiences. These traditional and nontraditional jobs, along with organizing with Harlem trade unionists during the depression, deepened her understanding of economic exploitation in racism. At the height of the depression, national production decreased by half, thousands were left homeless due to bank foreclosures, and millions were left jobless without compensation. By 1933 an estimated 66 percent of Harlem's potential labor force was unemployed.[39] Two years later over 2 million African Americans nationwide were on relief.

Experienced labor organizers by 1935, Baker and Cooke's "The Bronx Slave Market" describes sexual and racial exploitation unique to black female domestic workers. To research their essay, Baker and Cooke posed as domestic workers seeking employment in the "slave marts," where whites hired black day laborers. During their research, they were sexually solicited by white males and almost arrested by an undercover white policeman who assumed their ethnicity designated them as sex workers. Institutional sexism, racism, and segregation rendered black female employment—even for college-educated black women—synonymous to menial labor, particularly as domestic servants for whites. Thus Baker and Cooke easily assumed their roles as servants. Although a few African American men stood on line, waiting to be chosen for day labor, the slave markets were overwhelmingly reserved for African American women.

The auction blocks were located at 167th Street and Jerome Avenue and at Simpson and Westchester avenues in the Bronx (now the South Bronx). According to Baker and Cooke, black women exercised the least control over their labor and bodies at the Simpson slave market, which was the most dehumanizing of the two auction sites. Workers negotiated paltry salaries with employer(s) who paid little or, after the work was completed, nothing to women with few political or legal rights. African American women domestics were treated as "disposable."

Yet, in the 1930s, the overwhelming number of African Americans were trapped in domestic work. The depression forced middle-class African American women who previously had earned factory wages, or whose husbands' or fathers' salaries had enabled them not to work outside of the home, back into domestic "slavery." (Later, the availability of factory jobs first to white and then to black women during World War II increased the African American exodus from domestic service.) With fifteen million Americans without jobs and savings, the depression intensified the economic conditions tying African Americans to domestic and food service.

According to Baker and Cooke, while the depression eviscerated the conditions of middle-class and working-class black women, it elevated the social status of working-class white women, as it increased their access to African American servants: "Paradoxically, the crash of 1929 brought to the domestic labor market a new employer class. The lower middle-class housewife, who, having dreamed of the luxury of a maid, found opportunity staring her in the face in the form of Negro women pressed to the wall by poverty, starvation and discrimination. . . ."[40] Baker and Cooke describe white, working-class women employers who set their household clocks back an hour or two to cheat black female domestics of their wages. Ironically, even the wives of union activists engaged in these practices.

Subsistence levels of relief forced women into the slave markets. By providing a meager "safety net," relief allowed workers to negotiate for better wages: "As inadequate as emergency relief has been, it has proved somewhat of a boon to many of these women, for with its advent, actual starvation is no longer their ever-present slave driver and they have been able to demand twenty-five and even thirty cents an hour as against the old fifteen and twenty cent rate."[41] Yet the government neither regulated for decent wages to enable worker independence from relief nor provided adequate assistance to free workers from the need to "sell" themselves. Government emergency relief was riddled with inequities: Franklin Delano Roosevelt's policies excluded blacks from most of the Department of Labor's Federal Emergency Relief Administration assistance (for example, the Wagner-Lewis Social Security Bill failed to cover farm and domestic labor in which the majority of African Americans were employed); blacks received less relief assistance than whites; and the Federal Housing Administration denied mortgage financing to blacks seeking to buy homes in white neighborhoods. Federal administrators exacerbated racial inequities and fueled the black migration out of the South to the North by giving local racist southern officials overseer-powers in the distribution of federal funds.[42] Despite crucial federal aid, African Americans, dehumanized in seeking government assistance, were further debased in the free enterprise zones of the slave marts of contract labor.

African American female domestic workers had to contend not only with the government's indifference to their economic exploitation but also with the hostility and exploitation from employment agencies, their vehicle for gainful employment. Agencies tended to accuse female laborers in the slave markets of driving down wages, which reduced agencies' fees. Economic self-interest as well as class bias fueled the antiworker sentiments of employment agencies. Baker and Cooke report one agency's contemptuous view of women in the slave marts: "[D]eserving domestics are finding it increasingly difficult due to the menace and obstacles presented by the slavish performances of the lower types of domestics themselves, who, unlike the original slaves who recoiled from meeting their masters, rush to meet their mistresses."[43] Countering these stereotypes against the poorest of black women, Baker and Cooke suggest economic devastation, rather than slavish opportunism, as the primary motivation forcing women to auction themselves in the marts: "Who are these women? What brings them here? Why do they stay? . . . whatever their standing prior to the Depression, none sought employment where they now seek it. They come to the Bronx, not because of what it promises, but largely in desperation." The women also note that blacks seeking wages in the marts—which functioned as "auction blocks" where whites examined black females and "bought" them for the day—faced not only the derision of "respectable" wage earners but also exploitation from ineffective or fraudulent employment agencies: "Hours of futile waiting in employment agencies, the fee that must be paid despite the lack of income, fraudulent agencies that sprung up during the Depression, all forced the day worker to fend for herself or try the dubious and circuitous road to public relief."[44]

Although Baker and Cooke cite the positive role of some employment agencies that sought to curtail the activities of illegal agencies and to establish minimum and maximum wages for workers, they generally criticize agencies for neglecting workers' needs. Pointing out how government and employment agencies invest in workers' exploitation, the writers also addressed the public's general indifference toward black domestics, suggesting this public aloofness stemmed from its perception that desperate poverty was peculiar to "lower-class" domestics. Baker and Cooke chose instead to judge the workers' plight as an indictment of the economic system and systemic racism, arguing: "The real significance of the Bronx Slave Market [is that the]. . . 'mart' is but a miniature mirror of our economic battle front."[45]

Part of the social censorship and moral condemnation directed against the workers came from the fact that in the markets, women also sold sex to feed themselves and their families. Sexual exploitation and violence are, in general, an occupational hazard for domestics as control over women's bodies remains part of the dangerous terrain that maps out black women's work.

African American women generally warned their female children about sexual predators, given that many adolescent girls had to seek work as domestics. Proximity to white families brought dangers of sexual exploitation and violence, a fact particularly true during slavery. Ella Baker grew up hearing stories of how her grandmother's "demotion" from house to field slave brought an element of safety through greater distance from whites in the plantation house.

Rather than investigate sexual harassment or assaults of domestic workers, Baker and Cooke focused on women who "voluntarily" engaged in prostitution in the markets. Without moralizing, their descriptions of sexual trafficking within household wage labor emphasize economic constraints: "Not only is human labor bartered and sold for slave wage, but human love also is a marketable commodity . . . whether it is labor or love that is sold, economic necessity compels the sale."[46]

Forced by poverty into the marts to sell themselves to "mistresses" and "masters" who bought by the hour, day, or week, African American women grappled with dual commodification on the block as both domestic and sexual worker:

Rain or shine, cold or hot, you will find them there—Negro women, old and young—sometimes bedraggled, sometimes neatly dressed . . . waiting expectantly for Bronx housewives to buy their strength and energy for an hour, two hours, or even a day at the munificent rate of fifteen, twenty, twenty-five, or, if luck be with them, thirty cents an hour. If not the wives themselves, maybe their husbands, their sons, or their brothers, under the subterfuge of work, offer worldly-wise girls higher bids for their time.[47]

Euphemistically labeled, the "human love" purchased from "worldly-wise" women mirrored the southern sex trade that many African Americans had migrated north to escape. On the northern battlefront in the economic war, they found the same struggles and countered with the same tactic: selling, at subsistence wages, their bodies for survival.

As evidenced by its inadequate provisions for relief, the government shared much of the public's deep indifference toward black women trapped in domestic and sexual labor. Baker and Cooke recount their own experiences with a white male plainclothes detective who attempted to entrap and arrest them for prostitution while they were posing as domestics. Their story intimates the hypocrisy within punitive and protective aspects of the "law." Police entrapped or demanded bribes from black women domestics while ignoring white johns, pimps, and employers who sexually and physically abused or robbed the women workers; police punishment was as selective and discriminatory as police protection.

Despite the obstacles posed by state agencies, economic institutions, and debilitating labor, African American women resisted. In the slave marts, they created an "embryonic labor union." According to *The Crisis* essay, domestic workers forced black women who bargained for wages of less than thirty cents an hour to leave the market; they also organized workers to collectively demand thirty-five cents an hour on Jewish holidays. However, Baker and Cooke write that neither their conditions nor their nascent labor activism led these women workers to critically examine the political-economic structures that created the slave marts and drove black women to them.

The women were "largely unaware of their organized power," the writers note, but contradictorily they were "ready to band together for some immediate and personal gain either consciously or unconsciously," and they still clung "to that American illusion that any one who is determined and persistent can get ahead."[48] According to the authors, such beliefs in the limitless opportunities of free enterprise and the "American illusion" hindered the development of a broad-based, radical consciousness among black women.

Supplanting "American illusion" with labor militancy, Baker and Cooke maintained that the slave market would be abolished only when its causes were eradicated:

> The roots . . . of the Bronx Slave Market spring from: (1) the general ignorance of and apathy toward organized labor action; (2) the artificial barriers that separate the interest of the relief administrators and investigators from that of their "case loads," the white collar and professional worker from the laborer and domestic; and (3) organized labor's limited concept of exploitation, which permits it to fight vigorously to secure itself against evil, yet passively or actively aids and abets the ruthless destruction of Negroes.[49]

The oppressive conditions emphasized above, and the remedies based on labor activism as well as coalitions between "welfare" agencies, social workers, middle-class workers, and manual laborers, are important reminders of the centrality of economic struggles in antiracist organizing. They also point out the necessity of class alliances for the rights of African Americans in general and for black women workers in particular.

Theorizing on women's "multiple" oppressions, "The Bronx Slave Market" anticipated analyses of the intersections of race and class, and their relevance to progressive struggles, decades before black women's studies and cultural studies came into being.[50] Although the conditions surrounding contemporary black women's work differ, patterns of job segregation, economic exploitation, and sexual violence persist, reflecting the sexism and racism in labor practices of previous generations.

Social inequities still make domestic labor an economic mainstay for black women. For centuries, significant numbers of black females neglected their own homes and families to care for those of whites. In the "freedom" of emancipation, they sought to escape but were consigned to labor as surrogate wives and mothers in millions of white households. According to author Carole Marks, over 50 percent of African American women employed outside the home in 1920 were domestics. That figure increased to 60 percent in 1930 and fell to 33 percent in 1960; in the 1980s, 13 percent of black women worked in this area. In 1980 more African American women were employed as domestics than as professionals. Not only white but African American abuse of black women's labor also determines the constraints surrounding women's work.

Affluent blacks may employ and exploit domestic laborers, while African American men of all economic backgrounds benefit from black women's exploitation. African American women work more hours outside the home than do European American women and receive less pay due to employment segregation and wage and educational hierarchies; like most women, they also labor, without pay, more hours inside the home than their men. For many, black women's work means double shifts: unpaid domestic work inside the home and inadequate compensation for wage labor outside the home or some, the poorest, work triple shifts; two jobs plus domestic work when they arrive at home. Present-day "slave marts" expand within prisons and the underground economy. Prisoners and undocumented workers lack civil rights and face grotesque forms of exploitation in the sex trade, sweatshops, fields, and homes.

Racist and state violence and exploitation as "public" overshadow the "private" violence and exploitation within black families in antiracist rhetoric and organizing.[51] Focusing on structural racism and sexism in the economic market, Baker and Cooke make no reference to sexual violence or domestic abuse/exploitation within African American families and communities. Nevertheless, they provide a window for viewing the multiplicity of struggles faced by African American workers. They relate the occupational hazards for black women workers: poverty, under- or unemployment, labor and sexual exploitation, social contempt, and government indifference. We can add to these: depression, domestic violence, ill health, lack of job safety, and community "burn-out." Redressing these hazards entails expanding upon their analyses to deconstruct neocolonial sites.

Fifty years after Baker and Cooke exposed the slave marts, black academic Judith Rollins posed as a domestic worker to research her book *Between Women: Domestics and Their Employers.* Using "colonized" as an analytical category rather than as a metaphor, Rollins presents a context for examining the status of African American domestics:

> Are the conceptual leaps from the mistress ignoring the presence of her servant to Asians being portrayed as non-humans in films to the colonizer treating the colonized as an animal or an object too great? I think not. . . . all of these behaviors are manifestations of similar mental processes. . . . having been socialized into cultures that define people of color as worth less than whites and having observed material evidence that seems to corroborate this view of them as inferior, whites . . . , to varying degrees, devalue the personhood of such people. This devaluation can range from the perception of the persons as fully human but inferior, to conceptualizing of them as subhuman [Frantz Fanon's colonized "animal"], to the extreme of not seeing a being at all. And though this mechanism is functioning at all times when whites and people of color interact in this society, it takes on an exaggerated form when the person of color also holds a low-status occupational and gender position—an unfortunate convergence of statuses for the black female domestic servant.[52]

The subordination or devaluation of African American women's labor appears in: childbearing or biological reproduction; raising children/household management or social reproduction; wage labor; sexual commodification; and volunteerism in church, civic, community activism. Overwhelmingly, African American women sustain and lead parent-teacher associations, religious charitable work, community development, and environmental activism in black communities; sociologist Cheryl Gilkes refers to this as a gendered "occupationalization" of black liberation.

The work of Ella Baker and Marva Cooke suggests that moving from discourse about social work for ameliorating black underdevelopment to political activism requires that labor organize around the conditions of exploited workers. Such a movement would also require strengthening relationships among black activists, laborers, the unemployed, and street and institutional intellectuals.

Like Wells, Baker's protofeminism offers a black feminist theory of violence. She analyzes gender in relation to state and economic oppression in black life.

CONCLUSION

Expanding on the tradition within which Maria Stewart struggled, ancestors Ida B. Wells and Ella Baker challenged racial-sexual violence and exploitation. The women addressed the gendered as well as the racialized dimensions of oppression and violence and resistance. Dylan Rodríguez notes that Wells and Baker made a serious philosophical intervention on common sense conceptions of violence and resistance. For Rodríguez, a doctoral candidate in ethnic studies, pundits and activists often describe women of color's experiences with violence as simply domestic or "private," and then almost always at the hands of super-patriarchal and uniquely misogynistic men of color; Baker and Wells re-focus theoretical attention on the state and capital as the primary agents of women's suffering. Walking between worlds of privilege and disenfranchisement shaped by race, class, gender, and violence, they collectively projected into the twentieth century enduring forms of liberation practice that would infuse black feminist politics. Their legacy of protofeminism countered fetish and female and black victimization. Both women are associated with, respectively, the male-identified antilynching and civil rights movements. Yet each was a key leader, perhaps the single most significant organizer and strategist of her respective movement. Through antiracist struggles, both women made unique contributions to fighting sexual violence and framing liberation limbos.

Some of the most provocative and transformative of feminisms are tied to African American struggles. From the nineteenth-century abolitionist movements and post-Reconstruction, fin-de-siècle antilynching crusades to the midcentury civil rights and later black liberation movements, black women shared and shaped political methodology while redefining and building community. Movements tend to radicalize intellectual and political formations so that their emergent black feminisms, within the context of militant activism, are foreign to conventional politics. Multiracial and working-class feminist and antiracist groups are superseded by middle-class concerns because elites possess the resources to shape debate and agendas. Such elites have promoted a liberalism that has transformed the radical intent of civil rights and feminist movements, mainstreaming demands into institutionalized politics.

The often-unacknowledged contributions of abolitionist Maria Stewart, antilynching crusader Ida B. Wells, and civil rights militant Ella Baker mean that such women continue to inhabit gray areas in political memory. Shadowing American politics, the diversity of black female leadership and radicalism reveals critical perspectives on white supremacy, exploitation, and sexism. Gender-progressive politics play a role in contemporary struggles, where the black life span, which already is less than that of whites, is declining and where black poverty, which is greater than that of whites, is increasing. In a nation where blackness symbolizes pathology and violence and where feminism is increasingly viewed as either "antifamily" or anachronistic, limbos mark innovative political responses to marginalization and disempowerment.

FOUR

Radicalizing Feminisms from "The Movement" Era

In order for us as poor and oppressed people to become a part of a society that is meaningful, the system under which we now exist has to be radically changed. This means that we are going to have to learn to think in *radical* terms. I use the term radical in its original meaning—getting down to and understanding the root cause. It means facing a system that does not lend itself to your needs and devising means by which you change that system. That is easier said than done. But one of the things that has to be faced is, in the process of wanting to change that system, how much have we got to do to find out who we are, where we have come from and where we are going.

—Ella Baker

ROOTS

"The Movement" era largely existed from 1955 to 1975 and includes the black civil rights struggles, the American Indian Movement (AIM), Chicano activism, and Puertorriqueño insurrections, and militant feminism. During the height of the black liberation and black power movements, veteran activist Ella Baker's cogent assessment of the political contradictions of liberalism among black elites advocating civil rights distinguished between attempts to become "a part of the American scene" and "the more radical struggle" to transform society. According to Baker, "In . . . struggling to be accepted, there were certain goals, concepts, and values such as the drive for the 'Talented Tenth.' That, of course, was the concept that proposed that through the process of education black people would be accepted in the American culture and they would be accorded their rights in proportion to the degree to which they qualified as being persons of learning and culture. . . ."[1] For Baker, the common belief, that "those who were trained were not trained to be *part* of the community, but to be *leaders* of the community," implied "another false assumption that being a leader meant that you were separate and apart from the masses, and to a large extent people were to look up to you, and that your responsibility to the people was to *represent* them." This precluded people from acquiring their own sense of values; but the 1960s, according to Baker, would usher in another view: "the concept of the right of the people to participate in the decisions that affected their lives."[2]

Political agitation and movements historically have increased the scope of black leadership; however, African American participation in political decisions has historically been translated through corporate, state, or philanthropic channels. A century ago the vision and resources of the American Baptist Home Missionary Society (ABHMS) allowed wealthy, white Christian missionaries to support the black elite Talented Tenth as a shadow of themselves as influential, liberal leaders and to organize privileged black Americans to serve as a buffer zone between white America and a restive, disenfranchised black mass. During the Reconstruction era, funding elite black colleges such as Spelman and Morehouse (named after white philanthropists) to produce aspirants suitable for the American ideal, the ABHMS sought to encourage the development of race managers rather than revolutionaries.[3] To the extent that it followed and follows the funders' mandate, the Talented Tenth was and remains antirevolutionary. Supported by white influential liberals, the Talented Tenth historically included women. It therefore liberalized or deradicalized the protofeminism of historical black female elites. Contemporary black feminist politics as pursued by elites imbued with the bourgeois ideology of "race uplift" evince the same antirevolutionary tendency as the early Talented Tenth. Vacillating between race management and revolutionary practice, black feminisms are alternately integrated into or suppressed within contemporary American corporate-consumer culture.

Yet as Baker noted, the 1960s ushered in a more democratic, grass-roots–driven form of leadership. The new "wave" of black feminisms originating from that time invariably connects with historical antiracist struggles in the United States. Black women created and continue to create feminisms out of militant national liberation or antiracist movements in which they often function as unrecognized organizers and leaders. Equally, their contributions to American feminisms are inadequately noted even among those who document the history of contemporary radical feminism. Emerging from black militant groups, African Americans shaped feminist politics. These sites of emergent antiracist feminism influenced the more radical dimensions of black feminisms despite their inherent contradictions. For instance, the Combahee River Collective traces its origins to political formations now generally perceived as uniformly sexist:

> Black feminist politics [has] an obvious connection to movements for Black liberation, particularly those of the 1960s and 1970s. Many of us were active in those movements (Civil Rights, Black nationalism, the Black Panthers), and all of our lives were greatly affected and changed by their ideologies, their goals, and the tactics used to achieve their goals. It was our experience and disillusionment within these liberation movements, as well as experience on the periphery of the white male left, that led to the need to develop a politics that was antiracist, unlike those of white women, and anti-sexist, unlike those of Black and white men.[4]

The Combahee River Collective took its name from the June 2, 1863, guerrilla foray led by the black revolutionary Harriet Tubman in South Carolina's Port Royal region that freed hundreds of enslaved people and became the first and only military campaign in the United States planned and executed by a woman. During the Civil War, Tubman, the first American woman to lead black and white troops in battle, headed the Intelligence Service in the Department of the South. Before making a name for herself as a military strategist and garnering the people's title of "General Tubman," the formerly enslaved African woman had proven herself to be "a compelling and stirring orator in the councils of the abolitionists and the anti-slavers."[5] Tubman's distinct archetype for a black female warrior belies conventional narratives that masculinize black history and resistance. Although males remain the icons for black rebellion embattled with white supremacy and enslavement, women also engaged in radical struggles, including the strategy of armed self-defense. As fugitives with bounties on their heads, they rebelled, survived, or became casualties of state and racial-sexual repression.

Despite being designated "outlaws" and made outcasts because of their militancy, historical or ancestral black women such as Tubman have managed to survive in political memory. A few have been gradually— marginally—accepted into an American society that claims their resistance by incorporating or "forgiving" their past revolutionary tactics for humanitarian goals. Tubman's antebellum criminalized resistance to slavery, like Ida B. Wells's post-Reconstruction antilynching call to arms, typifies a rebellion that later became legitimized through American reclamation acts. The contradiction is that the nation's racial progressivism seeks to reclaim black women who bore arms to defend themselves and other African Americans and females against racial-sexual violence in a culture that continues to condemn black physical resistance to political dominance and violence while it supports at the same time the use of weapons in the defense or expansion of the nation-state, individual and family, home and private property.

Seeking explicitly to foster black female militancy in the 1970s, without the reservations of ambivalence that national culture exhibits toward black insurrectionists, Combahee black feminists selected an Afra-American military strategist and guerrilla fighter as their archetype.

Their choice of Tubman over her better-known contemporary, Sojourner Truth, suggests an intent to radicalize feminism. Truth, not Tubman, is closely identified with feminism because of her work as a suffragette and collaboration with prominent white feminists of her day. Tubman is identified with black people—men, women, and children—and military insurrection against the U.S. government. Her associations with white men are better known than those with white women; for instance, she actively planned to participate in John Brown's raid on Harper's Ferry despite the warnings of the prominent abolitionist and profeminist Frederick Douglass. With this African warrior and freedom fighter as their feminist model, the Combahee River Collective emerged in 1977 to contest the liberalism of the National Black Feminist Organization (NBFO) that preceded it.

In its manifesto, the collective expresses its "serious disagreements with NBFO's bourgeois-feminist stance and their lack of a clear political focus" and offers an activist alternative.[6] The collective, which included feminist authors and educators Barbara Smith, Gloria Hull, and Margo Okazawa-Rey, would later organize against a series of murders targeting black girls and women in the Boston area. Combahee's black feminist manifesto emphasizes radical activism rather than liberal politics: "Although we are feminists and Lesbians, we feel solidarity with progressive Black men. . . . Our situation as Black people necessitates that we have solidarity around the fact of race, which white women of course do not need to have with white men, unless it is their negative solidarity as racial oppressors. We struggle together with Black men against racism, while we also struggle with Black men about sexism."[7]

Given the prevalence of antiradical bias in American society, and despite writer bell hooks's definition of feminism that evokes the collective's ideology, Americans must continue to wade deeply beyond the mainstream to retrieve critiques such as the following issued by the Combahee River Collective:

> We realize that the liberation of all oppressed peoples necessitates the destruction of the political-economic systems of capitalism and imperialism as well as patriarchy. We are socialists because we believe that work must be organized for the collective benefit of those who do the

work and create the products, and not for the profit of the bosses. Material resources must be equally distributed among those who create these resources. We are not convinced, however, that a socialist revolution that is not also a feminist and antiracist revolution will guarantee our liberation.[8]

IDEOLOGY AND FEMINIST IDENTITY

Black feminists faced the challenge of how to maintain Combahee's integrative analyses—combining race, gender, sexuality, and class—with more than rhetoric, the challenge, that is, of how to express their critiques in viable political practice amid organizing in nonelite communities. Rhetoric notwithstanding, all antiracist and antisexist politics are not equally ambitious or visionary in their confrontations with state dominance and in their demands and strategies for transforming society by rechanneling economic and political power. Conservative attempts to bring "closure" to or contain the black revolutionary struggles that fueled radical black feminism such as Combahee altered the transformative potential of black feminist ideology.[9] "Closure" itself is likely an illusory pursuit, given the continuance of repressive conditions—impoverishment, abrogation of rights, racial and sexual denigration—that engendered revolutionary struggle.

Although the greatest opponent to antiracist and feminist revolutionary struggles has been the counterrevolutionary state (arguably, in the twentieth century, embodied by the United States),[10] black feminist writings often pay insufficient attention to state repression and the conflictual ideologies and divergent practices (from liberal to revolutionary) found within black feminisms. This may be partly due to the considerable energy that some focus upon the marginalization of black feminisms in European American and African American culture (as well as in African and Latin American cultures) and partly due to the often-obscured antiradical tendencies found within black feminisms.

Liberal, radical, and revolutionary black feminisms may be presented as ideologically unified and uniformly "progressive" while simultaneously being viewed as having little impact beyond black women.

Sorting out progressive politics within black feminisms, we may distinguish between ideological trajectories that reveal the at times compliant, often ambiguous, and sometimes oppositional relationships of black feminisms to state hegemony. Delineating ideology works to place in context black feminist attitudes toward institutional and political power. In the blurred political spectrum of progressives that broadly includes "liberal," "radical," "neoradical," and "revolutionary" politics and their overlap, all of these camps change character or shape-shift to varying degrees with the political context and era. For instance, no metanarrative can map radical or "revolutionary" black feminism, although the analyses of activist-intellectuals such as Ella Baker serve as outlines. Some reject while others embrace the self-proclaimed "revolutionary" that manifests through rhetorical, literary, cultural, or conference productions. "Revolutionary" denotes dynamic movement rather than fixed stasis within a political practice relevant to change material conditions and social consciousness. As the revolutionary has a fluid rather than a fixed appearance, its emergence remains episodic. As conditions change, what it means to be a "revolutionary" changes. "Revolutionaries" or "radicals" are not disembodied; rather they are understood (and so definable) only within context. (As a result, the articulation of a final destination for radical or revolutionary black feminisms remains more of a motivational ideal; and the pronouncement of an arrival at the final destination is a depoliticizing mirage.)

Despite ideological fluidity and border crossings, some useful generalizations can be made. Black feminisms that accept the political legitimacy of corporate-state institutional and police power but posit the need for humanistic reform are considered *liberal*. Black feminisms that view female and black oppression as stemming from capitalism, neocolonialism, and the corporate state are generally understood to be *radical*. Some black feminisms explicitly challenge state and corporate dominance and critique the privileged status of bourgeois elites among the "left"; those that do so by connecting political theory for radical transformation with political acts to abolish corporate-state and elite dominance are *revolutionary*.

Differentiating between liberalism and radicalism—or even more so between "radical" and "revolutionary"—to theorize about black feminist liberation politics is extremely difficult but essential for understanding some limitations of "left" politics and black feminisms. Part of the difficulty in delineating the "left" of black feminisms stems from the resurgence of the right and its modification of liberal and progressive thought.

New terminology denotes the pervasive influence of conservatism, as "neo" becomes a standard political prefix for the post–civil rights and postfeminist movements era. The efficacy of a rightist conservatism has led to the coupling of reactionary with conservative politics to construct the rightist hybrid "neoconservative"; the merger of the conservative with liberal politics to create the right-leaning "neoliberalism"; and the marriage of liberalism with radicalism to produce "neoradicalism" as a more corporate form of radical politics. Alongside "neoconservatism" and "neoliberalism" can be found "neoradicalism." All denote a drift toward conservatism. This drift has led to deradicalizing trends that include the hegemony of bourgeois intellectuals within neoradicalism and the commodification of the "revolutionary" as performer who captures the attention and imagination of preradicalized masses while serving as storyteller for apolitical consumers. Responding to revolutionary struggles, the counterrevolutionary, antirevolutionary, and neoradical surface to confront and displace activism, inspired and sustained by vibrant rebellions.

Neoradicalism, like liberalism, denounces draconian measures against women, poor, and racialized peoples; and, like liberalism, it also positions itself as "loyal" opposition to the state. Therefore, what it denounces is not the state itself but its excesses—prison exploitation and torture, punitive measures toward the poor, environmental degradation, counterrevolutionary violence, and contra wars. Abolition movements, directed by neoradicals, rarely extend their rhetoric consistently to call for the abolition of capitalism and the corporate state. Movements led or advocated by those representing the disenfranchised are marked by the appearance of the symbolic radical.

All black feminists, including those who follow conventional ideology to some degree, share an outsider status in a commercial culture. That marginalization is not indicative of—but often confused with—an intrinsic or inherent radicalism. Ideological differences among African

Americans belie the construction of black women or, even more significantly, black feminists as a "class." Refusing to essentialize black women or feminism, writers such as bell hooks have noted the conflictual political ideologies found among black women. In 1991 hooks's "Must We Call All Women 'Sister'?" questioned feminist championing of Anita Hill that made little mention of the fact that the then Reagan-Republican had promoted antifeminist, antigay/lesbian, antidisabled, and anti–civil rights policies at the Equal Employment Opportunity Commission (EEOC) under the supervision of Clarence Thomas.[11] The gender solidarity that surrounded Hill obscured her support for ultra-conservative policies. Prior to her courageous testimony at the Senate Judiciary Committee hearings—hearings that eventually confirmed Thomas as a Supreme Court justice—Hill had implemented reactionary attacks on the gains of the civil rights and women's movements—movements that had enabled nonactivists such as Hill and her former supervisor to attend Yale Law School.

Legal theorist Kimberlé Crenshaw has noted the consequences of African Americans' failure to distinguish and discuss political ideologies among black public figures. Crenshaw criticizes a racial uniformity in black solidarity that includes reactionaries. At a July 1998 gathering of black lawyers critical of the American Bar Association's invitation to Thomas to keynote its annual meeting, Crenshaw gave a scintillating critique of black support for Thomas. She contended that because of his race, African Americans paid little attention to his right-wing politics and so failed to distinguish between "conservative" and "reactionary" ideologies. (The endorsement by neo-Nazi David Duke of Thomas's appointment to the Court underscores the affinity right-wing ideologues felt for the Republican replacement to Justice Thurgood Marshall.[12]) According to Crenshaw, ideological distinctions eroded black opposition to former President George Bush's Supreme Court nominee, but if black Americans had maintained and sharpened the distinction between conservative and reactionary positions, more would have actively opposed Thomas's appointment.

Crenshaw's argument has merit. Conservatism has some respectability among black women and men immured in the "race uplift" of Booker T. Washington's black capitalism (even though they are not fully compliant with his prohibitions against competing with whites). Reactionary politics, however, hold no respectable public place among African Americans. Historically viewed as extensions of white supremacy and racial dominance, reactionaries have been considered anathema for black and female lives. Yet African Americans seem unwilling to publicly, critically discuss black reactionaries in service to the state and to distinguish their *counter*revolutionary service from the *anti*revolutionary disavowals of black liberals and neoradicals. (In similar fashion, maintaining distinctions between revolutionaries and radicals appears to be equally problematic.)

Just as blurring the lines between black reactionaries and conservatives politically accommodates reactionaries by reclassifying them as respectable "conservatives," some black feminisms have erased distinctions between liberalism and the radicalism that incited dynamic, militant formations (like the Combahee River Collective). Given that liberalism has accrued the greatest material resources and social legitimacy among progressives, the coalition of liberals and radicals to foment neoradicalism means that respectability has been designated to dual beneficiaries. Liberal black feminism garners the image of being on the "cutting edge" by appending itself to symbols of radicalism and hence increases its popularity as "transformative." Radicals are able to maximize their visibility and the market for their rhetoric via legitimization through association with liberalism. The terms for merger may be weighted toward the more privileged liberalism, and its offshoot neoliberalism, than radicalism or neoradicalism. Liberalism also allows black feminisms to increase their compatibility with mainstream American politics and with mainstream African American political culture.

From their strong fidelity to the Democratic Party (which under the Clinton administration increased police powers and punitive measures against the poor), it may be inferred that African Americans generally do not favor political "extremism."[13] Shunning reactionary or revolutionary politics, most black Americans support a progressive liberalism (left of center) that has a greater social conscience, and therefore moral content, than that of the general society. Yet this—and their sometimes outraged, and at times outrageous, condemnations of white supremacy—consequently places most African Americans outside narrowly construed conventional politics and allows them to be portrayed as political "extremists."

With centrism the conventional political stance, some black feminisms have reconfigured radicalism to fit within liberal paradigms.[14] Doing so enables a black feminist erasure of revolutionary politics and a rhetorical embrace of radicalism without material support for challenges to transform or abolish, rather than modify, state-corporate authority. An analogy for black feminist erasures can be made with the framing of a painting. The mat establishes the official borders for viewers. Often matting crops off the original borders of the picture. If incorrectly done, the mat encroaches upon the image itself and the signature of the image-maker. In framing black feminisms for public discourse and display, the extreme peripheries of the initial creation are often covered over. Placing a mat over the political vision of black feminisms establishes newer (visually coordinated) borders that frequently blot out the fringes—revolutionaries and radical activists—and allow professional or bourgeois intellectuals and radicals to appear within borders as the only "insurgents." With layered or overlapping mats that position rhetoric as representative of revolutionary struggle, the resulting portrait will leave liberals or neoradicals in the position of gender and race "rebels."

RESHAPING RADICALISM

Although a great impetus for the development of black feminisms came from black liberation movements, antiradicalism within American feminism (as well as masculinism among American radicals) obscured black female militancy. Antiradical sentiment, which has led some black feminist writers to dismiss black women's ideological critiques of black feminist politics as "sectarian," raises the issue of the place of revolutionary and antirevolutionary thought within progressive black feminism.

Black feminist liberation ideology challenges state power by addressing class exploitation, racism, nationalism, and sexual violence with critiques of and activist confrontations with corporate-state policies. The "radicalism" of feminism recognizes racism, sexism, homophobia, and patriarchy but refuses to make "men" or "whites" or "heterosexuals" the *problem* in lieu of confronting corporate power, state authority, and policing. One reason to focus on the state rather than on an essentialized male entity is that the state wields considerable dominance over the lives of nonelite women. The government intrudes upon and regulates the lives of poor and incarcerated females more than it does bourgeois and nonimprisoned ones, determining their material well-being and physical mobility and affecting their psychological and emotional health. Never the primary economic providers for black females, given the history and legacy of slavery, un- and underemployment, and racialized incarceration, the majority of black men exert little economic control over female life, although they retain considerable physical, sexual, and psychological dominance.

Radical black feminists' liberation theories address their nemeses: political violence, in both its private and public manifestations; counter-revolutionary state-police repression; and liberal antirevolutionary discourse that portrays radical black feminism as an idealistic maverick in order to contain radical feminism. Radicalizing potential based on incisive analyses, autonomy from mainstream and bourgeois feminism, independence from masculinist or patriarchal antiracism, a self-critique of neoradicalism, and most important, activism (beyond "speech acts") that connects with "grass-roots" and nonelite objectives and leadership all mark a transformative black feminism.

Revolutionary action or radical sentiments of "The Movement" era were not discarded by progressives solely because they became "anachronistic." These actions proved to be dangerous and costly in the face of state and corporate opposition and co-optation. The attacks launched against militancy had to do with its effectiveness or its potential to effect radical change.

Today in American politics in general and in black feminisms in particular there occurs the "mainstreaming" of radicalism as a form of resistance to radical politics. Formerly radical means—such as protest marches and demonstrations disrupting civic and economic affairs—are increasingly deployed for nonradical or liberal ends such as the maintenance of affirmative action. Likewise, formerly radical causes—such as prisoners rights' activism and advocacy to abolish the "prison industrial complex"—are increasingly administered through conferences, research, and social service centers financed by corporate philanthropy seeking to influence policy objectives.

In corporate culture, gender and race are filtered through class to juxtapose and contrast "workers" and "professionals." To the extent that corporate culture has infiltrated U.S. progressive movements, the polarities of worker/manager resurface to foster a resistance to or reshaping of radicalism embodied in a "corporate left." Those able to raise large sums of money through corporate largess to institutionalize their political formations and identities as astute "organizers," maintaining a political leadership that reflects the style of chief executive officers and mirrors state-corporate sites (among which academia is included), would qualify as members of the corporate left. Their status as sophisticated politicos often goes unchallenged because of the material resources they garner. Sites of the corporate left and their corresponding political styles are not known for being accountable to disenfranchised communities or democratic processes. Rather they are known for funding alternative entities to diffuse radical movements viewed as irrelevant by some progressives. Socialist Joan Roelofs argues that "One reason capitalism doesn't collapse despite its many weaknesses and valiant opposition movements is because of the 'nonprofit sector.' Yet philanthropic capital, its investment and its distribution, are generally neglected by the critics of capitalism. . . . Some may see a galaxy of organizations doing good works—a million points of light—but the nonprofit world is also a system of power which is exercised in the interest of the corporate world."[15] Whether through the academy, government agencies, or private foundations, an emergent "corporate left" has helped to deradicalize feminism and antiracism and thus antiracist feminism or feminist antiracism. Distinguishing between the "revolutionary" and the postmovement hybrid "neoradical" places a finer point on analyses of progressive black feminist politics and their contradictions.

Questions of co-optation and integrity are audible to those who listen attentively for sounds of political independence from corporate-state influence. The din can be confusing given that conflictual allegiances abound in American politics and culture. For instance, the oxymoronic wit of PBS "public service announcements" that validates corporate-state funders while broadcasting acquiescence to business elites reappears in progressive projects funded by state or corporate entities and severed from nonelite, community leadership. Searching for political independents, we find that liberalism competes with and censures radicalism while radicalism competes with and censures revolutionary action. Both forms of censorship seem to be guided by an amorphous framework of what constitutes responsible "left" politics delineated within a rapacious corporate world that funds the political integration of "radicals" on terms that follow, as a prime directive, the maintenance of stability and the accumulation of capital.

Corporate culture oils radicalism's slide into neoradicalism. According to consumer advocate Ralph Nader, being raised in American culture often means "growing up corporate." (For those raised "black," growing up corporate in America means training for the Talented Tenth.) A person need not be affluent to grow up corporate; he or she need only adopt a managerial style. When merged with radicalism, the managerial ethos produces a "neoradicalism" that as a form of commercial "left" politics emulates corporate structures and behavior. As corporate funders finance "radical" conferences and "lecture movements," democratic power-sharing diminishes. Radical rhetoricians supplant grass-roots organizers and political managers replace vanguard activists. Within this context, feminist "radicals" are discouraged from effective oppositional politics to social and state dominance and organic links to nonelite communities. Instead, they are encouraged as progressives to produce "ludic feminism" that, according to feminist theorist Teresa Ebert, "substitutes a politics of representation for radical social transformation."[16] Ludic feminism has a curious relationship to black feminisms because the latter has been shaped and contextualized by radical movements.

IN THE POLITICS OF "SISTERHOOD"

In the late 1960s, liberal bourgeois feminism among white women gradually expanded to include black women. This emergent multiracial "sisterhood" transferred the nineteenth-century white missionary mandate—promote elite leadership to serve as interpreters of and representatives for racialized and marginalized nonelites—to white bourgeois feminists. The result was a political paradox. Black feminisms pushed white feminisms (in their various ideologies) to repudiate ethnocentrism and racism and so to some degree "radicalized" America's dominant feminisms. The more financially endowed white cultural feminism supported and "mainstreamed" black feminisms by rewarding liberal politics within it; thus, to some degree, black feminist politics was deradicalized by normalizing its liberalism. This logically follows the historical trajectory of white radical feminism in contemporary American politics.

Amid the political battles waged by white middle-class women in "The Movement" era, Alice Echols's *Daring to Be Bad: Radical Feminism in America, 1967–1975* notes three forms of activism.[17] First, there emerged the "politicos" who worked in civil rights organizations such as the Student Nonviolent Coordinating Committee (SNCC), antiwar and radical youth groups such as Students for a Democratic Society (SDS), and revolutionary or underground spinoffs such as the Weathermen. Out of these formations emerged radical women who became disaffected because of the sexism of male-dominated organizations and who, as "radical feminists," subsequently developed organizations, such as Redstockings, opposed to the state's dehumanizing domestic and foreign policies.

"Cultural feminists" accrued gains from the concessions that radical feminists were able to wrest in the 1960s; according to Echols, cultural feminists, as liberal feminists, benefited from the militancy of radical feminists whom they later excised in order to consolidate an image of respectability and to garner corporate support for mainstream feminism. Women such as Gloria Steinem, Robyn Morgan, and other founders of *Ms.* magazine came to represent the cultural feminism that, unlike its radical rivals, defined men, not the state, as the primary "enemy" of women. *Radical* feminists acknowledged that men needed to change sexist attitudes and behavior, writes Echols, but emphasized structural critiques of capitalism and the state. Radical feminists became increasingly marginalized and eventually supplanted by cultural feminists who expressed politics less critical of, and so more compatible with, the state and its financial centers. In fact, *Ms.*'s early funders were white corporate males who—while categorized as women's "oppressors"—nevertheless became the financiers of mainstream feminisms.[18] (Given their accommodationist politics and access to state and corporate resources, such feminisms, whether conservative or liberal in ideology, might be considered "state feminism.")

Echols's depiction of cultural feminism, supplanting radical feminism because of its complementarity with state hegemony, resonates with the black liberation struggles of the period she analyzes.[19] This analysis raises important questions about the aspirations and dimensions of today's black cultural feminism and its relationship to black radical feminism. For instance, we might ask if a cultural form of black feminism (one that essentializes or generalizes African women or women of color) functions as a buffer against revolutionary feminist critiques that cite capitalism and the state as primary obstacles to black and therefore female advancement? Can cultural black feminism exist as a hybrid heavily invested in political appearances of revolutionary symbolism and representations shaped by ludic feminism rather than political organizing with nonelites for revolutionary action?

If the answer to either or all of these questions is "yes" or even "perhaps," then race, gender, or class is not the radicalizing impetus or deradicalizing tendency influencing black feminisms. Political ideologies shape feminist assimilation. As it is more assimilable, liberal black feminism remains more likely to be promoted into the political mainstream as normative among gender-progressive African Americans. Like the general society, mainstream feminism allows scant political space for revolutionary antiracists, even if they are white feminists, whose militant critiques of state power contest the assumptions (and funding) of liberal feminism. Cultural or liberal black feminism wields more influence in bourgeois, European American feminism than revolutionary white antiracist feminism does. Compatible ideologies allow white liberal feminist politics transracial privileges that mask its alienation from or antipathy toward radical antiracism. New forms of multiracial feminism allow dominant white feminists such as Gloria Steinem to "privilege" black female political celebrities like Alice Walker over white female political prisoners like Marilyn Buck. Revolutionary, antiracist white women, rarely referred to by feminists (or by black militants and white antiracists), are even more isolated than the white radical feminists and groups described by Echols.

The low visibility granted antiracist revolutionary white women in mainstream feminism coexists with their marginalization in discursive "critical white studies" and "abolition of whiteness" and "race traitor" movements, where whites challenge the existential if not always material benefits of white supremacy. Often in feminist and political discourse there is little mention of whites who viewed racism, patriarchy, and economic exploitation as embedded in state power and so who as revolutionaries resisted the state. Few liberal feminists or antiracists know much about Sylvia Baraldini, an Italian national convicted of aiding black revolutionary Assata Shakur to escape from prison. She and white female revolutionaries Susan Rosenberg and Marilyn Buck (and black male revolutionaries), who were also convicted of assisting Shakur, are serving sentences of between thirty and seventy years. (Baraldini received an additional three years for refusing to testify before a grand jury investigating the Puerto Rican Independentista movement.)[20] Likewise, the case of Judy Bari, the white feminist EarthFirster!, garners little attention in liberal feminism, black or white or multicultural, perhaps because it points to the continuance of COINTELPRO (under the guidance of FBI veteran Richard Wallace Held) in policing white female radical environmentalists.[21] Bari, a nonviolent activist who died from breast cancer in March 1997, survived a May 1990 car bombing, which, according to her attorneys was never seriously investigated by the police and FBI. She offered analyses that connected FBI repression of the Black Panther Party and the American Indian Movement with the repression of environmental radicals. The meeting and embrace between Bari and Ramona Africa, who survived the Philadelphia police's 1985 bombing of the African organization MOVE in which eleven African Americans (including four children) died, reflect radical forms of transracial "sisterhood" and political solidarity.

Revolutionary feminist politics are more likely than liberal feminist politics to note the political ramifications of radical alliances for "sisterhood" and antiracist feminisms. Such politics are also more inclined to scrutinize coalitions between radical and liberal black feminisms and white radical and bourgeois feminisms. While there has been considerable discussion of the interracial conflict between black and white women, some focusing on collaboration between the two groups, there has been little analysis of the ramifications of cross-ideological coalitions between African and European American women.

For instance, initially U.S. white feminists refused to participate in the Free Angela Davis campaign, one of the most publicized political trials in "The Movement" era, stating that Davis's case was not a "woman's issue."[22] The 1970 to 1972 campaign, co-led by black communist activist Charlene Mitchell, however, received an incredible opportunity to broaden its appeal and expand its base when Gloria Steinem agreed to chair the fund-raising committee of the National United Committee to Free Angela Davis. Steinem had by then emerged as an influential powerbroker and fund-raiser for institutional or state feminism. This made her a valued asset to some radical campaigns. On one level, this coalition between Steinem's and Davis's organizations appears as an act of solidarity in a sisterhood that transcends racial and ideological barriers. On another level, the association is problematic and politically confusing. That Steinem had previously headed an organization that received funding from the Central Intelligence Agency was public knowledge among progressives and Americans in general; according to Echols, Steinem responded to the disclosure of this information by *Ramparts* magazine by granting a *New York Times* interview to explain that she only worked indirectly with "liberal" elements within the agency. (Steinem's perception of what gains might accrue from such a relationship is of less interest for this discussion than what state police viewed as its potential benefits from alliances with liberal feminists).[23] The Free Angela Davis campaign was led by the Communist Party USA and supported by the Black Panther Party, nonrevolutionary organizations by 1971 whose "radical" politics mutated under state disruption of their internal operations and infiltration of organizational leadership and rank and file.[24] Both organizations advocated a militancy (and at times a patriarchy) seemingly incompatible with cultural or liberal feminism. Their curious alliance with anticommunist, bourgeois white feminisms may reflect either attempts to embrace feminism or a developing antirevolutionary sentiment.

The emergence of the "neoradical" persona as the symbolic rebel projects a form of cultural feminism that "radicalizes" conventional politics at the same time that it deradicalizes revolutionary politics. The "antirevolutionary" politics of liberals or neoradicals is not synonymous with "counterrevolutionary" state destabilization policies that include police repression, infiltration, and co-optation. Whereas the antirevolutionary also can be the antireactionary or antiright, seeking a centrist or center-left politics, the counterrevolutionary is pro-right or reactionary. Antirevolutionaries, though, may be incorporated into state or corporate counterrevolutionary initiatives. Within U.S. feminism and civil rights advocacy, anticommunism is such a cultural pillar that progressives who embrace this ideology find expedient alliances with corporate-state power and funds tenable. White feminists such as Steinem (who with hundreds of other prominent people signed a 1998 *New York Times* ad calling for a new trial for death-row intellectual and black activist Mumia Abu-Jamal; and who with the Ms. Foundation raised funds for "anti-prison-industrial-complex conferences") have no monopoly on conflictual political personas that offer contradictory images of resistance and allegiance to the state. For example, after the death of former Supreme Court Justice Thurgood Marshall in the 1990s, media reported that while serving as chief litigator for the National Association for the Advancement of Colored People during the 1960s civil rights movement, he had supplied names of young SNCC radicals suspected of "communist sympathies" to the FBI. Marshall's anticommunism and antirevolutionary views rooted him in the mainstream with other progressives.

CONCLUSION

The legacies of black female radicals and revolutionaries contest arguments that state repression and resistance to it are not "black women's issues" or are too "politicized" for "feminism." Such legacies also contradict contentions that feminism is inherently "bourgeois" and therefore incapable of an organic revolutionary politics. Yet even the "revolutionary" is marked in a corporate culture (where commercials at one time proclaimed that Revlon Corporation made "revolutionary cosmetics for revolutionary women"). Revolutionary black feminism transgresses corporate culture by focusing on female independence; community building/caretaking; and resistance to state dominance, corporate exploitation, racism, and sexism. Emphasizing economic and political power rather than social service programs for the disenfranchised, it challenges basic social tenets expressed in "law and order" campaigns. It does not restrict itself to political dissent channeled through lobbying and electoral politics or accept the corporate state as a viable vehicle to redress disenfranchisement.

In the United States, the blurred lines among revolutionary, anti-revolutionary, and counterrevolutionary politics allow for the normative political and discursive "sisterhood" that embraces conservative and liberal women of various ethnic backgrounds yet rarely extends itself to radical or revolutionary women. Adherence to mainstream political ideology appears key to any movement's general acceptance. Political marginalization generally follows challenges to repressive state policies (and critiques of female or feminist complicity in those practices). The revolutionary remains on the margin, more so than any other form of (black) feminism.

The symbiotic relationship between subordinate black feminists and the "white" masculinist state contests any presumption of a unified politics. Seeking a viable community and society, antiracist feminisms can serve as either sedative or stimulant. Conflicting messages about the nature of political struggle and leadership can be found within black feminisms, which function as "shadows"—both in the negative aspects attributed to them and in their subordinate status on the American scene. Ever present, often ignored but completely inescapable, their plurality is seen as monolithic and depicted as the antithesis of the "robust American" body. Fending their shadows as American alter political egos, black women paint varied portraits of the shadow boxer as radical: as lone warrior, successful corporate fund-raiser for and beneficiary of progressive issues, individual survivalist, and community worker receptive to the leadership of nonelites in opposing state-corporate dominance.

Progressive black feminisms face the predicament of struggling to maintain radical politics despite their inner conflicts. Yet this, after all, is the shadow boxer's dilemma: to fight the authoritative body casting the boxer off while simultaneously battling with internal contradictions.

FIVE

Revolutionary Icons and "Neoslave Narratives"

Over the centuries that America enslaved Blacks, those men and women most determined to win freedom became fugitives, fleeing from the brutal captivity of slavery. Many of their descendants who fought the Black liberation struggle also became fugitives. These men and women refused to endure the captivity awaiting them in retaliation for their systematic effort to win freedom. But unlike runaway slaves, these men and women fought for a more expansive freedom, not merely as individuals, but for an entire nation, and sought in the face of internationally overwhelming odds to build a more humane and democratic political order.

—Kathleen Neal Cleaver

As a slave, the social phenomenon that engages my whole consciousness is, of course, revolution.

—George Jackson

"NEOSLAVE NARRATIVES"

Historically, African Americans have found themselves corralled into dual and conflictual roles, functioning as either happy or sullen slaves in compliant conformity with or happy or sullen rebels in radical resistance to racial dominance. The degree to which historical slave narratives continue to shape the voices of their progeny remains the object of some speculation.

In his introduction to *Live from Death Row: This is Mumia Abu-Jamal,* Pulitzer Prize-winning author John Edgar Wideman argues that many Americans continue to encounter black life and political struggles through the "neoslave narrative" (popularized in the 1970s by the television miniseries *Roots* based on Alex Haley's fictional text of the same title).[1] Traceable to the nineteenth-century works that garnered considerable attention, this narrative is characterized by political traits that contextualize antiracist resistance in ways that at times mitigate black radicalism. First, it is marketed through literature (or cinema) accessible to liberal or moral (white) Americans, and so like its precursor, the slave narrative, it makes its appeal to the "moral conscience" of the dominant culture. Second, the neoslave narrative identifies fixed and therefore containable sites of freedom and enslavement. It juxtaposes the southern plantation against the northern city in the "free" or nonslave state. The former represents the site for the denial of freedom and democracy, the latter the site for the acquisition of same. In such narratives, the victorious "slave" must engage in flight—from the plantation, the South, the zones of black immiseration—in order to triumph.[2]

The successful escape then exists as physical and metaphysical fleeing of "blackness," understood as containment and debasement, toward "whiteness," perceived as an enlightened citizenry shaped by ethical and influential liberals safeguarding and expanding the promise of democratic ideals. In the neoslave narrative, the state, despite its limitations and abusive excesses, provides the possibility of emancipation and redemption. Consequently, it cannot be considered or constructed as inherently and completely corrupt, for the state permits and maintains the sites of freedom *and* enslavement. Flight and freedom are thus always contained within national borders, so that unlike Toni Morrison's

"Flying African" in *Song of Solomon,* freedom is not achieved in expatriation (through death), external migration "back to Africa," or internal migration toward a black "nation."[3] (Clearly this narrative does not lend itself to black nationalist discourse.)

Their assimilationist politics and loyal opposition to the racial state endear neoslave narratives to a general public that disparages radicalism. Such narratives moderate radical politics; as the sympathetic reader lives vicariously through the dangerous risk-taking that typifies the life of the slave rebel and fugitive, she is reassured of reconciliation with prevailing power structures that permitted the liberating, albeit tortuous, journey. That the narratives usually forgo calls for revolutionary struggle and armed resistance enhances their appeal within the "mainstream"—the majority of moral-minded women and men who are comforted by the fact that the narratives represent the state as reformable and so inherently democratic.

Nineteenth-century abolitionists and former slaves Harriet Jacobs and Frederick Douglass highlighted in their memoirs the racist barbarism of the South while reassuring that America works to fulfill on some level its democratic promise—despite its racial rages.[4] Their late-twentieth-century counterparts can provide a similar national function today. Redemption and safety continue to appear in African American narratives as a variation of black success stories tied to integration, encoded in flight from enslavement—now viewed as black, impoverished urban spaces or "inner cities"—that bring closure to black rebellion. The construction of fixed sites of enslavement and freedom means that rebellion cannot be an ongoing process, at least in this paradigm. Once a person disembarks at the Promised Land, the final destination of the "North" as geopolitical terrain or chair of the Democratic National Committee as prime political landscape, insurrection becomes "folly." (The irony of final destinations of safe haven, however, was never lost on African Americans who, confronting northern racism, coined the phrase "up South.")

As former Black Panther leader Kathleen Cleaver notes, there are differences between the fugitive slave and the insurrectionist. (There is also overlap.) Both rebelled against oppressive conditions and laws—one in flight and the other in resistance. (The state, predictably, reserves its

most severe punishment for those who fight it by advocating revolutionary struggle.) Not all contemporary black antiracist texts adhere to the
deradicalizing features of this progressive story, the neoslave narrative; as
Wideman argues, the writings of Abu-Jamal depart from the conventional politics of the neoslave narrative; for even if granted a new trial,
exonerated, and released from death row and Pennsylvania's SCI Green
prison, Abu-Jamal would still maintain that he is not *free* as long as U.S.
society and state institutionalize black oppression. Consequently, for
Abu-Jamal, there is no possibility of freedom without transformation—
that is, without revolution. As revolutionary and icon, "Mumia" stands
as a representative figure protesting the corruption of the current order
and proffering a vision for a new one. To Wideman's discussion of
narratives, which helps to demystify America's attraction to and/or
aversion for black revolutionaries, might be added an analysis of the state
violence, gender, and sexual politics that mark both neoslave narratives
and contemporary political struggles.

Gender analyses expand critical depictions of the neoslave narrative
and the historic role of black Americans as commodities or racial text
for white consumers and activists. Gender remains an integral part of
neoslave narratives and the construction of revolutionary icons. Influential male narratives have helped to masculinize the militant or the
black prisoner as political leader in the American mind and shaped a
genre of literature by "prison intellectuals." Nationally and internationally, the most prominently known black political prisoners or prison
intellectuals are male. The brief incarceration of Martin Luther King
Jr., in Alabama, in 1955, produced "Letter from Birmingham Jail" and
popularized civil disobedience to repressive laws and governments. The
imprisonment of Malcolm X for larceny and pimping in the 1950s
engendered the political man and *The Autobiography of Malcolm X* in
the 1960s.[5] The 1971 martyrdom of George Jackson, author of *Blood
in My Eye* and *Soledad Brothers: The Prison Letters of George Jackson,* who
was murdered by prison guards, helped to incite the Attica uprising that
met with violent and deadly repression by the National Guard deployed
by New York Governor Nelson Rockefeller.[6] Such racial rebels pro-
pelled the presence of black male prison intellectuals into the larger
American culture during "The Movement" era. More recently, former

Panther Geronimo ji Jaga (Elmer Pratt)'s release in 1997 after twenty-seven years in prison—the same length of arduous incarceration as that endured by African National Congress (ANC) leader Nelson Mandela (the Black Panther Party and the ANC were each at one time designated "terrorist" organizations by the U.S. government)—was heralded in black and progressive communities as a political victory.[7] Current organizing for a new trial for Abu-Jamal is galvanized by his radio commentaries and his writings—the incisive critiques of *Live From Death Row,* and the spiritual reflections of *Death Blossoms.* Each promotes his stature as an international cause célèbre or revolutionary icon. Yet celebrated women are associated with the iconography of revolutionary antiracism even though conventional political memory associates few women with armed resistance, political incarceration, or martyrdom stemming from struggles against enslavement or white supremacy. From the nineteenth century, recall military strategist Harriet Tubman. The twentieth century will remember Angela Davis and Assata Shakur because of their brief political but long-lasting symbolic associations with the Panthers. (Native American Anna Mae Aquash, killed in 1976 during the American Indian Movement occupation/defense of Wounded Knee, and Lolita Lebron, a former political prisoner of the Puerto Rican Independence movement, are significant but lesser-known figures in a national culture racially fixated on blacks.)

Notwithstanding the dominance of the elite and male presence in black and American radicalism, out of the recent volatile era of black insurgency, antiwar demonstrations, and women's liberation in the late 1960s and early 1970s, a few black women have become representational icons for female radicalism and black revolution. Although their connections with the rank and file and national leadership of the revolutionary period of the Black Panther Party (1966-1969) were tenuous or brief, Angela Davis, Kathleen Cleaver, Assata Shakur, and Elaine Brown have achieved international stature as revolutionaries through their real and symbolic associations with the Panthers. This is primarily because the Black Panther Party, not the Black Student Union, the Student Nonviolent Coordinating Committee (SNCC), or even the Communist Party—organizations with which the women were members—have come to embody revolutionary struggle for black freedom. The Black

Panther Party remains the organizational icon (with Malcolm X the individual icon) for black militant resistance to white domination and terror. (Today, political formations that may have little in common with the Panthers' revolutionary Ten-Point Program have appropriated that iconography.) Despite sexism and misogyny within its ranks, the party was instrumental in propelling select women into the national and international spotlight as revolutionaries.

Considering gender, it can also be seen that racial-sexual violence marks black women's bodies as spectacle. For example, Harriet Jacobs's *Incidents in the Life of a Slave Girl* narrative of a young woman who survives years of hiding in an attic to save herself from the white sexual predator known as her "master" adds a sexual dimension to antiblack violence and exploitation uncommon in male narratives. When sexuality is considered, the violator is both racialized and gendered: The narrator must survive not only white enslavers but also male predators. New depths in voyeuristic spectatorship can be uncovered when sexual violence is included in the accounts of the lives of black women associated with past militancy.

Violence, race, and sex shape the symbolism surrounding black female radical icons. Part of the narrative of the "conventional" female revolutionary is the prominence of the male comrade. A number of black female icons were recognized as the lovers or partners of black male revolutionaries, prison intellectuals who radicalized and linked them, at least in the public mind, to antiracist armed struggle. Kathleen Cleaver's tumultuous marriage to Eldridge Cleaver; Elaine Brown's devotion to her disintegrating, drug-addicted former lover, Huey Newton, who installed her as Black Panther Party Chair from 1974 to 1977; and Angela Davis's relationship with George Jackson, which began while she was organizing for the incarcerated Soledad Brothers—all serve as markers, promoting the image of black female militants as sexual and political spectacles. (Assata Shakur least fits this paradigm, given that she was already an incarcerated revolutionary when she conceived and gave birth to her codefendant's daughter.) African American male revolutionaries are not perceived as having been politicized through their romantic or personal relationships with female counterparts; rather, their speeches and deeds mark them for public recognition. The same cannot be said, to the same degree, for female black revolutionary icons. Not because they did not produce important works, words, and acts for liberation, they did; but because they were, and are, viewed as appendages to male initiatives and endeavors; and so their very appearance commingles in the conventional mind with that of the male revolutionary.

"PANTHER WOMEN":
ICONS AND ACADEMIC REBELS

Although the Deacons of Defense protected nonviolent civil rights organizers in the 1950s and 1960s, few in the United States belonged to any organization that publicly advocated armed self-defense against racist violence before they joined the Black Panther Party (originally named the Black Panther Party for Self-Defense in view of the fact that police brutality and killings of African Americans inspired its formation). The Panther party captured the national imagination (and its paranoia). The most celebrated African American women achieved their international iconic stature as revolutionaries through the militancy of their racial not their gender politics—and their real or symbolic connections to armed struggle (which poses an interesting dilemma for mainstream feminism). Their iconography so overshadows the tedious, mundane tasks of nonelite activists shaping political realities and history that it inevitably eclipses the stories of rank-and-file organizers. Paradoxically, some women activists who were reconstructed into political celebrities and identified with the Black Panthers spent comparatively short periods of time with its grass-roots constituency: urban, impoverished African Americans.

American cultural focus remains concentrated on the masculinized insurgent as warrior soldier. Consequently, the average American polit-ical spectator—black or white, red or brown or yellow—is more captivated by the Black Panthers' stance on armed self-defense and their battles with police—and resulting male martyrs—than with the social service programs largely organized and run by women. Thousands of women worked with and served in the Black Panther Party, comprising the rank and file that implemented the medical, housing, clothing, and

Free Breakfast and education programs. Female activists among the Panther ranks displayed an agency that reshaped American politics, although their stories recede in popular political culture before the narratives of elites who have become icons. (Before being forced underground, Assata Shakur routinely worked in the rank and file.) Iconic imagery and symbolism filter political history and memory so that what is often recalled is the image, not the specificity, of militancy.

Without diminishing the contributions of past activists in radical movements, the problematic aspects by which past activism becomes personified, and consequently distorted, in representations of elites can be highlighted. A select, elite group of African American women served with their male counterparts in the "central committees" that comprised Panther leadership before, during, and after the factionalism and infiltration, as well as state violence, that led to the party's demise as a revolutionary organization. The deradicalizing tendencies of iconography mask the diverse and significant contributions "Panther women" made under considerable difficulty and hardship. These contributions stemmed from the rank and file who in anonymity shared the risks of police persecution and bore the brunt of party discipline and organization, selling party newspapers on street corners for revenue, and delivering social services to impoverished and underresourced black communities. The elite (largely Oakland-based) leadership suffered state violence as they focused on representing the party, disseminating political ideology, and engaged in decision making. For iconic and rank-and-file women, the weight of representation would include sexualization.

Unlike their black female predecessors and elders in the southern civil rights movement—middle-age activists Fannie Lou Hamer, Ella Baker, Rosa Parks, and Septima Clark—Panther women leaders were romanticized as icons, noted for a particular form of physical appearance tied to "fashion," skin color, and youth that led to their commodification. The production of political ideas and leadership in the civil rights and black power movements reveals a striking paradox in terms of iconography. Key strategists for the southern civil rights movement included older women. For instance, Ella Baker, then in her fifties, was instrumental in the group "In Friendship" that supported the Montgomery bus boycott, and consequently she became the first de facto director of the Southern

Christian Leadership Conference and eventually the "godmother" of SNCC. Female SNCC leaders included Fannie Lou Hamer, a former Mississippi sharecropper, and the young Ruby Doris Smith Robinson. (Robinson, one of the exceptional young women who formed SNCC's national leadership, died at an early age from cancer.) Unlike the older celebrated women in the southern movement, the women who became national political celebrities in the Black Panther Party tended to be under thirty. (Intellectuals and former members have described the Panthers as a "youth organization.") Unlike their southern activist predecessors and peers, these particular women would be constructed by sectors of the media (and later Hollywood's blaxploitation cinema) as black femmes fatales.

The construction of elite black female radicals in the Black Panther Party as "revolutionary sweethearts" fueled their popularity with both males and females, particularly in segments of the culture that tended to idolize, and continues to revere, rather than critically engage with black radical heroes and heroines. Henry Louis Gates Jr.'s 1998 PBS Frontline documentary on class stratification and African Americans, *The Two Nations of Black America,* which offers no gender analysis, used archival footage to ridicule and disparage male Panthers. (Gates reports that when he was a student, the Panthers used him and other Yalies as "cannon fodder" in their battles with police around the New Haven Panther trial.)[8] Yet the documentary sexualizes the young Angela Davis and Kathleen Cleaver and resists demonizing them. While the narrator Gates confides that Martin Luther King Jr., and the southern civil rights movement held little attraction for him as a youth, the film flashes archival images of the "sexier" Black Panther Party, replete with the faces, bodies, and youthful beauty of Davis and Cleaver.[9] Paradoxically both women by virtue of their past activism, bring a "left" credibility to the neoliberal politics of a documentary hostile toward the organization that helped to propel them into the national and international spotlight (Davis also had the international platform of the Communist Party).

In much of the popular and academic discourse concerning gender politics and the Black Panther Party, discussions vacillate among female apologias protecting the reputations of male radicals, criticisms of an allegedly uniform sexism and misogyny, and feminist revisionism safeguarding the emergent iconic stature of "Panther women." Iconography remains central to most representations of the Panthers. For instance, a recent anthology, *The Black Panther Party [Reconsidered]*, features on its jacket only one female image—the cover of *The Black Panther* newspaper carrying a photo of Angela Davis, taken when she was not a member of the party. (Rejecting photographs of the lesser-known Brown and Cleaver or unknown rank-and-file women the book follows the American tradition of using female images for advertising.) The anthology's section entitled "Gender Dynamics" explores the roles of women in the party; except for an autobiographical essay by a former Panther in which the author recounts sexual harassment within the party, the issues of domestic violence by revolutionary or cultural nationalist leaders and the normative silence about battery and rape are not significantly explored.[10] (For example, there is no discussion of how the Oakland-based leadership broke that silence on domestic violence by publishing a photograph of Kathleen Cleaver's battered face in the party newspaper. However, this potentially feminist message was undermined by an ulterior motive; Huey Newton sought to discredit and "purge" Eldridge Cleaver from the party.) The issue of female abuse and battery by male leaders and the rank and file in the Black Panther Party, led by Newton and Eldridge Cleaver before the split, and its rival organization Us, headed by Maulana (Ron) Karenga, remains somewhat of a taboo among African Americans.

In addition, the issue of black women's complicity in violence and destabilization of a radical political group appears to generate little interest.[11] The counterfeminist and antirevolutionary aspects of female Panther leaders represented by former Black Panther Party Chair Elaine Brown go unexplored in her reconstruction as a "feminist" within the anthology.

In 1974, when Huey Newton expelled Bobby Seale as chair of the Black Panther Party and appointed Elaine Brown, the organization was no longer national or revolutionary.[12] (*All Power to the People!: The Black Panther Party and Beyond* argues that under the West Coast elite's deadly factionalism, the party became anti- if not counterrevolutionary.) In her 1993 memoir, *A Taste of Power: A Black Woman's Story,* Brown describes a "taste of power" that included an authoritarian female reign in what was essentially a local organization, heavily infiltrated and disrupted by the FBI, internal factionalism, and elitism.[13] (On some levels, her story mirrors a narrative of a woman taking leadership in an elite military unit.) A formidable supporter of Newton, even while he careened out of control, Brown had men and women "disciplined" with beatings and survived challenges to her reign and death threats. Black feminist reconstructions of Brown are often silent about her disclosures of her own sexual excess, manipulation, and deployment of physical punishment against African Americans.[14] In Brown's memoir, black women save themselves from predatory black male radicals and revolutionaries. This somewhat inverts Harriet Jacobs's slave narrative, given that the state, capitalism, and white supremacy recede from center stage in this black radical feminism where the "enemy" is viewed as dangerous black men. Brown's flight to freedom is in part an escape from abusive Panthers. Women's complicity in state and patriarchal abuses remains largely unscripted in her neoslave narrative.[15] For feminists, what appears to be most striking is her story of surviving male abuse and violence.[16]

Before becoming members of the Black Panthers, Cleaver and Davis worked with SNCC, which had been in existence since 1960 but was by this time on the wane as the "black power" ideology began to take root among black radicals and masses. A member of New York SNCC in 1966, Cleaver, the daughter of a U.S. Ambassador, dropped out of Barnard College; relocating to Atlanta to work in SNCC's national office, she began to organize support for incarcerated Panthers. In 1967 she married; during the height of Black Panther radicalism, she spent years in exile in Europe or Algeria with Eldridge Cleaver (who had violated parole and feared imprisonment and retaliation from Newton after the party split). While a graduate student at the University of California at San Diego (where she helped to form the Black Student Union), Davis joined SNCC's Los Angeles chapter as well as the Communist Party USA (CPUSA), where she would serve in its leadership for the next twenty years.

At the 1998 Black Radical Congress in Chicago, Angela Davis and Kathleen Cleaver were questioned by young activists about their roles in movements in the 1960s and early 1970s. Cleaver recalled that the poster which shows her posing with a rifle—a poster that promoted her international visual recognition and notoriety—was a tactical and symbolic challenge to police raids on the apartment that she shared with Eldridge Cleaver, who as an ex-convict could not legally possess weapons. According to Cleaver, soon after the photograph was taken, she left the country and had no control over the use of the image. Davis never posed with guns, although, having grown up on Dynamite Hill, she was raised in a house that stored them as a precaution against Klan violence and weapons registered in her name would be linked to Jonathan Jackson's tragic attempt to free his brother and other Soledad prisoners in 1970.

As former radical activists and current radical academics-intellectuals, Davis and Cleaver have become public "historians" analyzing past radical or revolutionary black movements. Identified with past revolutionary movements, their roles as historians of black radicalism have become central to their iconography as Panther currency has risen in American popular culture. As translators of cultural and political views and practices and as academics, these women offer important views of past revolutionary politics for contemporary audiences that complement, and contradict, current revolutionary politics. The most influential of contemporary public historians with experiential knowledge of black radicalism is Angela Davis, who is arguably in American popular culture the contemporary persona most commonly identified with black revolutionary struggle.

Viewed by some as a radical middle-class academic before her incarceration and later as an internationally known author and celebrity after her acquittal on murder and conspiracy charges and the publication of her 1974 memoir, Davis has benefited from the currency of cultural "hybridity" that marks influential black intellectual elites—a modicum of affluence and a suspension of revolutionary rhetoric connected to physical insurgency. Such cultural currency, compatible with the assimilationist ideology of the Talented Tenth, procures the title of "citizen," a desired recognition that has proved to be elusive for many disenfranchised peoples; and in fact, remains somewhat illusory for black icons and elites who retain the "suspicious" markings of a subordinate race.

In contradistinction to the political celebrity, Davis's co-defendant in the 1971 trial, before their cases were severed, Ruchell "Cinque" Magee (whose "free" name evokes the nineteenth-century African liberator of the slave ship the "Amistad"), has been stripped of the title of "citizen" and is not considered "embraceable" by mainstream Americans. He has remained incarcerated, in anonymity for three decades. While Davis has pointed out that Magee has not been forgotten, many still do not seem to recall his existence. A black male politicized into prison leadership while incarcerated for social crimes, Magee lacks noted literary accomplishments and thus is denied intellectual or celebrity stature and consequently a measure of social acceptance. In conventional culture, he has no story that many are willing to tell or listen to, one deemed marketable for mass consumption.[17] Magee will not reflect the successful assimilation of the black rebel. His class or caste works against recognition of him as a "revolutionary" icon in popular culture and therefore against his emancipation; as former Panther Geronimo ji Jaga notes, Americans are not predisposed toward supporting revolutionaries, or at least those lacking cult status.[18]

Although it was the Communist Party USA, not the Black Panther Party, to which she was a stanch member and long-time supporter, Davis's association with the Panthers and work with the Soledad Brothers and Soledad leader George Jackson, a Panther field marshal, would mark her as "black revolutionary." Thirty years ago Davis's political affiliations and her educational elite status made her *the* iconoclastic academic rebel in America, a status that she still retains despite punitive measures to erase her presence in American intellectual and political life. In 1969, the new assistant professor in philosophy at the University of California at Los Angeles (UCLA)—the first black woman to ever have held such a position—was recognized in the university system as a radical antiracist and a communist.

Her ability to influence middle- and upper-class youths with critiques of capitalism and white supremacy made her a formidable spokesperson and opponent to state oppression at the elite university; consequently, she was targeted by the California state and various police agencies. While defending her right to teach at UCLA, Davis began organizing a mass defense for the Soledad Brothers—George Jackson, Fleeta Drumgo, and John Clutchette. All three African Americans were leaders in the California prisoners' rights movement, and as activist prisoners were falsely charged with killing a prison guard in January 1970; they were acquitted of those charges in 1972. Through the Soledad

Brothers' Defense Committee, Davis met prison intellectual and revolutionary theorist George Jackson, who was later shot and killed by a
guard in what many activists viewed as a political assassination. The
August before Jackson's death in 1971, his younger brother Jonathan
attempted to free prisoners James McClain, William Christmas, and
Ruchell Magee from a Marin County Courthouse using a gun or guns
registered in the name of Angela Davis.[19]

During that incident, shots fired by guards led to casualties among
insurrectionists and hostages (standard California prison policy was for
guards to prevent escapes, even if it meant killing hostages). Under U.S.
law the defendants were charged with the killings. The state of California
issued murder and conspiracy charges against Davis who, maintaining
that she did not know of Jackson's plans, subsequently went underground, initiating one of the largest "manhunts" in FBI history. After
her arrest, activists effectively mobilized a massive, international protest
for a fair trial (protests included a telegram signed by all thirteen members
of the full Congressional Black Caucus). Like the Soledad Brothers,
Angela Davis was acquitted of all charges when the jury rendered its "not
guilty" verdict on June 4, 1972.

Davis's vindication in 1972 became viewed and understood by many
progressives as one of the infrequent "people's victories" against a
pervasive state power and domination. This victory created the political
space that permits left-liberals to "identify" with her today. (If she had
been convicted by the courts, presumably Davis would now be facing
either the anonymity of other U.S. political prisoners like Ruchell Magee
or the iconic stature of Mumia Abu-Jamal.) Angela Davis's 1972
acquittal *proves* to some liberals that the system works, and, conversely
for conservatives that it is dangerously flawed (Assata Shakur's 1979
escape from prison rejects the conviction that the judicial system is just).
The "cultural dialectic" in a society that was expanding to embrace past
radicalism (and in some ways condition it) coupled with her class
background and education to elevate Davis's status to American icon;
yet this same dialectic has not evolved to encompass incarcerated and
fugitive revolutionaries.

As progressive nonelite blacks invested in Davis's release and
exoneration, black women wittingly and unwittingly took risks to ensure

her survival and freedom. Some wore Afros hoping to serve as decoys during the FBI hunt for Davis. One African American professor who had helped to organize in the "Free Angela Davis" campaigns recounts that following a car accident at the time of the acquittal, she was rushed to the emergency room of a local New York hospital. While semiconscious on the gurney, she heard white hospital staff who surrounded but would not treat her, holding an impromptu debate. Having noted the "Free Angela Davis" button pinned to her jacket, they discussed their amazement that anyone could "support a murderess." Lifting her head, the injured black woman confronted white nurses and interns, saying that if she needed to take off the button to receive medical attention, they should let her know so that she could do exactly that. The same woman recounts her disappointment that Davis left "immediately" for the Soviet Union after her acquittal instead of traveling to thank African American communities for their support. Although anticommunism is a possible source for her supporter's criticisms, this narrative suggests and reflects some of the intense investment that black people had made into the persona and the political battles that Angela Davis represented.

The high expectations that black Americans displayed toward Davis as a political leader upon her acquittal surpassed the twenty-eight-year-old's training and experience. In some ways, her story parallels that of the young Huey Newton sans Newton's later grandiose pretensions. Davis's political career was tied to the Communist Party USA, as Newton's was to the Black Panther Party. Both articulate, formally educated young African Americans, they became charismatic draws for their respective parties and overlapping audiences. To ensure that Newton was not executed or imprisoned for life, Panthers developed a "Free Huey!" campaign that fostered a "cult of personality." Although Newton initially was a young student organizer and then a prisoner who spent considerable time in "the hole" (solitary confinement), upon his release many assumed he was capable of (and had always been involved in) national leadership of the Black Panther Party as a revolutionary movement. Davis spent several years removed from community-based organizing: first underground as a fugitive; later in prison for sixteen months (often in solitary confinement); finally out on bail, preoccupied with the trial and its defense strategy. Like Newton, she was the beneficiary of, but forcibly separated from, black, militant grass-roots activism. Unlike Newton, who attended Merritt Community College in Oakland and cofounded an urban black militant group criticized for its "lumpen" ideology, she spent decades in elite white schools and the CPUSA, which although integrated, had limited mass appeal or credibility among poor and working-class black communities and grass-roots revolutionaries.

In the early 1970s, ill-informed about insurgent organizations and antiracist radicalism (or the fact that the Communist Party USA was arguably not revolutionary), large segments of the public, influenced by sensationalist media coverage, assumed Davis to be a "black" revolutionary leader, although her organizing prior to the Jonathan Jackson tragedy was local or California-based. Davis garnered national and international attention because of anticommunist persecution on the part of the University of California Board of Regents who fired her from her position at UCLA. Governor Ronald Reagan's response to hearing that Black Panther Eldridge Cleaver had been invited to lecture at the prestigious University of California at Berkeley reveals the climate of that era: "If Eldridge Cleaver is allowed to teach our children, they may come home one night and slit our throats."[20] Reagan's histrionics illustrate how reactionaries perceived and propagandized the minuscule physical but significant intellectual presence of black radicals and revolutionaries on university campuses as "life-threatening." The conservative fervor to ban Davis from teaching at the University of California and to discredit her as an academic reflected her political efficacy as well as the rightist paranoias ably performed by Governor Reagan.

Davis's political impact would reside partly in her evolving status as a cultural icon. In symbolic representation, she signifies victorious opposition to state repression. Later her stature grew as an intellectual due to her antiracist feminist writings and lectures. Angela Davis's representational status and freedom from incarceration gave currency to the tenets of American democracy. Her ouster from the Communist Party[21] and subsequent renaming of herself as a "socialist" has also enhanced her standing in an anticommunist nation. Davis has a respected—for some progressives a revered—place on the American left, having participated in the leadership of mass struggle and provided a "bridge" between academia and street politics. One of her key successes continues to be in academe, where she has introduced and popularized social radicalism and analyses of race, gender, and class to elites or the sons and daughters of the bourgeoisie. University teaching remains a battlefield frequented by select black women, one in which they have made significant contributions. As an iconoclastic academic and radical intellectual, Davis represents the "revolutionary" for left liberals and progressives but not necessarily for radical activists or impoverished or working-class peoples. Her symbolic representation and appeal are both transnational and transracial.[22] Davis's public persona is partly fueled by her hybrid nature as a member of the elite Talented Tenth; this stature of bourgeois respectability was cemented by her 1990 appointment as full professor at the University of California and her 1991 expulsion from the Communist Party USA.

Noting the iconography surrounding her public image to detract from her politics, in "Afro Images: Politics, Fashion, and Nostalgia" Davis observes how many youths equate her political appearance with her physical appearance in the previous militant era. She writes:

> [I]t is both humiliating and humbling to discover that a single generation after the events that constructed me as a public personality, I am remembered as a hairdo. It is humiliating because it reduces a politics of liberation to a politics of fashion; it is humbling because such encounters with the younger generation demonstrate the fragility and mutability of historical images, particularly those associated with African-American history.[23]

For Davis, being known as "the Afro" is a by-product of "journalistic images" that highlight select individuals from the movement era; "the very segregation of those photographic images" transposed Davis into mainstream journalistic culture because of her "presumed 'criminality.'" Most black youths know her as a fashion statement via their encounters with her image in music videos, popular magazines and books, according to Davis, who writes that her hair has become a marker for "revolutionary glamour." For white women "big hair" is usually teased, a bouffant tied to fetish around white female beauty embodied in "Miss USA" pageants and frivolous and labor-intensive work to create hair that "won't move in the wind." Davis suggests other meanings for hairstyles. Photographic images were able to construct Davis as "fugitive" and impart meaning to black women's natural hairstyles in a way that criminalized both simultaneously. Davis recounts how when she was forced underground, the iconoclastic imagery supported the police search and progressive activism: "The circulation of various photographic images of me—taken by journalists, undercover policemen, and movement activists—played a major role in both the mobilization of public opinion against me and the development of the campaign that was ultimately responsible for my acquittal."[24] The *Life* magazine exposé (which Davis saw as free publicity for the FBI) reached 40 million readers, internationally and nationally. For Davis, it provides an occasion for a circumspect reading on assimilation and rebellion, the conflictual themes of neoslave narratives: "Illustrated by photography from my childhood years through the UCLA firing, the article probed the reasons for my supposedly abandoning a sure trajectory toward fulfillment of the middle-class American dream in order to lead the unpredictable life of a 'black revolutionary'."[25]

The FBI hunt for Davis, her imprisonment, and her trial made her a cause célèbre, one promoted on an international level by the Soviet Union and other communist states. Some, but not all, who celebrated her heeded her 1970 pronouncements on freedom before her incarceration:

> Liberation is synonymous with revolution. . . . A revolution is not just armed struggle. It's not just the period in which you can take over. A revolution has a very, very long spectrum. . . . Che [Guevara] made the very important point that the society you're going to build is already reflected in the nature of the struggle that you're carrying out. And one of the most important things in relationship to that is the building of a collective spirit, getting away from this individualistic orientation toward personal salvation, personal involvement. . . . One of the most important things that has to be done in the process of carrying out a revolutionary struggle is to merge those two different levels, to merge the personal with the political where they're no longer separate.[26]

HUNTING THE
REVOLUTIONARY AND FUGITIVE "SLAVE"

The "neoslave narrative" appears as somewhat normative in American society and is not based merely on rhetorical, political imagery or the imaginary of black nationalism. Slavery continuously re-creates itself under U.S. law. The Thirteenth Amendment to the U.S. Constitution codified rather than abolished slavery, designating involuntary servitude as permissible in cases were people were duly convicted of crimes. In the postbellum rise of the convict prison lease system, slavery manifested in vicious and virulent fashion; consider Louisiana's Angola prison, originally "Angola plantation," where emancipated blacks were worked to death. After the civil war, more African Americans died as public property in the state-corporate enterprise of the convict prison lease system than they did under the lash as the private property of individual plantation owners. Essentially, the U.S. outlawed slavery by restricting it to incarcerated criminals (under state or corporate management); then, through legislation (Black Codes and Jim Crow laws) and cultural imaging, it proceeded to criminalize blacks. Restricting "involuntary servitude" to prisons, which exist as largely black or racialized sites today (today some 70 percent of the nearly 2 million people housed in prisons, jails, and detention centers are "people of color"), filters the appearances of postmodern black revolutionary icons through the historical lens of antislavery battles. The neoslave narrative reemerges and recreates itself in response to continuing black disenfranchisement and racial exploitation.

Historically within the United States, black resistance, including nonviolent resistance, to white or state domination has been met with violence. The grim pronouncements of an "unfixed" freedom are linked to institutional antiblack violence. In the postslavery era, the most devastating forms of policing to undermine black advancement were mass incarceration and lynching (in which law enforcement officials occasionally participated). In the post–civil rights movement (called the "second reconstruction" by some), that policing takes the form of racialized incarceration and COINTELPRO, the FBI's clandestine and deadly campaign to undermine radicals and revolutionaries. Given that the state acknowledges no morality outside its laws, revolutionaries become legal criminals and social immorals.

The story of COINTELPRO lends itself neither to the redemptive aspects of neoslave narratives nor to the state's morality plays. Deployed since the 1940s in some fashion against communists and black civil rights activists, the illegal FBI counterintelligence program destabilized progressive political movements by targeting radicals and revolutionaries. The program remains in effect today with the continuing harassment and incarceration of its captives.[27] In 1968, when FBI Director J. Edgar Hoover designated the Black Panther Party as the "greatest threat to the internal security" of the United States, imprisonment as well as executions or assassinations of dozens of Panther leaders followed.[28] However, no concerted national outrage emerged in response to the state's violent repression of black insurgency. (American sympathy for persecuted blacks elicited by antebellum fiction such as *Uncle Tom's Cabin* would find no cultural counterpart for black revolutionaries persecuted by state violence a century later.)[29] The lack of concern was partly tied to ignorance and partly the consequence of negative media depictions of black revolutionaries. According to the U.S. Senate's 1976 Church Commission report on domestic intelligence operations: "The FBI has attempted covertly to influence the public's perception of persons and organizations by disseminating derogatory information to the press, either anonymously or through 'friendly' news contacts." Media stigmatization and state disinformation continue to influence American cultural perceptions of black militants. The "shadow" tracking black militant life took shape in violent policing as the hunt for black revolutionaries led to executions, jail cells, lockdown, and exile. Revolutionary icons do not all uniformly return to those grim realities.

COINTELPRO survivors are exiled or imprisoned militants. The most (in)famous are accused of killing white police officers. That particular criminal charge—the killing of white police attributed to black rebels—functions today in a manner similar to the rape charge—the sexual assault of white females by black males—did during the lynching era. This specific accusation, irrespective of evidence or facts, mobilizes intense, punitive sentiment and racial rage that supports police, prosecutorial, and judicial misconduct in order to achieve swift and deadly retribution. Yet contemporary progressive elites establish varying relationships with revolutionary icons in their advocacy for political rights and just trials for survivors of state violence. In the tradition of Ida B. Wells, a journalist who championed the most vilified of the criminalized at the turn of the century, prominent black writers and intellectuals, such as Alice Walker, Angela Davis, Manning Marable, Cornel West, Henry Louis Gates Jr., and John Wideman, have publicly called for justice for the best known of the criminalized at the end of the twentieth century: Political fugitive-exile Assata Shakur and death-row inmate Mumia Abu-Jamal were both convicted of killing white policemen in political trials where prosecutorial zeal and malfeasance denied defendants due process. That Walker and Gates offer support despite their antipathy to the Black Panther Party (from which both Shakur and Abu-Jamal resigned, given their own criticisms) suggests that black elite advocacy for African American political prisoners reflects not agreement with revolutionary ideology and/or tactics but a shared sensibility that resents and resists (largely through rhetoric) state repression of black rebellions.[30]

With the testimony of an unreconstructed insurrectionist, Assata Shakur's political life reworks the neoslave narrative to invert its deradicalizing tendencies. Standing as a fugitive "slave" for twenty years, Shakur represents the unembraceable: The state exercises severe punitive sanctions against anyone who offers her refuge. Nevertheless, Shakur's case has received support from ideologically disparate African Americans, ranging from incarcerated revolutionaries and prison intellectuals through political icons to neoliberal black studies professors. Her narrative, which is more that of the revolutionary slave than the slave fugitive, seems to construct Cuba, not the United States, as the site for (black) freedom. However, the fact that media reported in 1998 that the U.S. State Department was seeking to negotiate with the Cuban government to lift the crippling forty-year embargo in exchange for the extradition of Shakur and ninety other U.S. political exiles suggests that there exist no fixed sites for "freedom."

Shakur's political contributions to black liberation are enmeshed in high controversy and life-and-death crises. In his article of April 22, 1998, entitled "Black Political Prisoners: The Case of Assata Shakur,"

Manning Marable writes: "there is no question that if Assata Shakur is involuntarily returned to the US that she will be imprisoned for life, and very possibly murdered by state authorities. The only other Black Panther who survived the 1973 shoot-out, Sundiata Acoli, is 61 years old and remains in prison to this day. No new trial could possibly be fair, since part of the trial transcripts have been lost and crucial evidence has 'disappeared.'"[31]

Assata Shakur is less marketable in mainstream culture given that her life and writings present a narrative similar to that of Mumia Abu-Jamal; she is portrayed as the unrepentant rebel who calls herself "slave" (and rejects her "slave name," Joanne Chesimard), and therefore sees the white-dominated, corporate society and state as "slavemasters." Aspects of her narrative (found in the memoir, interviews, documentaries, and media reports) link her more to the underground Black Liberation Army (BLA) than to the Black Panther Party, which has become on some levels a cultural commodity. According to Shakur, she has never been "free"; and even in Cuba, where she has been exiled since 1984 and is valorized as a "black revolutionary," she remains a "slave" because of her status as a black or African woman, a status that she sees as inseparable from the state of subordinate Africans throughout the diaspora.

Shakur's iconography functions less as a political anachronism or celebrity and more as political embarrassment and irritation for the police and conservative politicians; conversely it also serves as political inspiration for radicals and revolutionaries. Just as those who worked above ground with the courts see in Davis's release a vindication of their political agency; those who worked underground through military operations see in Shakur's liberation from prison—which entailed neither casualties nor hostages—an affirmation of their political efficacy. Individuals and organizations that ideologically support her prison escape are thus placed into an adversarial relationship with the state.

Before being forced by the New York Police Department and FBI into the Black Liberation Army underground, Shakur organized in the student rights and anti-Vietnam war movements. Her memoir, *Assata: An Autobiography,* depicts a political persona hardly compatible with commodification. Rejecting the imago of violent black revolutionaries, it offers a complex portrait of a woman so committed to black freedom that she refused to reject armed struggle as a strategy to obtain it. Even during violent upheavals, community remains central to Shakur who, refusing to make revolutionary war synonymous with violence, writes of a "people's war" that precludes elite vanguards. *Assata* describes the limitations of black revolutionaries: "Some of the groups thought they could just pick up arms and struggle and that, somehow, people would see what they were doing and begin to struggle themselves. They wanted to engage in a do-or-die battle with the power structure in amerika, even though they were weak and ill prepared for such a fight. But the most important factor is that armed struggle, by itself, can never bring about a revolution. Revolutionary war is a people's war."[32] The "people's war," however, retained a military dimension for Shakur. She continues:

> I wasn't one who believed that we should wait until our political struggle had reached a high point before we began to organize the underground. I felt that it was important to start building underground structures as soon as possible. And although I felt that the major task of the underground should be organizing and building, I didn't feel that armed acts of resistance should be ruled out. As long as they didn't impede our long-range plans, guerrilla units should be able to carry out a few well-planned, well-timed armed actions that were well coordinated with aboveground political objectives. Not any old kind of actions, but actions that Black people would clearly understand and support and actions that were well publicized in the Black community.[33]

Over a decade after her arrest, trial, and incarceration for the 1973 killing of New Jersey state trooper Werner Foerster (Shakur maintains her innocence in the shooting),[34] Shakur's case was reintroduced to mainstream black America in the mid-1980s through a segment on a New York–based television talk-show, *Like It Is,* hosted by black journalist Gil Noble, who traveled to Cuba to interview Shakur. Archival footage of the civil rights and black liberation movements set the context for their discussions. Following the two-part segment, a panel was convened to talk about her case that included the Reverend Jesse Jackson.[35] In the 1990s Shakur would appear in various documentaries, including Cuban filmmaker Gloria Rolando's *Eyes of the Rainbow*, which intersperses images of a serene Shakur with African Orisha, or Yoruba female warrior deities and entities of love and community. Other narratives emerge to portray this revolutionary as political icon.

Shakur's image in Lee Lew-Lee's *All Power to the People!: The Black Panther Party and Beyond* appears with archival footage in an exposé on the murderous aspects of COINTELPRO—what Lew-Lee has labeled "death squads"—that operated against both the Black Panther Party and the American Indian Movement in the 1960s and 1970s. Former New York Panther Safiya Bukhari is one of the few black women in the documentary who sheds some light on the emergence of the Black Liberation Army as an underground offshoot of the Panthers.[36] According to Bukhari, New York Panthers, accused of breaking with the West Coast leadership, were caught between "a rock and a hard place": Huey Newton allegedly had put out a death warrant on their lives; the NYPD, assisted by the FBI, had done likewise. With the memories of Malcolm X's 1965 assassination tied to the Nation of Islam and its leader Louis Farrakhan's rhetoric, and the 1969 killings of Fred Hampton and Mark Clark by the Chicago police (and the FBI), the Black Liberation Army formed.

In the book, *Still Black, Still Strong: Survivors of the War Against Black Revolutionaries,* where Shakur is identified as a member of the Black Liberation Army, former Panther Dhoruba Bin Wahad offers insights into the underground organization.[37] *Still Black, Still Strong* provides an interview with Shakur that reveals the complex gender and race dynamics surrounding her flight as a fugitive, being shot and then brutalized by police. Later, shackled and chained to a bed, arms paralyzed and bullet wounds in her chest, Shakur was reportedly assaulted by New Jersey State Troopers who threatened to kill her. She recounts that after her capture medical staff kept her alive despite her wounds and the continuing trauma inflicted by her captors:

> The one who gave me the call button was a German nurse; she had a German accent. Some of the Black nurses sent me a little package of books which really saved my life, because that was one of the most difficult times. One was a book of Black poetry, the other was *Siddhartha*

by Hermann Hesse, then a book about Black women in white America. It was like the most wonderful selection that they could have possibly given me. They gave me the poetry of our people, the tradition of our women, the relationship of human beings to nature and the search of human beings for freedom, for justice, for a world that isn't a brutal world. And those books—even through that experience—kind of just chilled me out, let me be in touch with my tradition, the beauty of my people, even though we've had to suffer such vicious oppression. Those people in that hospital didn't know who I was, but they understood what was happening to me; and it makes you think that no matter how brutal the police, the courts are, the people fight to keep their humanity, and can really see beyond that.[38]

During the trial, Shakur was confined in a men's prison, under twenty-four-hour surveillance, without adequate intellectual, physical, or medical resources. She was relocated later to a women's correctional facility in Clinton, New Jersey, where she was housed with women of the Aryan Nation sisterhood, the Manson family, and Squeaky Frohm, who had attempted to assassinate former President Gerald Ford. In 1977, convicted of killing State Trooper Foerster by an all-white jury, Shakur was sentenced to life plus thirty-three years in prison. Shakur maintains that her escape in 1979 was motivated by a fear of being murdered in prison.

In a 1978 petition concerning political prisoners, political perse-cution, and torture in the United States, the National Conference of Black Lawyers, the National Alliance Against Racist and Political Repression, and the United Church of Christ's Commission for Racial Justice brought Shakur's case before the United Nations. The petition states that:

The FBI and the New York Police Department in particular, charged and accused Assata Shakur of participating in attacks on law enforce-ment personnel and widely circulated such charges and accusations among police agencies and units. The FBI and the NYPD further charged her as being a leader of the Black Liberation Army which the government and its respective agencies described as an organization engaged in the shooting of police officers. This description of the Black Liberation Army and the accusation of Assata Shakur's relationship to it was widely circulated by government agents among police agencies and units. As a result of these activities by the government, Ms. Shakur became a hunted person; posters in police precincts and banks described her as being involved in serious criminal activities; she was highlighted on the FBI's most wanted list; and to police at all levels she became a "shoot-to-kill" target.

Malfeasance was the norm during the trials.[39] The 1973 trial in Middlesex County was discontinued because of the blatant racism expressed in the jury room; the court ruled that the entire jury panel had been contaminated by racist comments like "If she's black, she's guilty." The New Jersey courts then ordered that a jury be selected from Morris County; one of the wealthiest counties in the country, 97.5 percent of its potential jurors were white. Most potential jurors believed the defendants guilty based on pretrial publicity. The trial was later moved back to Middlesex County, yet most whites continued to equate "black militancy" or a "black revolutionary" with criminality. Shakur's political affiliations as well as her race-ethnicity[40] would mark her as criminally culpable.[41]

In 1998, African American activist intellectuals S. E. Anderson, Soffiyah Jill Elijah, Esq., Joan P. Gibbs, Esq., Rosemari Mealy, and Karen D. Taylor circulated via e-mail "An Open Letter to New Jersey Governor Whitman." This letter to Christine Todd Whitman protested the $50,000 bounty she had placed on the head of political exile and fugitive Shakur. "In seeking her apprehension by methods that include 'kidnapping,' you have engaged in the kind of debased moralism that the former slave masters in this country resorted to when seeking the return of runaway Africans to slavery." According to the letter's authors, Assata Shakur "followed in the footsteps of Harriet Tubman, who instructed: There was one of two things I had a right to, liberty, or death; if I could not have one, I would have the other; for no man should take me alive; I should fight for my liberty as long as my strength lasted. . . ." In closing, the signatories admonish Whitman concerning her civic and political responsibilities: "The people of New Jersey, particularly people of African descent, other people of color and the poor, as well as your political aspirations, would be better served by your attention to reducing poverty, unemployment, underemployment, the incidence of AIDS, police brutality and corruption and improving housing, public education and health care."[42]

"My name is Assata Shakur, and I am a 20th century escaped slave" is how the "Open Letter from Assata Shakur" begins; it circulated in early 1998 concurrently with "An Open Letter to New Jersey Governor Whitman" on e-mail. In her letter, Shakur writes of herself and codefendant, Sundiata Acoli: "We were both convicted in the news media way before our trials. No news media was ever permitted to interview us, although the New Jersey police and the FBI fed stories to the press on a daily basis." Shakur's conflictual relationship with mainstream media was not new. On December 24, 1997, a press conference was held to announce that New Jersey State Police had written a letter (which was never released publicly) to Pope John Paul II asking him to intervene on their behalf and to aid in having Shakur extradited back to the United States. In response, Shakur wrote to the Pope explaining her story. Then in January 1998, during the Pope's visit to Cuba, she granted an interview with NBC journalist Ralph Penza. For this three-part "exclusive interview series," NBC advertised on black radio stations and placed notices in local newspapers. The series erased or distorted much of the information Shakur and other progressives had presented concerning her case.[43]

However, most striking in the context of the neoslave narratives explored here is the bizarre polarization of female identity with images so diametrically opposed that the only comparable extremes in American cultural iconography are that of the white plantation mistress and the black field slave. In a media interview, Governor Whitman expressed "outrage" at Shakur's happiness about being a grandmother and her haven in Cuba. Shakur's rejoinder notes that she has never seen her grandchild; she argues that if Whitman considers "50 years of dealing with racism, poverty, persecution, brutality, prison, underground, exile and blatant lies has been so nice, then I'd be more than happy to let her walk in my shoes." Responding to an NBC interviewee's statement that the New Jersey police would do everything to extradite Shakur from Cuba, including kidnapping and bounty hunters, Shakur writes in her "Open Letter":

I guess the theory is that if they could kidnap millions of Africans from Africa 400 years ago, they should be able to kidnap one African woman today. It is nothing but an attempt to bring about the re-incarnation of the Fugitive Slave Act. All I represent is just another slave that they want to bring back to the plantation. Well, I might be a slave, but I will go to my grave a rebellious slave. I am and I feel like a maroon woman. I will never voluntarily accept the condition of slavery. . . .

Perhaps the most unsettling passage in the letter is where Shakur echoes Martin Luther King, Jr.'s April 3, 1968 eschatological vision in which King states that he does "not mind" dying because he has been to the "mountaintop." Shakur observes:

Everybody has to die sometime, and all I want is to go with dignity. I am more concerned about the growing poverty, the growing despair that is rife in Amerika. . . . our younger generations, who represent our future. . . . [and the] one-third of young black [men who] are either in prison or under the jurisdiction of the 'criminal in-justice system.' I am more concerned about the rise of the prison-industrial complex that is turning our people into slaves again. . . . about the repression, the police brutality, violence, the rising wave of racism that makes up the political landscape of the US today. Our young people deserve a future, and I consider it the mandate of my ancestors to be part of the struggle to insure that they have one.

Arguing for young people's right to "live free from political repression," Assata Shakur urges the readers of her letter to work to free all political prisoners and abolish the death penalty, offering up "a special, urgent appeal" for struggle for the life of Mumia Abu-Jamal, the only political prisoner on death row.[44]

CONCLUSION

The "rehabilitative" reconstruction of revolutionaries as icons makes them more palatable to mainstream American culture. Left-liberals who purchase the neoslave narrative and its surrogate insurrections are invested in these icons. Institutions which harbor and give new identities to former freedom fighters absorb dissidence with their ability to accommodate political "difference" and subvert transformation.

The "true" revolutionary and icon can coexist in the same personas. Which raises the question: In revolutionary struggles, to what extent does the icon disrupt her/his iconography and with what effect on political practices? To use iconography is not in itself a conservative act. Mumia Abu-Jamal's increasing iconic stature has likely prolonged his life. His use of his social standing to educate about human rights abuses and humanity in prisons has inspired activists. The same can be said of Angela Davis and Assata Shakur.

Conversely, the revolutionary icon can also in fact be antirevolutionary. That does not mean that she or he is not progressive, or even not radical; rather, it suggests that she or he no longer believes in the viability of revolutionary struggles on a material, rather than purely theoretical or rhetorical, level. This anti-revolutionary sentiment can, as discussed in chapter 4, facilitate alliances between neoliberals, neoradicals, and state institutions to the detriment of revolutionary movements or organizations. Given the state and dominant culture's drive to either rehabilitate or eliminate insurgents, it is remarkable that revolutionaries survive, whether behind concertina wire or stage microphones. Perhaps what is even more striking is how organizers and critical thinkers manage to evade the seductive powers of iconography.

Historically icons were objects of uncritical devotion; now, in the computer age, they also represent symbols displaying technical options. Icons, then, have both devotional and instrumental functions as romanticized representations of "respectable" political citizenry, racial and female identity contextualize political dissent in the racial state. On one level, revolutionary icons challenge conventional beliefs with an iconoclasm that disrupts the veneration of bourgeois political practice and symbolism. Paradoxically, iconoclasts who take the political risks to establish an alternative norm may eventually become icons themselves. As revolutionary icons, they are presented as the new authoritative "radicals" to be revered, transgressed, or transformed in struggles with the state.

The political appearances of black revolutionary icons, fugitives, prisoners, and insurrectionists may be contextualized in the dramatic polarities between black/white, slave/master, fugitive/hunter. In a larger framework, today those increasingly targeted by police, grand juries, and the FBI for their political resistance are peace activists, independentistas, and environmental radicals. An estimated ninety activists from the Black Liberation, Puerto Rican Independence, and the white American anti-imperialist movements exist in a precarious Cuban exile while over one hundred of their counterparts remain incarcerated in U.S. prisons. Most are anonymous to the general American populace in the "Free World" and even to the progressive communities that revere the names of political prisoners and icons Abu-Jamal or American Indian Movement activist Leonard Peltier.

Progressive icons are significant because they function to popularize political movements and struggles. However, this popularization partly reflects selective political memory and representations skewed toward elite leadership and symbolism. Selective memory, masked by an uncritical valorization of icons, shields the contradictions of black political leadership from scrutiny while it deflects attention from revolutionary politics and rank-and-file leadership.[45] Those who welcome the chiseling of a marble pantheon of (black) political celebrities likely believe any chipping away at reification to be icon vandalism; yet that "crime" is continuously perpetrated within a racial state indifferent to or implicit in black impoverishment, one that meets political "resistance" with repression.

Contemporary progressive culture is a consequence of past movement battles; yet it does not prevent the public from distancing those it wishes to claim as celebrated political insurgents from those who cannot or will not be mainstreamed. Every neoslave narrative is a freedom story. The diversity of politics within such narratives—whose ideologies range from neoliberal to revolutionary—suggests that revolutionary personas could be as mercurial and impermanent as fixed sites for freedom.

SIX

Depoliticizing Representations: Sexual-Racial Stereotypes

American filmmakers deployed images of Black women which adopted the ideological strata-gems of the jungle films and the plantation genre. Just as the white heroine had served as a canvas upon which was inscribed the nature of her race's supposed virtues and the conflicted construct of her gender, Black women were impersonated (to use [D. W.] Griffith's term for acting) to display the hidden and perverse nature of Blackness, and the essentially savage erotic impulses of Black women.

—Cedric Robinson

Political scientist Cedric Robinson notes that the image of Angela Davis as fugitive (we might also add former Panther leaders Kathleen Cleaver and Elaine Brown) became commercialized and sexualized in the Coffy/Cleopatra Jones blaxploitation films of the 1970s—the armed, revolutionary black woman as embodied by the stereotypes (and phenotypes) projected on celluloid of the "murderous mulatta."[1] This icon, a standard feature in film, has mutated and expanded in the 1990s to encompass domesticity. Whereas the 1970s featured the radical black woman confronting political violence, the 1990s circulate the depoliticized images of the black femme of private fantasy and wish fulfillment.

Consuming images performed by blacks but largely scripted by and for whites, nonblack viewers encounter African Americans primarily through movies and television. Consequently, most representations of radical black women and their iconoclastic feminism are culturally subordinate to the film fetish surrounding black females. Even in contemporary, "progressive" cinema, films project the idea that intermingling with "blacks" increases the possibilities of excitement for whites while promising opportunities for the expression of white humanity and self-restraint. Popular interest in films that feature black females and males is partly tied to racialist, sexual obsessions. The political portraits of militant black female leaders discussed earlier are constantly distorted by the fetishistic images of consumer culture that shape a desire fixed on taboos.

Feminist Audre Lorde has written that "Eros is your joy." Yet given the ways in which racism, heterosexism, and violence shape understandings of sexual desire in the United States, at times what passes for Eros seems more pain-filled than joyful. Americans often discuss themselves and others, local gossip or national news, in relation to sex and violence. Often familial, social, and national debates on violence and safety are filtered through race. Our narratives reflect obsessions and denials about racial and sexual politics in a country long fixated on, repelled by, or attracted to blackness. Present-day crises and confusions concerning racial and sexual violence are traceable to historical coded and explicit taboos that consumers savor.

Writer Patricia Storace notes the hydra-like manifestations of racial-sexual prohibitions that romanticize old racial hierarchies. Describing the literary and cultural accolades for Margaret Mitchell's *The Birth of a Nation* spinoff, she writes that *Gone With the Wind* ranks behind the

Bible as one of the world's most translated books. Its appeal is woven into the warp of a southern tapestry of racial-sexual mastery. According to Storace:

> The seething bitterness of defeat was a part not only of southern family life, but of its political and sexual psychology. A rage at defeat underlay white supremacist platforms; whites could still be masters with or without slaves; the humiliation of defeat increased the virulence of whites toward blacks, who had after all, explicitly or implicitly, been on the winning side . . . [as] knowledge of defeat added variants to the white terror of interracial sex. The defeated white southern men had begun the war as masters, boasting of their virile invincibility in battle and failed before the witness of white women to back these boasts up. . . .[2]

The boastful virility in battle echoes today throughout the rhetoric and violence of neo-Nazis, Klansmen (and women), and White Supremacist skinheads and throughout the "civilized" racism of the white Citizens' Councils whose current-day manifestation, the Council of Conservative Citizens, has included Senate Majority leader Trent Lott (R-Mississippi) and Congressman Bob Barr (R-Georgia).[3] Literature and cinema fuels its contemporary currency as the American fetish for racial-sexual taboos and purity replays throughout popular culture.

Film scholar and critic Donald Bogle satirizes the obsession with interracial sex in *Toms, Coons, Mulattos, Mammies & Bucks: An Interpretive History of Blacks in American Films.* His description of D. W. Griffith's 1917 Klan eulogy offers useful applications for black feminism:

> Matters in *The Birth of a Nation* reach a heady climax later when the renegade black Gus sets out to rape the younger Cameron daughter. Rather than submit . . . she flees from him and throws herself from a cliff into the "open gates of death." Then the mulatto Silas Lynch attempts to force the white Elsie Stoneman to marry him. Finally, when all looks hopelessly lost, there emerges a group of good, upright Southern white men, members of an "invisible empire," who, while wearing white sheets and hoods, battle the blacks in a direct confrontation. Led by Ben Cameron [the white father] in a rousing stampede,

they magnificently defeat the black rebels! Defenders of white womanhood, white honor, and white glory, they restore to the South everything it had lost, including its white supremacy. Thus we have the birth of a nation. And the birth of the Ku Klux Klan.[4]

Bogle's satire of racial stereotypes focuses on males and females. Of the former, he writes that

it was the pure black bucks that were Griffith's really great archetypal figures. Bucks are always big, baadddd niggers, oversexed and savage, violent and frenzied as they lust for white flesh. . . . Griffith played on the myth of the Negro's high-powered sexuality, then articulated the great white fear that every black man longs for a white woman. Underlying the fear was the assumption that the white woman was the ultimate in female desirability, herself a symbol of white pride, power, and beauty.[5]

Bogle's humor shapes his commentaries on black film actress Dorothy Dandridge:

Tarzan's Peril (1951) was typical jungle fare with one twist. In a crucial episode, Dandridge, as a kidnapped African princess, was tied to the stakes by a warlike tribal leader. As she lay with legs sprawled apart, heaving and turning to break loose, it was apparent that never before had the black woman been so erotically and obviously used as a sex object [in film]. From the way Lex Barker's Tarzan eyed the sumptuous Dandridge, it was obvious, too, that for once Tarzan's mind was not on Jane or Boy or Cheetah![6]

He also notes that *Island in the Sun* (1957) functioned as a political intervention for integration liberalism: "Today some might think it totally unimportant that Dorothy Dandridge was the first black woman ever to be held in the arms of a white man in an American movie. Yet because she was permitted to bring integrated love to the mass audience in an age about to erupt in chaos over the issue of integration, she remains a socially significant figure in this film."[7]

We should also note that black female love interests for white males appeared before the civil rights era. Josephine Baker in *Jungle Queen* as well as black and white women playing black women in *Showboat, Band of Angels,* and *Kings Go Forth,* featured white men whose love connects them with the black female body. As moral and legal codes against miscegenation gradually fell into disrepute, black/white love stories featuring black men and white women during the civil rights movement displayed the restrained sexuality of the black (well-educated) male protagonist, portrayed by Sidney Poitier in *Guess Who's Coming to Dinner?* and similar 1960s spinoffs; these images allowed black male and white female bodies to be publicly intertwined.

Part of the racialized attraction or aversion for "the black" in a society obsessed with race, sex, and violence is the appeal of exotica tinged with racial savagery and perversity. In politics, cinema, and music, "being black" is often bound up in the antiblack stereotype of the criminal or hypersexual deviant. Toni Morrison describes how the American literary "white imagination" appears fascinated with "Africanisms" or antiblack racial stereotypes. Functioning as the "marker and vehicle for illegal sexuality, fear of madness, expulsion, self-loathing," according to Morrison, these stereotypes divide the sexually degenerate from the sexually civilized: "Just as entertainers, through or by association with blackface, could render permissible topics that otherwise would have been taboo, so American writers were able to employ an imagined Africanist persona to articulate and imaginatively act out the forbidden in American culture."[8]

What is "forbidden" in American culture often seems to be projected outward onto the outsider or scapegoat. The forbidden, as a volatile mix of race, sex, and violence, seems to enthrall Americans. Media routinely turn civil or criminal proceedings (for instance, Justice Clarence Thomas's Supreme Court confirmation hearings and the Mike Tyson and O. J. Simpson criminal trials) into titillating spectacles. Many consume this mix in novels and films (such as Warren Beatty's *Bulworth,* discussed later). Blackness has come to represent sex and violence in the national psyche. Although they gain notoriety as the most infamous perpetrators of unrestrained and criminal sexuality, African Americans are given little recognition in media, crime reports, or social crusades as being victims of sexual violence. Because of this cultural bias, more than a few African Americans steadfastly refuse to publicly denounce blacks accused, convicted, or guilty of committing sexually violent acts. To do so, some argue, would be an act of racial betrayal that legitimizes the national equation of blackness with sexual deviancy.

Yet silence or irrational denials prove disadvantageous. Rather than counter racial stereotypes, they work with them to deflect concern from a cultural acquiescence to the convergence of race, sex, and violence, particularly in assaults against black females. Audre Lorde's adage "Your silence will not protect you" suggests that not only does silence not protect (innocent and guilty) black males and communities, it increases the likelihood of black victimization. Silence ensures low visibility of sexual or domestic violence against black females. Stereotypes of blacks as sexual savages promote antiblack violence, social indifference to sexual assaults against black women, and the imago of American cultural "savages."

TRACKING THE SEXUAL SAVAGE IN AMERICA

U.S. narratives about the alleged unrapeability of black females stem from the racial-sexual ideologies of colonial settlers and slave societies. After the abolition of slavery, these narratives were reshaped by rhetoric that justified lynchings during the Reconstruction era. In the twentieth century, they have been recycled into pornographic icons and prostitution, which are marketed to symbolize black female sexuality. In each era, the dominant narratives obscure sexual violence against black females while constructing these women as property and/or sexual outlaws.

In the early settler state, the changing legal status of Africans—from humans to subhumans and property—determined the physical and sexual treatment of women. Writer Paula Giddings traces the devolving status of African and African American women in the colonies to the establishment of a bride sale price in 1619 that distinguished between, and placed a price tag upon, "corrupt" and "uncorrupted" women. In 1661, referring to enslaved (or free) African women as "nasty and beastly," the state of Virginia officially recognized slavery. Under the new slave laws, children assumed their mother's status (a situation that proved profitable to white males, who could impregnate black females to create new "crops" of enslaved workers).

By the end of that century, laws became more restrictive and repressive. In 1691, Giddings reports, white marriages to indigenous or African Americans were banned. Maryland passed laws to enslave women for the lifetime of their husbands; but because white women were also being legally reduced to the status of slaves, the laws were amended. By 1705 the term "slave" became synonymous with people of African descent.[9] A century later legislation had emerged to institutionalize slavery with provincial codes and codified racism. The Civil War was fought to deinstitutionalize slavery. Despite the Thirteenth (which restricted rather than abolished slavery), Fourteenth, and Fifteenth amendments to the Constitution, the slave codes mutated into the Black Codes in the South, whereby a racialized caste became reduced to racial-sexual servitude.

Throughout the descent of colonial American law toward slavery, advocates for black enslavement made arguments that implicitly or explicitly centered on the alleged sexual "difference" of the enslaved. Their images of "nonwhite" sexualities played an immense role in the idealizations European immigrants and their descendants held of themselves. Authors John D'Emilio and Estelle Freedman observe: "European settlers attempted to justify their superiority over native peoples in terms of a need to civilize sexual savages, and whites imposed on blacks an image of a beast-like sexuality to justify both the rape of black women and the lynching of black men."[10]

The stereotypes of sexual depravity originating with the white middle classes were shaped and reinforced by class and racial hierarchies and not limited to women of African descent. Historically, Mexican and Native American women were also depicted as sexually savage and promiscuous, and therefore the female representatives of uncivilized races. The "good" colored woman, as the beautiful, noble primitive who befriends whites, was epitomized in historical imagination by Pocahontas. (Centuries after her first appearance as cultural icon, Disney's 1995 animated film of the same name omitted the negative aspects of John Smith's abduction of the teenager.) The image of the red princess was rivaled by the red "whore" or "the savage and promiscuous squaw" just as nineteenth-century laws solidified the status of blacks as slaves.[11] An African American female, unlike her Native American counterpart, would not find herself romanticized in national mythology as a protective heroine for whites, one sexually desired by—even considered a potential bride for—white males.[12] (The image of the protective black female is the asexual, physically unattractive "mammy.") European American taboos against race-mixing were more strongly held against black women than red women. Although both black and red women were sexually vilified, they were assigned different roles in the U.S. imagination. In colonial and neocolonial America these taboos were part of a legal system that forced only black females to mate with black or white males. This system logically had to blind itself to its complicity in sexual coercion and violence against black females documented in slave narratives and would have no stereotypes depicting them as princesses. Sexual violence included forced breeding, rape, incest, battering, and pornography. Black women, as sex commodities, lived or died under the brutalities not only of racial slavery but of sexual slavery as well.

During the Civil War, black females found themselves confronting new forms of sexual violence. As customary in warfare, soldiers used rape as a weapon to terrorize girls and women, undermine communities, and demoralize males whom they battled. Throughout the war, African American females were vulnerable to sexual abuse not only from Confederate soldiers and renegades but also from their "liberators." Union soldiers, like their southern counterparts, considered black females sexual spoils of war. The nominal protection racialized females had as the legal property of elite whites during slavery dissipated after the Emancipation Proclamation, which perversely increased white male license for antiblack sexual abuse.

Following the withdrawal of federal troops with the aborted Reconstruction, defeated southerners of various classes waged a clandestine race war against freed men and women and male enfranchisement. Racial terrorism against African American communities and sexual assaults against black women reached epidemic proportions. In their 1866 Memphis race riot, "whites attacked and killed black people, burned their homes, robbed and gang raped former slaves, raped several other black women at gun point, and attempted to rape a black child."[13] In addition to rioting, whites expressed a raging racism by transforming their antiblack hatred and prejudices into law.

In the postbellum era, black women, seeking to establish inheritance rights for their interracial children, brought paternity suits against white men. Demanding child support from white fathers, the dismantling of concubinage, and promotion of legal marriages between white men and black women, they engaged in some of the earliest efforts to force "deadbeat dads" to assume their legal and moral responsibilities as parents. In response to this early black feminist organizing, southern states passed so-called antimiscegenation laws banning interracial marriages. Courts and vigilantes prosecuted those who engaged in interracial marriage, as new laws blocked African American women's attempts to find safe havens in marriages with white men.[14]

Intraracial marriages offered little refuge. The notion of property and rape, familiar to slavery, appeared in black marriages: Women in general were not legally protected from rape and sexual assault from their husbands. Nor were their children legally protected from family violence, given that incest was usually represented as the girl or child's "seduction" of the male. Newly emancipated black women could now freely and legally marry black men and would confront the dilemma of domestic nightmares that legally wedded white women survived. Yet, in addition to domestic violence from their black partners and family members, black females had to guard against white sexual predators who were virtually immune to legal prosecution.

The imaginary, collective, racial ownership of women as "our women" by black or white men functions like the property contract of marriage, which maintains that a man cannot rape what he allegedly owns. If a socially-constructed race of men really believes that it "owns" the women of their ethnic group and refers to them as "our women," then intraracial rape is considered less heinous than interracial rape. In this construct, only the latter is a violation of the property rights of "owners." Whereas other males were legally restricted and socially prohibited from heterosexual unions (or transracial "ownership"), white males wielded a proprietary hold over black women and an economic dominance over other women that represented their right to interracial sexual relationships.

Ida B. Wells's controversial demystification of rape and sexual abuse, discussed earlier, provided a cornerstone for moral and political resistance to racist violence that was justified as prosecuting or preventing sexual violence. It is helpful to recall and expand upon her analysis. Lynchings embodied the antithesis of rape prevention or prosecution. As sites of sexual violence and sexual mutilations, they functioned as exorcisms to entertain as well as pacify the white mind haunted by black sexual demons. The sexual savage invariably appears in an American shadow play with racially assigned roles. Portraying European American women, particularly those from middle- or upper-class families, as inherently virtuous absolved them of breaking taboos against interracial sex or "miscegenation" and premarital and extramarital sex. Depicting European American men, particularly those with property, as inherently chivalrous absolved them of sexual violence. Identifying African American men as rapists and African American women as whores—innately promiscuous women who could not be violated since they had no sexual virtue—absolved U.S. society of its indifference to white-on-black violence. Racial-sexual mythology, on one hand, and a white code of chivalry, on the other, worked hand-in-glove (or hand-in-rope), orchestrating a deadly duet of bipolar stereotypes: Following the script for this shadow play, people reasoned that a white man, by definition a "gentleman" (in comparison to black men), would not rape a lady (white woman) and could not rape an object (black woman). Racial logic dictated that a white woman, by definition a "lady" (in comparison to a black woman), could not desire a brute and would not join antisexual violence coalitions with black females who were culturally imbued as immoral.

The myth of black sexual pathology justified rape and masked the reality that, overwhelmingly, white women were and are raped by white men.[15] By the early twentieth-century, mob prosecution gave way to legal executions. However, lynchings did not disappear. The most severe retribution for rape, capital punishment, was disproportionately reserved for African American men: "Between 1930 and 1964, ninety percent of the men executed in the United States for rape were black. . . . black men convicted of raping white women received prison terms three to five times longer than those handed down in any other rape cases. . . . at the same time that black-on-white rape evoked the most horror and outrage, it was by far the least common form of violent sexual assault."[16]

Black sexual assaults against black females were treated lightly in courts that considered only interracial sexual violence against white women heinous enough to warrant the death penalty. The racialization of the death penalty for selective, antiwhite acts of sexual violence reflected the different values the state and society placed on both white and black lives and white and black sexuality.

Contemporary black feminists deride the American obsession with black sexuality and the paranoid hypocrisy of its sexual mores concerning violence. In doing so, they often invoke the legacy of black women in the antilynching campaigns. In mocking defiance, Toni Morrison's Sula, a black female character in the novel by the same title, offers a black male character her wry, satirical commentary on twentieth-century American culture's obsessions:

> I mean, I don't know what the fuss is about. I mean, everything in the world loves you. White men love you. They spend so much time worrying about your penis they forget their own. The only thing they want to do is cut off a nigger's privates. And if that ain't love and respect I don't know what is. And white women? They chase you all to every corner of the earth, feel for you under every bed. I knew a white woman wouldn't leave the house after 6 o'clock for fear one of you would snatch her. Now ain't that love? They think rape soon's they see you, and if they don't get the rape they looking for, they scream it anyway just so the search won't be in vain.[17]

Sula's mockery does not negate the reality of black male sexual assaults against white females. Rather it challenges a society that elevates this form of sexual assault as pervasive and uniquely demonic. As earlier noted, the FBI reports that less than ten percent of rapes are interracial; of those assaults, *white*, not black, males are the greatest reported percentage of assailants.

African Americans might ridicule white society's hypocrisy concerning interracial sex and violence without addressing the duplicity in their own sexual treatment and condemnation of black females. Black racial-sexual codes and double standards brand black females as "whores" for engaging in behavior that black males consider a sexual conquest, political defiance, or transracial love in the face of white supremacy. Even when black females do not consort with white males, the accusation, like the charge of "lesbian" or "dyke," functions to police and discipline black female sexuality, securing it as the property or investment of black males. *Sula* relates the black male opprobrium (frequently shared by black females) that censors black females:

> It was the men who gave her the final label, who fingerprinted her for all time. They were the ones who said she was guilty of the unforgivable thing—the thing for which there was no understanding, no excuse, no compassion. The route from which there was no way back, the dirt that could not ever be washed away. They said that Sula slept with white men. . . .
>
> Every one of them imagined the scene, each according to his own predilections—Sula underneath some white man—and it filled them with choking disgust. There was nothing lower she could do, nothing filthier. The fact that their own skin color was proof that it had happened in their own families was no deterrent to their bile. Nor was the willingness of black men to lie in the beds of white women a consideration that might lead them toward tolerance. They insisted that all unions between white men and black women be rape; for a black woman to be willing was literally unthinkable. In that way, they regarded integration with precisely the same venom that white people did.[18]

Having a markedly different relationship to prosecutorial mobs and law enforcement, blacks could not and did not punish voluntary interracial sex as "rape" with the same venomous vigor as whites. Their anger would be focused not at the white male but at the assailable black female who could be ostracized and punished for violating the sexual taboos that black males wanted enforced. (Black male consumption of sexually violent pornography and black male assaults against black females in some ways reflect this anger.) Given the history of racial-sexual slavery and lynching, some argue, it is understandable that African Americans might condemn black female liaisons with whites. However, it is not just historical memory of past atrocities at work here.

The issue of ownership and sexual property remains a deciding factor as all women in a racialized and racist society function on some level within the category of "racial property" belonging to "their" men. Black women who associated with white men for emotional and/or financial support, or those who expressed their sexuality with whomever pleased them, were easily labeled, castigated, and ridiculed as "prostitutes" by black Americans. The slur "whore" was also applied to sexual assault survivors who accused socially powerful black men. White America had categorized black women as a group as sexually immoral and therefore "deserving" violence or harassment. Ironically, African American communities would dismiss black women's reports of sexual harassment or rape as just deserts. Held to stricter standards of sexual conduct in both interracial and intraracial sex, black females continuously confronted images of themselves as actual or potential whores and prostitutes embedded in "white" and "black" minds.

IMAGES OF BLACK SEXUAL PATHOLOGY

Societies that tend to denigrate women often represent them as subnormal and female sexuality as corrupting and pathological. Racialized capitalist cultures tend to have hierarchies in their devaluation of women. On society's color polarity chart, white women may be viewed with suspicion as potential sexual contaminants who swing between the white whore - Madonna icons. But women with dark coloring and African features are depicted as the virtual antithesis of the sublime, ranking the lowest on the visual rating scale for sexual virtue. Unsurprisingly, many women believed that their prospects for social power, esteem, and safety derived from their distancing themselves from the female image whose appearance signified that of the sexually seductive polluter.

Theoretically, only the "lady" is exempt from rhetoric that designates her as a worthy target for sexual abuse (and therefore unworthy of protection). African American women struggled for several centuries to dispel the stereotypes that marked them as the antithesis of the lady. They battled with the stereotype of the sexually free and eager black female. (Ironically, their descendants market in their music this same stereotype to white consumers.) Black women aspired to, and were excluded from, participation in the nineteenth-century Victorian cult of femininity fostered among white, middle-class women. Using race and class divisions to draw the line between the "lady" and "woman," the cult also set the hypothetical boundaries for sexual vulnerability and safety. It demarcated the space for social outrage at any assault directed against a lady and social contempt for violence against the so-called common woman or whore. Allegiance to the cult often determined a girl or woman's credibility in charges of sexual abuse. The imaginary power of the cult to protect "respectable" women explains in part why so many black women eagerly sought to join it as emancipated women, although the cult of femininity was originally a bourgeois, whites-only club.

Racial stereotypes stigmatizing black women as beyond the pale of sexual virtue and restraint appear to be remnants from a dead past. Yet today a white woman may lose her status by openly engaging in sexual choices, particularly those that cross the color-line. "Colored" women, however, are collectively denied that status by virtue of their appearance, not their actions. As an older black woman bitterly observes in Lorraine Hansberry's play, *To Be Young, Gifted and Black,* she could be "Jesus in drag" and still have white males proposition her in the street.[19]

Racially subordinate women are "sexual primitives" and racially privileged women are "sexually civilized" in a society where race, class, and sexual orientation—and secondarily individual behavior—still largely determine whether a woman (who so desires) can pass as a "lady." Lesbians, prostitutes, "nonwhites," prisoners, and poor women are categorically excluded from the caste of civilized sexual beings and the chimerical rewards of being ladylike—protection from social ridicule and sexual abuse.

Exclusionary gender cults, racist images, and social narratives historically were not the only mechanisms working in the United States to construct black females as sexual targets. Like other poorer females, black women were sometimes economically (in order to feed themselves and their families) or physically (through pimps) coerced to work in the sex trade. Discrimination and need have led some women to make unpopular and dangerous choices, choices that appear to reinforce stereotypes of black females as inclined toward impersonal sex with multiple partners. Nowhere is this appearance more reified than in prostitution.

Sex for sale in the United States is historically racialized with unique implications for black women. Before the Civil War, black women and girls were sexual slaves. In the postbellum years, they were sexually terrorized by white males. (Unlike today, where they are overwhelmingly victimized by black males.) After Reconstruction, more than a few were forced to work as sexual laborers, selling the only commodity they possessed to mostly white buyers. Black women who work as prostitutes or sexual laborers exist under different constraints than those of women in general who live as sexual objects. Since the seventeenth century, black females have existed as sex workers largely in service to whites.

This service was codified under slavery and criminalized after emancipation. Just as the most severe penalties for rape convictions targeted black males disproportionately, arrests for prostitution targeted black females. Black females were more visible to arresting officers gazing through a distorted social lens in New York City in the 1930s, where they constituted over 50 percent of detainees and were arrested at a rate ten times higher than that of white women. Police were more likely to arrest black women in the company of white men, whereas white women, who did not generally appear in the company of black men, approached white men in relative safety.[20]

Unlike white prostitutes who tended to have more access to houses of prostitution, black women forced into the lower levels of prostitution worked the street. Black females who were not engaged in the sex trade but were merely walking the streets could be harassed by police. Whether any crime had been committed or not, black females were linked with sexual vice, just as activists Ella Baker and Marvel Cooke were harassed by an undercover policeman from the vice squad as they investigated the Bronx slave marts.

The high visibility of black women as prostitutes mirrored their low visibility as victims of sexual assaults. Punishment of illicit sex was as selective and discriminatory as police "protection" as police entrapped or demanded bribes from black women while ignoring johns and pimps who abused them. Prostitution generally served white men, who expected black females to be "sexually freer" than white females. Malcolm

X once observed about the sex trade in northern cities that what a white person could not or was too ashamed to ask for or demand from a white counterpart he or she brought to a black person. The former hustler contended that in the 1940s Harlem night world, blacks "catered to monied white people's weird sexual tastes."[21]

Sexual violence is a routine occupational hazard in prostitution. Although girls and women who use their bodies as a source of income rarely contract to be brutalized, sex workers garner the least sympathy and concern when they are assaulted. Social indifference stems from the women's violation of conventional sexual mores and from notions of property and contract tied to the white male. What the john pays for, he owns or rents; he may treat his property as he wishes. Given the social inequities framing U.S. prostitution, it is not surprising that most police target prostitutes (poorer, darker-skinned females) while ignoring their customers (nonpoor white males).

Black women who escaped overt prostitution tended to find themselves confronting sexual violence in other areas of employment. As noted earlier, sexual exploitation and violence are occupational hazards for domestic workers, particularly dark-skinned, immigrant females. During slavery and its aftermath, African American women generally cautioned female adolescents to avoid work as house slaves or domestic servants for proximity to white families increased the likelihood of sexual abuse. In their migratory flight from the South, black women sought living wages and an escape from sexual violence. However, the North proved to be "up south," making African American women vulnerable to abuse through job segregation, low wages, and menial labor in domestic service, factories, prison, sweatshops, and agricultural fields.

PORNOGRAPHIC TREATMENT AND SEXUAL SAVAGES

When sexual objectification and racial spectacle meet, an explosive combination for sexual violence usually ensues. Feminist Tracey A. Gardner traces the history of pornography to European travelers in Africa who linked "the dark skin of the people with that of the ape population [and] even imagined that Africans had sex with apes."[22]

Within racist cultures, any "ethnic" women historically considered as consorts with animals (and so tied to bestiality) will not be seen as vulnerable to sexual abuse. In the 1810s in Europe, the South African Sarah Baartman, the so-called Hottentot Venus, was first displayed for upper-class pornographers. After her death, she was dissected and her genitalia put on display in Paris's Musée de l'Homme. In the United States, during Baartman's lifetime, black women were chained in slavery to sexual commodification and relegated to the low status of sex objects for white spectators, voyeurs, and buyers.[23] In twentieth-century popular culture, the dated spectacle reappears in France in the 1920s with Josephine Baker's jungle femme fatale and in American cinema in the 1980s with Grace Jones's sporting a furry tail as Arnold Schwarzenegger's sidekick in *Conan the Barbarian*.

Patricia Hill Collins writes that American society treated African American women as "pornographic objects" or "sexualized animals," sanctioning rape "with the myth of the Black prostitute as its ideological justification."[24] Although coexisting with, and preceded by, the visual sexual exploitation of European and indigenous American women, the "pornographic" slave auctions of black women are likely America's most graphic and visceral image of sexual commerce combined with racial violence. Today the sexualized auction block is supplanted by largely white-dominated pornography and prostitution industries marketing to their clientele of choice—white men.

Referring to pornography as a "direct denial of the power of the erotic" which "emphasizes sensation without feeling," Audre Lorde describes the devaluation of Eros and ways in which those contemptuous of erotic power trade it for porn.[25] Porn imaging is white-dominated irrespective of sexual orientation. Adam Thornton's work on images of black men in white gay pornography documents brutality and bondage as central recurring themes.[26] Heterosexual men are, of course, not the only male purveyors of racialized pornography. Gardner writes of the ambivalent responses of gay and heterosexual African American men to pornographic stereotypes.[27]

Some men "appear to accept and indeed play up to white expectations and assumptions," according to Gardner, who notes that some "myths about black male sexuality are maintained not by the imposition of force from above, but by the very people who are dominated by them."[28] In the popular black women's magazine, *Essence,* journalist Robert Santiago asks "What happens when we absorb the toxic waste of a pornographic culture?"[29] Writing that porn videos featuring black and interracial couples appear designed for white male viewers, Santiago refers to video writer-director William Margold, who states that, for him, any appeal to black male viewers "is purely accidental." Santiago then quotes Marigold: "When I put Blacks in my videos, I project my fantasies, not theirs." African Americans need not depend on (or only denounce) whites for porn production. Black magazines such as *Players* (which offered a special issue in the 1980s, "Daddy's Little Girls," promoting incest) market sexual abuse and exploitation among African Americans.

Blacks share with gays and prostitutes the stereotypes of being "naturally" and primarily sexual. In fetishized representations, they are all aberrational sexual beings who court their own abuse. This stereotype doubly rebounds on black gays, lesbians, and bi- and transsexuals. Caricatures fuel the image of racialized groups serving as racialized sexual spectacles and entertainers for majorities. Progressives critique the images that justify racial-sexual violence and exploitation. Interestingly, among black men, some of the most incisive critiques come from black gay writers and cultural critics, such as James Baldwin, Marlon Riggs, Kobena Mercer, and Isaac Julien, who demystify racialized sexuality and its links to social violence. In his documentary *Ethnic Notions,* Riggs illustrates U.S. black female objectification as either the hypersexual whore or asexual caretaker. These bipolar stereotypes were paired with those depicting African American men as either aggressively oversexed in the image of the black rapist or as neutered family retainer, the Uncle Tom. Cultural representations of African Americans as degenerate "sexual others" inspired and rationalized antiblack exploitation and lynch law at the same time the image of the servile black pacified the white mind.

Antigay stereotypes and homophobic sexual violence depicted in Riggs's documentary *Tongues Untied* intersect with misogynist violence. Riggs investigates black sexual stereotypes and homophobia in which "references to, and representations of, Negro faggotry seem a rite of passage among contemporary black male rappers and film makers."[30] Referring to skits from the TV comedy series *In Living Color,* he contends that "Negro faggotry is the rage! Black gay men are not." Sexual reductionism, applied to both blacks and gays, doubly rebounds on black gays as racism and heterosexism represent blackness and gayness as symbols of impurity, sexual degeneracy, and disease. For some, black Eros or sexuality is the rage—in dance, music, physical features (silicon-injected lips and fanny-lifts—the postmodern Hottentot accessories), while black people are not.

For some blacks, the image of black women—as mulattas bearing the hybridity of white and black females, Afrocentric Nubian queens, or gangsta bitches and "hos"—is the rage, while black females in their individual humanity and subjectivity are not. For Riggs, the "obsession with Negro faggotry" represents "the desperate need for a convenient Other within the community, yet not truly of the community" who can be blamed for "the chronic identity crises afflicting the black male psyche." In light of Riggs's observations, we may also add that the national obsession to discipline, or be serviced by, "compliant" black female sexuality amid indifference to black female abuse represents the desperate need for a convenient Other as a receptacle for sexual anxieties. Black women survive as the Others upon which black male rage and contempt can be displaced and white insecurities and paranoia about civilized sex and family values exorcised.

Kobena Mercer and Isaac Julien describe an "'essentialist' view of sexuality" within a racist framework in which the European construction of sexuality converges with imperialism to portray the colonized as "savage" identifiable by physique and physicalness; this "Other" represents "an open, frank and uninhibited 'sexuality'—unlike the sexuality of the European which was considered to be fettered by the weight of civilization." Critiquing depictions that designate people of African descent as "most natural" when sexual, the black British writers contend that nineteenth-century medicine made identity "equivalent to sexuality" and note how this ideology reappears in "post-60s 'permissiveness.'"[31]

Mercer and Julian argue that European antiblack racial fictions may become "empirically true" through the responses of black males: "the mythology of 'black macho' is maintained by black men who have had to resort to certain forms of force in order to defend themselves and their communities"; they add that the "stereotype of the threatening black 'mugger' is paradoxically perpetuated by the way black male youth have had to develop macho behaviors to resist harassment, criminalization, and the coercive intrusions of white male police forces into their communities." Sometimes those objectified by the stereotypes appropriate them, claiming a liberatory politics. Mercer and Julien argue against "a version of sexuality which says that what is needed to undo the history of homosexual repression is some kind of metropolitan gay savage whose sole purpose is to express his naturalness, his sexuality, for he is at his most natural when he is most sexual."[32]

The black urban savage is considered "most natural when most sexual" and most sexual when savage. That these images have such a wide appeal among middle-class white males (young white suburbanites are the greatest consumers of "gangsta rap" and its pugilistic misogyny) suggests that they serve a cathartic role. The dependency that mainstream American culture has upon the appearance, the hypervisibility, of the black sexual character allows the white "civilized" sexual the normative body. This body is only able to appear, however, when juxtaposed with its racialized negation, given that "whiteness" cannot manifest without "blackness"; it also rarely appears without antagonism toward its most unassimilable element. Predictably, when that "whiteness" and "blackness" are commingled, the resulting hybridity offers possibilities for reconciliation, but usually on the terms of the dominant racial persona. When that commingling is sexualized, then the terms usually depend on the objectification of the racialized female.

CINEMA BLACK FEMMES FATALES

The most controversial films revel in the appearance of violating racial-sexual taboos. Such cinema intends to be thought-provoking, even shocking, in its unconventionality and moral repudiations of racism and repressive sexuality. However, its cultural clichés contradict the repudiations. In formulaic cinema, scripts rely on the familiar, stereotypical mix of sex, race, taboo violations, and violence. The reappearance of "Africanist" characters, described in the previous chapter, undermines the liberal politics of films that commodify racialized sexuality. Historically, cinema has promoted subtle as well as overt reinforcements of racial-sexual stereotypes, projecting the illusion of social transgressions. Those that feature the morally deviant "white" male mated with the biological aberration "black" female recycle hierarchies of racialized sexuality.

Racial-sexual politics have existed since the emergence of American cinema. Donald Bogle describes how the "mulatto came closest to the white ideal," observing that following director D. W. Griffith's use of the mulatta in *The Birth of a Nation,* a "sexy black woman" in movies became "cinnamon-colored" with "Caucasian features." For Bogle, the tragic mulatta Lydia in *The Birth of a Nation,* "the part-black woman—the light-skinned Negress—was given a chance at lead parts and was graced with a modicum of sex appeal. . . . Whether conscious or not, Griffith's division of the black woman into color categories survived in movies the way many set values continue long after they are discredited."[33]

Transracial love permits honor in societies where miscegenation is neither legally enforceable nor fashionable. In transracialism it is safest to love the "woman" one creates: in these Pygmalion films, mulattas. It is routine to love within one's caste. It is noble to love, in fact, champion, those from subordinate castes, particularly the "deviants" within the "lower" races. Racist sexual taboos are directed not at "lust" itself but at where "lust leads to the development of a committed relationship between white males and black females."[34] Rather than break racist and sexist mores, in many films death or prison inevitably severs interracial relationships.

At some point, most moviegoers or video viewers have seen the "tragic mulatta," perhaps without fully comprehending its historical origin and cultural function in American cinema. The mulatta remains the literal and symbolic embodiment of "miscegenation,"[35] or historical racial-sexual violence and the transgression of racist sexual taboos. Like black women in general for a racialist and racist state and society, miscegenation symbolizes decadent sexuality. The mulatta presented an antithesis for the romanticized "healthy," white female sexuality that reproduced children for the patriarchal white family and society (while enslaved black women were forced to reproduce children as commodities). The mulatta's appearance during slavery revealed the hypocrisy of European/American marital vows, sexual moralism, and familial incest taboos. It also illustrated white men's attempts to re-create themselves as Pygmalions by creating a new species of woman through "breeding" enslaved black women to produce near-white black women. "Breeding" also was a new iconography of objectified female beauty. The mulatta, as hybrid, supplanted both the African and European woman in representations of female sexual fetish. In contemporary film, this hybridity surfaces to shape perceptions of interracial desire and black female sexual "power" that deflect from black female political agency.

Visible in the liberal racial politics of mid-twentieth-century America is the tragedy of the mulatta, depicted in films such as *Imitation of Life*, whose seductress attempts to "pass" and is tortured by her unrequited love for white men. In late-twentieth-century liberal race politics, the mulatta represents the transitional figure for the postracial society. This society has finally "overcome" its racial divisions through the ultimate integration—welcomed hybridity. The racial liberalism of Warren Beatty's *Bulworth* works to popularize integration via the sexualization of the black female.

The significance of *Bulworth* is not based on its artistic qualities (which are limited) or its mass appeal (it was considered a box-office failure). Rather, its reception as a political intervention to buttress racial liberalism against the dominance of racial conservatism at the end of the twentieth century makes it noteworthy. *Bulworth* is a political farce about the venality of contemporary electoral politics and a semitragedy about an aging, wealthy white senator who finds a new lease on life by hanging in "the hood" and whose final self-acceptance unfolds as he transforms into a "black man."

Married to a "classy" WASP, with a young adult daughter he loves but never sees, dismayed and disgusted by the vacuity of Washington, D.C., Bulworth takes out a contract on his own life and negotiates a $10 million insurance policy, with his daughter as beneficiary. In June 1998, as *Bulworth* was released in movie theaters, the Supreme Court issued a ruling that opened the way to a dismantling of the federal program that mandates that insurance companies provide services to the poor and working class. In *Bulworth* it is an insurance corporate executive, a white southern good-ol' boy patterned after former House Speaker Newt Gingrich, who—in order to obtain the senator's opposition to a pending bill mandating that insurers provide coverage for poor, inner-city blacks—issues the policy. This CEO eventually assassinates Bulworth after the senator reneges on their deal. Warren Beatty coproduced, wrote, and directed *Bulworth*. Beatty, who has an eclectic history as an actor and filmmaker, has to his credit films as diverse as: *Shampoo; Reds,* an epic docufilm on European American communist John Reed; and *Dick Tracy* (which co-starred Madonna).

"The White Negro," Harvard professor Henry Louis Gates Jr.'s eloquent endorsement of Beatty the man and *Bulworth* the satire, makes little reference to the movie's representations of black women, as it establishes Beatty's credentials with black intellectuals and rap entrepreneurs.[36] The article discloses that Beatty has associated with Amiri Baraka (who appears as a wandering street sage in *Bulworth*), Cornel West, Snoop Doggy Dog, and Dr. Dre and reports that Beatty knew James Baldwin, Alex Haley, and Robert Kennedy. In fact, according to Gates, conversations with Baldwin and Haley in the late 1960s provided the occasion for Beatty's first thoughts on doing a movie "about race." The wall of Senator Bulworth's office in the opening scenes of the film displays photographs of Malcolm X, Martin Luther King Jr., Rosa Parks, Robert Kennedy, and Huey Newton with Elaine Brown. According to Gates, the photo of a young Bulworth with Bobby Kennedy is really a young Beatty with the slain senator and American martyr.

The film's progressive slant impressed more than Gates. In the June 15, 1998, issue of Colorado's "Building Bridges: Progressive Politics Network News," a community newsletter, editors urged readers to go see Beatty rapping in *Bulworth*. According to the article, *Bulworth* is "not a perfect movie, but it's the only mainstream film outside of Michael Moore's *The Big One,* which played a lot fewer venues, where you'll see ideals like that so overtly expressed." The ideals referred to appear in stanzas of a rap delivered in the movie by Bulworth and reprinted in "Building Bridges" that equates "one man one vote" with the television game show "Let's Make A Deal," while disclosing that large contributors garner the loyalty of politicians. Although Gates contends that "'Bulworth's rapping, as a senator on the edge of a nervous breakdown, is more akin to the 'rhythmic rhyme' of 'Dr. Seuss than Dr. Dre,'" he writes that Beatty himself defends rap "from critics who attack it as misogynistic."[37] (This suggests Gates's own self-defense after his public support of the rap group Two Live Crew generated considerable controversy among black feminists.)[38] Gates supports Beatty's position that gangsta rap represents "black rage" and therefore has legitimacy despite its sometimes retrogressive depictions of women; yet he fails to mention that it is *male*, not *female*, rage that is presented as *black* rage. In fact, neither Gates nor other male writers mention if Beatty ever interviewed black women intellectuals or artists for his screenplay. Beatty's political pedigree in liberal antiracist politics is more impressive than his gender politics. Feminized black "ghetto" culture provides the license for sexual free speech. Most reviews of *Bulworth* made little mention of the role of women in black urban culture in the redemption of Bulworth's (aka "the white man's") political soul.[39] Yet women provide the bodies upon which racial divisions are to be resolved. Beatty's one-dimensional representations allow blacks to "save" or redeem the souls of whites. The young, independent, urban sophisticate light-skinned African American "Nina" is contrasted to the aging, yet still handsome, wealthy and powerful "insider." Like other Hollywood films that undermine their stated progressive politics, this film promotes bipolar stereotypes for white male moral subjects and black female sexual objects. In *Bulworth*, the black female is indispensable in the moral advancement of the white male protagonist. Yet the black female is herself a cultural caricature that provides the stimuli of taboo sex and violence. As stereotype, a creation of white males, the "mulatta" as vamp and seductress wields a peculiar power in patriarchal culture. Some black women welcome these screen images of sexual allure where "power" is not synonymous with political agency but dependent on the desires of male suitors. Ironically, the murderous mulatta is part mammy as alienated, despairing men pursue more than sex: They desire emotional sustenance encased in love or lust for the black female. The lack of love and belonging leads to "antisocial" behavior, while uncritical acceptance and sexual affection tied to the black feminine form brings some form of salvation or respite.

Bulworth reveals a white male liberal political strategy for vanquishing white supremacy and racial antagonism. Screenwriter Aaron Sorkin sums up the position of Beatty's character. Apologizing for the crude language, he relates the movie's premise: "the only way for us to overcome on this debilitating racial thing is simply . . . for everybody to fuck everybody else. Warren [Beatty] spent many, many hours trying to convince me that that's what was actually happening, even showing me census data about it."[40] (It is unclear how seriously this position, in a film released during the reconciliatory Presidential Race Initiative, is taken as a political option by the filmmakers.)

At least in theory, sexual politics is at the heart of racial reconciliation and white redemption. (Although Bulworth's miscegenation or interracial mating resonates with antebellum scripts: The whites are propertied males, the blacks are impoverished and "ghettoized" females; there are no images of white females with black males, or poor whites with affluent blacks.) As in Gates's interview of Beatty, most "progressive" accounts of the movie focus on its racial or economic politics without critically examining its gender and sexual politics.[41]

As the "Great White Hope" in a conservative age melding two major parties, *Bulworth* presents a Kennedyesque liberalism that unintentionally replays the worst aspects of the private life of John F. Kennedy while emulating the liberal antiracism of his younger brother, Robert, for whom Beatty had campaigned. Robert Kennedy's concern for impoverished people also reappears in this film, which juxtaposes the lifestyles of the (white) rich and famous with that of the (black) "ghetto." In south-central Los Angeles, the white male counterhero encounters enlightenment and death. *Bulworth* suggests *Reds* without its historical and intellectual substance and cultural nuances to maintain the centrality of a "class war" fought on sexual-racial grounds.

Bulworth first introduces Nina, played by Halle Berry, in a black church in south-central Los Angeles, where she is sucking on a red blow pop. Black church members and community members are packed into the church for a photo opportunity for their Democratic senator. Nina comes up to his car with her female companions to congratulate the senator on his blunt address (in which he informed the group that if they were less concerned with chicken wings and a black football star who murdered his wife they would get better political representation). When the sleep-deprived, inebriated Bulworth first sees her, he woofs and barks. Later in conversation with the senator, Nina reveals a radical intelligence partly inherited from her mother. In a rebuttal to one of Bulworth's monologues where he laments that most black youths do not know about the Black Panthers, Nina informs him that her mother worked in a breakfast program alongside Huey Newton.[42] Nina's politically conscious mother, as an older militant black woman, is absent from the screen. So is her father. But the surrogate father of the house full of play kin in which she lives warns her against associating with the senator, reminding her that a white man ruined her mother's life and "drove her crazy." This suggests that Nina, the lightest in skin color among the extended family, is a racial hybrid. Nina's maternal, familial role, particularly toward her younger brother who defaults on a loan from a local drug dealer, depicts her as black matriarch, although she is only twenty-six years old. Engaged in the underground economy, a hired assistant assassin in the contract Bulworth took out on his life, she uses her sexuality to set him up for his recanted death wish. As the "prostitute" who promises but never delivers sex, motivated by altruistic motives to save her brother from being brutalized by his creditors, she appears on screen as the hooker with the heart of gold.

Berry (who earlier spoofed the treacherous mulatta in the film, *The Flintstones*) is the central "lust interest" in *Bulworth*. The movie offers puerile obscenities and genitalia obsessions as the wealthy white male protagonist (and presumably viewers) relishes breaking social prohibitions by savoring "dirty" words. Rather than black men, black women—Nina's two girlfriends and her grandmother—introduce ribaldry. (Nina herself is spared verbal lewdness and thereby becomes dignified and more "desirable" in comparison with the other black women, despite her provocative attire.) The working-class black women in the film flirt with middle-class white men, providing them with attention and release from Euro-bourgeois social constrictions through black female sexual aggression.

Senator Bulworth is shot before he can engage in "race suicide" by partnering with Nina. He is killed by the good ol' boy who refers to blacks as parasites on welfare and crack, while reserving approval for entertainers Michael Jordan, Oprah Winfrey, and patriot Colin Powell. The film's political dreamer dies with the political dream, echoing the 1968 assassinations of Martin Luther King Jr. and Robert Kennedy. However, the dreamer's mulatta love interest had pronounced his benediction moments before the execution: "Bulworth, you know you my nigga."

CONCLUSION

Historical narratives and contemporary cinema have each projected racial-sexual stereotypes wrapped around the black female body. Such packaging works to overshadow the political images of black female activism and agency. Black feminist discourse has critiqued the use of the black female body as object or victim of the white male sexual gaze or aggression. What has garnered lesser attention is how black male political performances and activism "protecting" the black female from this sexually "predatory" relationship have inspired distinct forms of counterfeminism that deny black women's power while promoting their dependency. Countering protector narratives that mask black sexism, gender-progressive males have produced antiracist feminisms that challenge old racial-sexual stereotypes. Their writings and analyses remain marginalized within popular culture. Still, they manage to inspire debate and reflection on black or antiracist gender coalitions in feminist politics.

SEVEN

Fostering Alliances: Black Male Profeminisms

The distinctions between black men championing black females as patriarchal protectors and black men championing feminism to challenge sexism are easy to see.[1] Patriarchal politics exemplifies the protector's stance, while profeminist advocacy explicitly disavows sexism and patriarchal privilege. As chapter 5 on black female revolutionary icons sought to demonstrate, recognizing the contributions of black progressives does not necessitate uncritical acceptance of them. In the alliances being fostered between black feminists and their male counterparts, profeminists often appear to overshadow black feminist politics and radical agency. Evident obstacles to black revolutionary feminism stem from historical sexual-racial stereotypes that thrive in popular culture and from black male demagoguery disguised as racial chivalry that usurps the voices and agency of black females. Profeminist males present an alternative. For those efforts they are sought out as allies in the "gender wars." However, profeminists also may contribute to the diminishment of radical black feminism, and so comrades in struggle may present problematic gifts.

AN ACHILLES HEEL

There exist very few viable female "support roles" for antiracist male feminists. As a result, the "male feminist" takes on an indeterminate appearance and shadowy form. His appearance alters conventional language so that the terms "feminism" and "feminist" for females and "profeminism" or "profeminist" are required for males to maintain gender distinctions among advocates for gender equality. Some women, desiring female autonomy and leadership, are reluctant to concede the use of the label "feminism" for men, although the existence of antiracist whites just as the existence of antisexist males disavows rigid identity politics. Reluctance to cede the identifier may stem partly from the new necessity of qualifiers—such as *female* feminist—to distinguish between men and women who advocate ideology associated with females. Perhaps an uneasiness with the term "male feminists" is tied to a desire to biologize feminism. Or perhaps some women are merely wary of the possibility of benign paternalists or Pygmalions as the Trojan horse on gender battlefields.

Like racial or economic elites, as gender elites, males are able to bestow a largess to females in political struggles. This political and material support simultaneously repudiates and reinscribes their structural superiority and advantages as political allies. Both nonprogressive and progressive males, including profeminist writer-academics, wield undue privileges over women. Patriarchal privileges are structural or institutionalized. Consequently, the authoritative voice, irrespective of ideology or advocacy, remains male. (In similar fashion, white supremacy has constructed the "responsible" voice on race as white, while capitalism has designated the informed speaker on economics and class issues as bourgeois, from Keynesisan to Marxian.) Academe, where first women's studies and now gender studies struggle to achieve institutionalization, clearly reveals patrimonial legacies. In 1998 the journal *Chronicle of Higher Education* noted that 43 percent of women in academe had never published a journal article compared with 23 percent of men; women's work is less widely read; women are more likely to teach undergraduates and less likely to hold advanced degrees from prestigious institutions.[2] The academy continues to allow the subordination of women while it supports the development of male profeminist writers. Among academic writers, at least, feminist and profeminist progressive politics shelter conflicts and contradictions.

Emergent feminisms partner males and females, asking for a shadow dance set by unspoken expectations that feminist women uncritically support their male counterparts. In an antifeminist society, one increasingly marred by strident voices in the backlash against feminism, women may eagerly respond partly from solidarity and partly from a desire to be "rescued" by male allies from the ignominy of ideological wallflowers.[3] Missteps are inevitable in a novel tango. In uncritical partnerships, collective movements—two steps forward, one back; one forward, two back—spare only the very agile the frustration of faltering. In an uneasy and unequal match, the mere ability to not stumble and remain upright rarely constitutes progress even when validated as such.

On a limited level, progress is measured by the increasing numbers of male feminists. The quality of their political ideologies and their commitments to critically examine racism, corporate capitalism, and heterosexism are often unmeasured. No doubt, a democracy needs more profeminist males just as it needs more antiracist whites, and greater numbers of the affluent to struggle for socialism and dominant sexuals to battle heterosexism. The necessity for profeminist males, some argue, comes from a need to halt the abuse and degradation of women and girls as well as the need to grow community where a thick skin of sexual isolation can be shed for a translucent one of connection. This shared membrane is seen in black men's critical contributions to antiracist feminist thought, but it can be frayed by a feminism appended to male privilege. Male privilege, of course, is not universally and equally shared among males; color and caste have always mitigated and in some instances radicalized its power.

Black male feminists appear and likely are inherently more progressive than mainstream ("white") male feminists by virtue of their subordinate social status and, black male feminists have argued, "matriarchal" or "nonpatriarchal" family structure prevalent among African Americans. Dominant society has constructed black men or "men of color" as less civilized, as hypermasculinized and counterfeminist. Black male feminists, however, understand themselves to be "feminized." Some of male feminism's most thoughtful and challenging expressions are found among Latino and African American males.

Not only do black profeminists not share the same structural, patriarchal authority and dominance of white males—the supreme fathers—they simultaneously struggle against racism and feminism. Their progressive positions on class and sexuality are less clearly demonstrated. Regardless of gender, most mainstream feminists rarely give priority to, or seriously acknowledge, antiracist feminism. This is why "black male feminism" is so appealing. Black women, identified with black communities, collectively have more in common with black male feminists than they do with white feminists who are not radical antiracists. Some antiracists even argue that black women have more in common with black masculinists or sexists than with racist or Eurocentric white feminists, suggesting race not gender as the dominant politicizing element.

The antiracist endeavors of male feminists benefit black women as *women* in a patriarchal society, while their profeminist endeavors assist black women as *blacks* in a white supremacist state. (If it seems that I have erred in reversing the emphasis here, consider how antiracism benefits women and how profeminism uplifts a race.) Given the progressive nature of profeminist politics, it is difficult to argue against naturalizing coalitions between black feminists and profeminists. Still, a healthy suspicion questions coalitions between black feminists and even the most progressive profeminists. A recollection of the gender contradictions of progressive males inhibits any uncritical embrace. The antiracist feminisms in Michael Awkward's literary criticism, in Lewis Gordon's philosophy, and Devon Carbado and Richard Delgado's critical race theory provide models for male feminism that posit and complicate alliances between black men and women.[4] These models offer insights into gender-progressive or liberal politics. At the same time, they frame the limitations of some male advocacy for gender parity.

A BLACK MALE FEMINIST MANIFESTO AND THE FEMININITY OF BLACKNESS

In "A Black Man's Place in Black Feminist Criticism," Michael Awkward presents a black profeminist manifesto:

Black womanism demands neither the erasure of the black gendered other's subjectivity, as have male movements to regain a putatively lost Afro-American manhood, nor the relegation of males to prone, domestic, or other limiting positions. What it does require, if it is indeed to become an ideology with widespread cultural impact, is a recognition on the part of both black females and males of the nature of the gendered inequities that have marked our past and present, and a resolute commitment to work for change. In that sense, black feminist criticism has not only created a space for an informed Afro-American male participation, but it heartily welcomes—in fact, insists upon—the joint participation of black males and females as *comrades*.[5]

Awkward argues that the value of male black feminism lies in its anti-patriarchal stance and self-reflexivity in its relations to, rather than reproduction of, a feminism that focuses on "the complexities of black female subjectivity and experience." For him, the abilities of male feminists to expand the range and use of feminist critiques and perspectives include a critical discourse on obstacles to a black profeminist project and new constructions of "family" and black male sexuality.[6]

Awkward reassures his readers that male feminists are trustworthy. His manifesto issues a code of conduct to ensure that they become or remain so. First he notes feminist Alice Jardine's concern that male feminists do not imitate feminists: "We do not want you to mimic us, to become the same as us; we don't want your pathos or your guilt; and we don't even want your admiration (even if it's nice to get it once in a while)."[7] Then Awkward advocates a form of male feminism that neither appropriates nor dominates feminism; rather it seeks to reassure female feminists that they need not fear the increasing entry of profeminist male voices as authoritative in feminist discourse.

Aware that our hierarchical society translates biology into social dominance or subordination, Awkward comforts the uneasy by dismissing the political clout wielded by an ascending profeminism: "Surely it is neither naive, presumptuous, nor premature to suggest that feminism as ideology and reading strategy has assumed a position of exegetical and institutional strength capable of withstanding even the most energetically masculinist acts of subversion."[8] Yet his pronouncements are not entirely reassuring.

Male faculty have gained an increasing presence within the discipline of gender studies, a discipline that has begun to supplant sites labeled "women's studies" in academe. This in itself is not a sign of counterprogressive politics. Yet the "institutional strength" Awkward heralds for women's feminism could be overstated in order to serve as a defensive maneuver to preempt critiques of the advantageous position of male feminism. Historically, marginalized and oppressed groups such as Native, African, Latino, Asian, Arab Americans, and women struggled in social movements that altered academe. Where they have survived in the post - mass movement era, such studies have become institutionalized and mainstreamed. Originally considered to be marginal, and unsuitably politicized, these studies became legitimized by the inclusion of dominant elites who express interest or become authorities in the areas of ethnicity-race studies.

Those who welcome the departure of exclusionary disciplines and Manichean depictions of the oppressed and their oppressor(s) are still left with an uncomfortable perception. The validity of an area of knowledge—for instance, women's studies or ethnic studies—garners legitimacy partly to the extent that privileged intellectuals, such as men or whites, shape the discourse. Therefore, the exegetical and institutional strengths that allegedly safeguard against subversion or mutation are not as powerfully entrenched as Awkward would have us believe. Setting aside his injunction "not to worry," perhaps what concerns feminists is the ascension of male literary feminism.

Author Michele Wallace expresses reservations about black male feminists in "Negative Images: Toward a Black Feminist Cultural Criticism." According to Wallace, Henry Louis Gates Jr., who is coeditor of *The Norton Anthology of Afro-American Literature* and editor of the Oxford series on black women writers, is "single-handedly reshaping, codifying and consolidating the entire field of Afro-American Studies, including black feminist studies." Given his influential literary and academic status as director of Harvard University's W. E. B. Du Bois Institute of African American Studies, Gates wields considerable clout. This institutional power, writes Wallace, means that Gates

> demonstrates an ability to define black feminist inquiry for the dominant discourse in a manner yet unavailable to black female critics.

The results so far are inevitably patriarchal. Having established himself as the father of Afro-American Literary Studies, with the help of *The New York Times Book Review,* he now proposes to become the phallic mother of a newly depoliticized, mainstreamed and commodified black feminist literary criticism.[9]

Wallace mentions Gates's statement that "learning to speak in the voice of the black mother" is the objective of the Other's discourse. In literary production, men still have greater access to publishing and authority as intellectuals and thinkers. The greatest literary achievements of African American women in feminism are in fiction. Men—whether masculinist or profeminist—define the social and intellectual parameters of gender politics through literary *non*fiction. Male writers who highlight the significance of female contributions can nevertheless engage in an opportunistic feminism. Men who profess feminism may acknowledge the "exceptional" woman as their intellectual equal just as whites who profess antiracism validate the "exceptional" black or person of color. Yet the "exceptional" is an aberration. Such men see most women as supporting helpmates or damsels to be succored; such views complement the images of male competency and heroism.

Sensitive to black feminist criticisms, as expressed by Wallace and others, Awkward cautions black men who desire to be productive feminists not to reproduce dominance or erasure of females in their discourse about black feminism and women. Instead, he argues that they should deal with the specificity of their gender as males. The self-interest at work here, according to Awkward, is not selfish or narrow but self-enlightened and enlightening, for profeminism furthers men's ability to explore male identity and masculinity. (A parallel construction and argument exists in critical white studies or antiracist discourse that provides opportunities for Euro-Americans to explore white identity and "whiteness.")

Illustrating his point, Awkward offers an insightful reading of Toni Morrison's *Sula.* He describes the relationship between the character Eva's infanticide of her adult son—a drug addict who she feared was attempting to reenter her womb—and black male sexism. Awkward asks: "Beyond its heterosexual dimension, can the 'female' truly come to represent for a traditional black male-in-crisis more than a protective maternal womb from which he seeks to be 'birthed' again?"[10] For him, redefining manhood means neither re-creating the domestic and uterine enclosure of black women nor emulating the acquisitive power of dominant elites.

Awkward's profeminism presents the black male as linked to women by virtue of race-ethnicity. His black male is a gender hybrid. He uses Alice Walker's term "womanist" to juxtapose the black-community-centered womanist or black feminist with the white or mainstream feminist:[11] "'Womanist theory' is especially suggestive for Afro-American men because, while it calls for feminist discussions of black women's texts and for critiques of black androcentricism, womanism foregrounds a general black psychic health as a primary objective."[12]

For Awkward, probably the "most difficult task for a black male feminist is striking a workable balance between male self-inquiry/interest and an adequately feminist critique of patriarchy."[13] Framing womanism rather than "nonblack" feminism as his model, he argues for the place of the black male feminist as noninterloper. This is not because he pronounces himself with "insider" status but because womanism constructs him as such: It is a people, not merely a gender, that preoccupies womanist discourse.

Offering the progressive intellectual stance of black male feminism against an undifferentiated sexism, Awkward presents patriarchy monolithically. Yet he variegates male identity. Using Hortense Spillers's "Mama's Baby, Papa's Maybe: An American Grammar Book," he discusses how black male identity evolves in a feminine matrix.[14] In Awkward's case, we may also add differentiation. His autobiographical narrative discloses that as a consequence of having been raised by his mother who was brutalized by his father, he attempted early in his life to construct an identity not based on male privilege and violence.[15]

As Awkward reconstructs Spillers's argument, we see the familiar premise that black males are denied full patriarchal privileges due to racism, the same racism that engendered the much-maligned "female-headed household." Awkward concurs with and quotes Spillers: "It is the heritage of the *mother* that the African American male must regain as an aspect of his own personhood." This heritage constitutes a form of "power" that Spillers describes as "the female within," which is not defined. Awkward writes that the idea needs more exploration as to what it signifies in the lives of black males' "repressed female interiority."[16] The "female within" appears strongly tied to a black identity. Although Awkward rejects the thesis of the black matriarch, propounded by Daniel Patrick Moynihan in his writing, single black women seem to possess a special essence.[17] They are the designated source of this hybrid male who recognizes the mother's strong character and will.

What can be said of black men raised by "nonblack" women, black men with white, Latina, Asian, or Arab mothers? How do they obtain this cultural strength typical of Awkward's matriarchal black communities? In *Get on the Bus* (1996), director Spike Lee fictionalizes a black male pilgrimage to the 1995 Million Man March. His film character Gary, the son of a black father and a white mother, embodies both a strong black identity and a feminized consciousness. Art imitates life: African American males raised by white females display a "black identity" (as nebulous and contested as that may be). They also exhibit the feminization of blackness both in its positive aspects celebrated by Awkward and its negative aspects critiqued by Lewis Gordon.

Awkward concludes that for black male feminists, the "Father's law [is] no longer the law of the land."[18] Yet he does not say who and what have replaced the father and the father's law. Surely not the mother or her law. And anarchy does not rule. Perhaps the emergent son, the hybrid with the interiority of the female, supplants the patriarch. But how did the new son, or the son for the new age, ascend? In a transgender, nonviolent, safe-sex oedipal drive, the feminist male may supplant not only the father but also the mother (and the sister). He thereby proves himself superior to the patriarch based on his claims—buttressed by the authority of his masculinized feminist speech—to having transcended the female/male dichotomy of mother/father.

Given that Awkward has stated that black female subjective experience is not the focus of black male feminism, he need not address the mother's law or the liberation of the "male interiority" of the female/sister. Sans patriarch and matriarch, forgoing anarchy, it is unclear if leadership and the law are to spring from the progeny's transgender consciousness. The "law" or ideology of the hybrid male, the feminized man, differs from that of the hybrid female, the masculinized woman, the "sistah." Conflict or coalition is inevitable. In disagreements and battles among heterogeneous feminists, the hybrid male retains some unspoken advantage in conflict resolution. He is the beloved of the interiorized mother (or, in the words of black gay writer Hilton Als, the "antiman" or "negress"). Yet he seems to possess the latent, institutional power of the patriarch, remaining the he (she) who is heir apparent to the father. Not every male advocate of feminism actually relinquishes latent power. Awkward fails to explore the degree to which profeminists transcend or jettison rather than merely feminize or share their patriarchal privileges.

While Michael Awkward illuminates the black man who is not really a "man" because of his feminine interiority, Lewis Gordon reflects on the black man who is not truly a "man" because of his feminized exteriority. In "Effeminacy: The Quality of Black Beings," exploring sex and gender within Jean Paul Sartre's *Being and Nothingness*, Gordon notes the nuances "of antiblack and misogynous worlds" and their coextensive appearances.[19] Discussing blackness as femininity, he writes: "Our descriptions of sexuality in an antiblack world pose a gender problem. From the standpoint of an antiblack world, black men are nonmen-nonwomen, and black women are nonwomen-nonmen."[20]

According to Gordon, this position is premised on European Americans "—white men and white women—being both human, being both Presence, and our premise of blacks, both black men and women, being situated in the condition of the 'hole,' being both Absence." He notes that this dichotomy raises "a gender question concerning black men and a metaphysical one concerning black women. Blackness is regarded as a hole in being. Black men are hence penises that are holes; and black women are vaginas that are holes—holes that are holes. If blackness is a hole, and women are holes, what are white women, and what are black men in an antiblack world?"[21]

This exploration of the "nature" of black males and white females in an antiblack world offers important insights. For instance, Gordon argues that white women as "indeterminate" choose between their "Presence" biologically embodied in their whiteness and their "Absence" determined, again in biology, by their femaleness. He maintains that the choice that white women have for Absence is doubly reified by their racial transgressions, transgressions viscerally marked for the racist by the ability of white women to bear "black" children. In this argument, Gordon reinforces critical feminist analyses. For example, film critic Rhona Berenstein also notes the element of contamination embedded within film's projection of a mystic virginal whiteness embodied by the European (American) woman:

> A range of jungle films align monstrosity with darkness and position the white woman as the figure who negotiates the chasm between the white and black worlds. Her role is ambiguous. She is under threat and in need of white male care and she is liminal, aligned with and likened to monsters, blacks, and jungle creatures. The figuration of white heroines in jungle narratives underscores the slippage of race and gender traits in these pictures, and highlights the terrifying and monstrous results of transgressions of the conventional boundaries of sex, species and race.[22]

Where biology connotes Presence or Absence, race and gender become determining markers. "Effeminacy" contends that, for the antiblack racist, the "'essence' of blackness . . . is, if you will, the hole, and the hole is the institutional bad-faith mode of the feminine"; antiblack racism is therefore "intimately connected to misogyny." Gordon's feminism depicts with evocative imagery the suspect-status of white women in a racist world:

> [T]he white woman should not be regarded as the jewel of the antiblack racist. For hidden in her whiteness—like the secret blackness of milk, the secret abundance of blackness, the fertility that so outrages Manicheanism with its propensity to split apart and weaken the Light—is the antiblack racist's suspicion of her blackness. She stands as a white blackness, as a living contradiction of white supremacy. Out of her comes every white, placing a question mark on the notion of the purity of whiteness in the flesh. Unlike the black woman, out of whom only black children can be born, she can bear both white and black children. Because of this, the white woman ultimately stands on

the same ontological level as slime in an antiblack world. She is regarded as a frightening substance that simultaneously attracts and repels.[23]

According to Gordon, "As pure Presence, masculinity is an ideal form of whiteness with its own gradations; the less of a hole one is, the more masculine one is; the less dark, the more white." Therefore, the less dark, or more white, the less feminine. This equation allows him to maintain that the black man "embodies femininity even more than the white woman." For Gordon, a "black man in the presence of whiteness stands as a hole to be filled; he stands to the white man in a homoerotic situation and to the white woman in a heterosexual erotic situation with a homoerotic twist; she becomes the white/male that fills his blackness/femininity."[24]

Gordon goes on to argue that whiteness can be worn as a phallus: "The 'phallus,' against which and upon which gender analyses often focus, needn't be and possibly no longer is a penis. In an antiblack world, the phallus is white skin."[25] That assertion aptly describes an antiblack or "white" world to some degree; although it might be pointed out that the white female's phallus operates on some levels as a prosthetic. Significantly, though, Gordon's argument says nothing about the phallus in a "black" world. It may be doubted whether, in their relationships with black women and girls, black men and boys are feminized (subordinated) in the same manner in which they appear to be in the "nonblack" world.

Gordon writes that the black man "cannot reject his femininity without simultaneously rejecting his blackness, for his femininity stands as a consequence of his blackness and vice versa." Black men disavow their connection to black women by asserting their "maleness." For him, the black male "has a connection to the black woman in virtue of his blackness, but he can deny who he is by asserting what limited connection to maleness he may have."[26] Here black men betray their femininity, which is based in blackness, a femininity in some ways purely negative in its construct. This form of blackness is externally defined and delimited as the antithesis of whiteness and/or maleness (which are conflated in this argument), a white maleness extended to white women by racial proxy.

What the black woman embodies as doubly feminized by race and gender is unclear here. Despite the essay's incisive analysis of white patriarchy and supremacy, readers may be left wondering, "What are black women in an antiblack world?" Gordon's discussions of black male and female relationships never fully develop. Given its primary focus upon black men and white women, his analysis appears to overlook the issue of where the black male stands in relationship to the *black* female. Gordon is not completely silent about the black female. However, his remarks juxtapose her with the white male and female, not the black male. According to Gordon, "The black woman stands as the reality of sweet, seductive, open femininity" in an antiblack/misogynist world. By "sweet and seductive," he refers to, in the dominant culture's sensibilities toward black females, the putrefying rancidity of rotting fruit. He notes in reference to academic Hazel Carby that the black woman appears as "an exotic figure of solution."[27] Her reconstruction as the sugar tit of consolation masks the abhorrence people feel toward her as a source of fecundating decay. "Effeminacy" fails to note that it is not only blackness that constitutes femininity as debased phenomenon. Femininity is more than blackness, just as masculinity is more than whiteness.

Given that Gordon's work is on antiblack racism, his black male feminism need not explore the ways in which patriarchy reasserts itself in black forms against black females. That racism contributes to sexism, that white women have patriarchal power invested in their wearing of skins/phalluses, are important points to be made. And Gordon does so with turns of language and ideas that illuminate and disturb. Still, the defensive murderous rages and desperate protective measures of black females against black males range from Eva's immolating her son to restraining orders. What transpires as black men disavow their connections to black women to assert or deny "maleness" can often be misogynist.

Both Gordon and Awkward see black males as suspect masculine beings, not truly "male" in an antiblack or racist world. This view speaks in part to a sense of severance from traditional and historical constructs of a humanized rather than animalized existence and a connection to femininity embodied in the black, not the white, female. Likely, black male femininity is a racialized gender construct (or sexualized racial construct). Both writers evoke the kinship of shared skin. Each directly or indirectly refers to Spillers's "captive community" where, on some level, blacks seem to occupy the same skin, uncut by gender and blood. In "Mamma's Baby, Pappa's Maybe" Spillers maintains that an enslaved African American female "shares the conditions of all captive flesh" as the "entire captive community becomes a living laboratory." For such women, according to Spillers, the theft and mutilation of the body create a special condition in which "we lose at least gender difference in the outcome, and the female body and the male body become a territory of cultural and political maneuver, not at all gender-related or gender-specific."[28]

These shared conditions of racial oppression do not erase the female body as a site for sexual violence. Spillers, Awkward, and Gordon do not argue for black gender essentialism. But their works overlook differences separating black males and females. Instead, the writers emphasize commonalties between the racialized genders. Tensions, strife, and divisions between black women and men garner the attention of spectacle in American culture. Awkward's discussion of ties based on a shared femininity from familial conditioning for the male feminine interiority and Gordon's analysis of a shared femininity based on the racialized epidermal in a racist society respond to the felt need and desire to stress what black men and women have in common. However, those commonalities cannot efface the battles that cut through ties. Despite the realities and ideals concerning the female within or blackness as Absence, tense relations and distrust are frequently normative. Nowhere are the frays between black women and men so stark than as in the arena of domestic violence.

THE PITFALLS OF
GENDER COALITION POLITICS

Legal scholar Devon Carbado explores the issues of coalition politics and antiessentialism from a black male feminist perspective. In "Race, Domestic Abuse, and the O. J. Simpson Case: When All Victims Are Black Men and White Women," he notes that to "the extent that black men ignore the particularities of black women's racial experiences or exclude themselves from discussions about gender dynamics in the black community, they are unlikely to come to terms with . . . the patriarchal privilege they wield. Nor are they likely to challenge the notion that black men, and not black women, represent the paradigm of black being."[29]

Carbado is clearly writing about black masculinists, or sexists. But to some degree his critique can be applied to black profeminists whose progressive gender politics or feminization via racism may shield them from their own participation in patriarchal privilege. Carbado's black feminism emphasizes and elevates the status of black women. It is hoped that most black profeminists and feminists are unlikely to agree that black women should "represent the paradigm of black being" even if they agree that black men should not be constructed as such a metaparadigm under patriarchy. Patriarchy makes men representative of humanity. Must profeminism make women—and antiracist profeminism make *black* women—representative of humanity? Such an argument seems to engage in romanticism or patronage. Even the feminized paradigm remains some form of Foucauldian carceral or containment waiting to be dismantled or traded in for a more expansive worldview.

Carbado's article focuses on the status of black women in two 1995 media "events," the O. J. Simpson case and the Million Man March. As spectacles, each generated and continues to incite heated debates about black gender politics. Using the Simpson case, Carbado raises questions about civil rights advocacy and how the black male "subordinating experience is perceived to have enough cultural currency to represent victimhood for a specific political or legal battle cry." Carbado notes what is generally acknowledged among progressives, that the "racial battle cry" in black antiracist struggles has been gendered male. His essay identifies "unmodified antiracism" as a form of black male essentialism that "derives from intentional sexism and/or functional sexism in antiracist discourse." Functional sexism for Carbado is a strategy in instrumental politics that confronts racism by privileging the male. He argues that "there is no justifiable basis for treating the subordinated status of young men as more deserving of black political solicitude than the subordinated status of young black women."[30] Unmodified antiracism reduces discussions of "black community" or "black people" to references to black males and the struggle against racism to essentially a struggle against black male subordination. (We could add reductionism of "black rage" to one gender or rhetoric about black males as an "endangered *species*.") It presents explanations of antiblack racism directed against males as able to address antiblack racism against females. Carbado provides an example of unmodified racism in the Million Man March injunction for women to support the march financially yet stay at home and take care of children in order to facilitate males' experiences to assert themselves as the head of households.

He also describes unmodified racism stemming from black women as he recounts the domestic violence workshop at the July 1995 African American Women in the Law Conference. In the workshop, black women argued against the incarceration of black male batterers for domestic abuse "because such abuse stemmed from black men's collective and individual sense of racial disempowerment."[31] Using his experiences in that workshop, he reflects on the ways in which black women—those who do not avail themselves of Eva's homicidal remedy—render their own experiences secondary and in service to, or protection of, black males. This self-sacrifice, or Catch-22, that some black females face mirrors social expectations on their performance in relationship to black males. Women survivors weigh the need not only to protect themselves from violence but also to shelter the black men who brutalized them.

For Carbado, dominant historical narratives on the unfair treatment of black males in the criminal justice system "contain political and legal symbols of race and gender that function to construct O. J. Simpson as a victim of racism in a way that obscures that he was a perpetrator of domestic violence." The dominant narrative of the domestic abuse workshop, that of protecting violent black males, shows women's common marginalization: "Blackness (which Simpson represents) and not Nicole Brown is the victim." Carbado notes with irony the reductionism in response to the racialized and feminized jury acquittal in the criminal trial: "While we, and not the jury, were exposed to the most emotional and sensational aspects of the trial, it is the jury that is being accused of rendering a decision based on emotion."[32]

Examining how black communities view racial subordination in a gendered fashion, Carbado uses communal narratives and journalistic and autobiographical accounts. The use of the latter is very much in keeping with Awkward's observation about black male feminist narratives: "to speak self-consciously—autobiographically—is to explore, implicitly or explicitly, why and how the individual male experience (the 'me' in men) has diverged from, has created possibilities for a rejection of, the androcentric norm."[33] The male-centered paradigm obviously shifts in Carbado's feminism to privilege black women. What this represents for coalitions with "nonblack" women is unclear. His work does not provide a theory for gender politics in a larger context connected to the issues he highlights in his denunciation of black antifemale violence. If he created or imagined his dialogues, Carbado might tell other stories.

Carbado's narratives are nonfiction, unlike the tales of fellow profeminist legal theorists who use the fictional narratives of Derrick Bell and Richard Delgado, who acknowledges his inspiration from Bell. Delgado's "Rodrigo's Sixth Chronicle: Intersections, Essences, and the Dilemma of Social Reform" discusses coalition politics in ways that both highlight and minimize the presence of black women. The narrative presents protagonists Rodrigo, a black male law student whose father is African American and whose mother is a white Italian, and "the professor," a progressive male legal scholar, a "man of color" who serves as Rodrigo's intellectual mentor and foil. After being ousted from a women's law caucus meeting (and criticized by his female partner, Giannina) because of an uninvited lecture he makes assessing the antagonistic relations between women of color and white women, Rodrigo seeks out the professor for counseling. As they discuss the limitations of coalition politics or "the perils of making common cause," the two debate the role of profeminist men in women's liberation struggles.

Rodrigo first notes that essentialism appears to be "the usual response of a beleaguered group" seeking "solidarity in a struggle against a more powerful one." For him, essentialism appears in "three guises"— the meaning of words, the theory of coalitions, and the canon of knowledge—that all "share the search for narrative coherence." To identify relational essentialism, the law student cites the example of black women joining white women because "they stand on the same footing with respect to patriarchy" and share the need to be freed from it.[34] Through Rodrigo's pronouncement Delgado paints a rather distorted view of patriarchy. In fact black women do not stand on the same footing with white women in relation to patriarchy.

Rodrigo discusses intersectionality, or the interconnections of gender, race, and class, in order to examine the place black women occupy as women and as members of an oppressed ethnic group, given that "blackness" has been masculinized and "femaleness" racialized white. Because he acknowledges only race and gender, the place of class and sexual identity in this intersectionality remains obscured. He does remark, quoting his partner, that a relatively disempowered person, such as "a lesbian single mother," jeopardizes her power base by engaging in strategic coalitions with a more privileged group.[35]

Paradoxically, the "Sixth Chronicle" notes the importance of alliances between black and white women in a passage that represents black women as an afterthought, depicting them as the rank and file in coalitions rather than the impetus behind feminist and antiracist social movements and coalition politics: "Change comes from a small, dissatisfied group for whom canonical knowledge and the standard social arrangements don't work. Such a group needs allies. Thus, white women in the feminist movement reach out to women of color; Black men in the civil rights movement try to include Black women, and so on."[36] Although the historical record reveals that a number of black women pioneered the civil rights and feminist movements, their agency disappears in this profeminist essay.

Rodrigo critiques the assumed progressivism of coalitions between white women and women of color: "Gains are ephemeral if one wins them by forming coalitions with individuals who really do not have your interest at heart. It's not just that the larger, more diverse group will forget you and your special needs. It's worse than that. You'll forget who you are. And if you don't, you may still end up demonized, blamed for sabotaging the revolution when it inevitably and ineluctably fails."[37] He cites two reasons against coalition politics. First, often in coalitions strategic essentialism leads to a Gramscian "false consciousness" in which "the oppressed come to identify with their oppressors."[38] Second, the pitfalls of "interest convergence" are a constant liability. For instance, in

Brown v. Board of Education, black civil rights gains progressed only to the extent that they coincided with the interests of dominant whites who mitigated these rights. Rodrigo surmises that under interest convergence between subordinate and dominant groups: "Rights won are generally constrained and those with the least power are scapegoated."[39]

A certain pessimism informs the essay's observations concerning interest convergence and coalition politics for disenfranchised groups: "Rights, once won, tend to be cut back. And even when part of them remains, the price of the newly won right is exacted from the most marginal of its beneficiaries." For Rodrigo, people must remain oppositional (despite socialization toward collegiality and civility); he reasons that a "nationalist, counter-essentialist course" benefits both more privileged groups and the outsider group. "Justice first, then peace" becomes Rodrigo's epigraph and motto. (In radical demonstrations, the chant "No justice . . . no peace!" is often heard.)[40]

What are the interest convergence politics of male and female feminists in sexual liberation projects? With the growing appearance of the articulate male feminist, what sustains coalitions between male and female feminists? Do profeminists, who are more institutionally empowered than their female counterparts, align themselves with feminists only to the extent that the interests of both groups converge? Equally as important, when do coalition politics become caretaking politics for subordinate women aided by the patronage of feminist men? (Analogies to people of color and liberal whites abound.)

CONCLUSION

It is difficult to measure "equality" between male and female feminists. The works of Awkward, Gordon, Delgado, and Carbado foster gender egalitarianism among antiracists (and, it is hoped, racial equality among feminists). The proliferation of new profeminist writings, and the promising intellectual and political currency that is shaping the literary and academic market, creates the opportunity to examine deradicalizing tendencies within feminist discourse. For instance, the exploration of "self" or male identity in profeminism creates tangible contributions to feminist struggles. It may also paradoxically lead to narcissistic solipsism, a tendency that appears in the ambivalent relationship of critical white studies toward antiracist radicalism.

The femininity of the black male in a state where "whiteness" is worn as "phallus" enhances feminist analyses that address the points where sexism and racism meet. Still, the disappearance of the black female in such discourse is a possible by-product of a profeminist, antiracist paradigm. Focusing on the conditions of black women, male feminists can elevate the black female above the black male by putting her on a pedestal. Such an analytical framework addresses domestic abuse, but inadequately analyzes institutional violence. It also incompletely refers to the selective manner in which dominant society and the state apparatus demarcate the "legitimate" spheres in which black males may exercise and abuse masculine power. Perhaps coalitions are inevitably and inherently flawed, particularly if the pitfalls of transgender, multiracial coalitions dominated by the interests of whites or males replace political parity for inclusivity. The stance of profeminists in relation to feminists determines how closely their interests converge.

A feminist appreciation for the work of profeminists may coexist with a cautious concern. A growing feminist discourse or interest convergence needs not always signal a shift in gender power. Men who work and live as "feminists" will be ostracized and marginalized in some sectors and validated in others, just as antiracist whites are. Yet increasingly their authoritative male voices (particularly if their feminism is filtered through conventional ideologies) will allow them to be promoted as the source for the most rational, informed speech. At its best, the feminization of male discourse confronts gender hierarchy, inextricably linked to heterosexism, racism, classism, *and* the institutional privilege of the feminized male voice. At its worst, in the absence of a radical practice and theory, profeminism will foster a coalition politics that stops before full justice is achieved. Consequently, its politics will downplay disputes between professed feminists, adding to the restive uneasiness among profeminism's natural allies.

EIGHT

Conclusion: Black Shadow Boxers

National cultures relegate their subordinated and marginalized peoples to the role of stigmatized Others—the lesser shadows of the "greater" normative bodies. To the extent that they resist and fight for the legitimacy of their appearance and attendant rights, Others become shadow boxers. They have their own internal hierarchies and contradictions marked by caste, class, race, sexuality, and gender. In American society, the most pronounced "seen invisibility"[1] against the white landscape is the "black." In the obscured background, the doubly eclipsed tend to be female, poor, lesbian/gay or bi/transsexual, and two-spirited.

Among the marginalized, black males are perhaps the most influential petitioners and pugilists in contemporary American race politics. Their ideological span stretches from the reactionary positions of California's antiaffirmative action czar Ward Connolly and Supreme Court Justice Clarence Thomas's anti-civil rights activism through the liberalism and reconciliation politics of historian John Hope Franklin, who headed Clinton's President's Race Initiative to the neoradicalism of elite black academics. Sexism, misogyny, and battery exist irrespective of the political differences from "right" to "left," among black males and their "nonblack" counterparts. Unsurprisingly, black women's lives reveal complex relations to African American males who battle against them.

Images of antiracist resistance cross the ideological spectrum to elevate the black male, fostering among African Americans the transgender appeal of and at times aversion to the masculine black fighter.[2] In a "pugilistic culture,"[3] the visible disappearance of images of political black females presents ambivalence and irony. Although exceptions were made for exceptionally extraordinary women, historically, recognized "freedom fighters" have been masculinized, a fact that furthers the erasure of black women activists.

As interposed opaque bodies, black females partially emerge from double-paned obscurity because of their "reflections" of others—generally whites or black males. Even in space devoid of light, mainstream Americans see the distorted figure of the "mammy" who in combative stance transforms into her stereotypical antithesis, the "sapphire." Projecting either inferiority, maternal domesticity, or animalistic hostility, American culture inscribes upon black females their appearance as shadows, marking them as imperfect imitations of feminized Europeans or masculinized Africans. These projections haunt the public and private lives of black females.

Suspicious of and uneasy with the black female fighter, national culture restricts her to near invisibility. America prefers to view her shadow as either a shelter entrapped in the body of the mammy or as sexual or verbal excess in the forms of the debased seductress or abrasive sapphire. Conversely, white America has loved and enshrined or hated and hounded, obsessed over, the black male fighter (who despite the deadly risks seemed to relish the attention). Not only white America is fixated. Black America, including African American females, is captivated as well, particularly when the black fighter represented the "race man," historically the African American working against social injustice and discrimination for the advancement of blacks. Through these "race men," black women mitigated their conditions of involuntary servitude.

Recollecting childhood memories, Maya Angelou describes how in the 1930s, in Stamps, Arkansas, local blacks gathered in her grandmother's country store to hear the radio broadcast a Joe Louis championship fight. After a nerve-wracking battle against the white contender emotionally drained the all-black gathering, the announcer proclaimed Louis the victor. Angelou recalls the intense, collective pride, jubilation, and protected euphoria that followed:

> Champion of the world. A Black boy. Some Black mother's son. He was the strongest man in the world. People drank Coca-Colas like ambrosia and ate candy bars like Christmas. . . . It would take an hour or more before the people would leave the Store and head for home. Those who lived too far had made arrangements to stay in town. It wouldn't do for a Black man and his family to be caught on a lonely country road on a night when Joe Louis had proved that we were the strongest people in the world.[4]

Before Louis, Americans first obsessed over Jack Johnson. At the turn of the century, the best white boxers refused to fight blacks, or at least one particular African American: Jack Johnson. By 1907 Johnson had defeated all major black challengers. Attempting to galvanize a European-American defender of both boxing and the notion of white superiority, reporter Jack London wrote, "The White man must be rescued." But it was only after the white boxer Tommy Burns was offered $30,000 that a challenger was found for the black fighter. Overnight the 1908 interracial battle for heavyweight champion turned the frontier settlement of Reno, Nevada, into a city as thousands gathered for the first "fight of the century."

This battle for, or against, white supremacy as American manhood also proved the struggle whereby blacks would either recede into the shadows of American culture or step out fully into the spotlights of its center ring. Johnson performed brilliantly, flamboyantly, and mercilessly. When the bout ended, thousands of white spectators, as if in a funeral entourage, departed in silence, stunned by the sudden death of the iconography of white male masculinity. In the "race riots" that soon followed, whites killed African Americans in New York, the Midwest, and throughout the South. (In the wake of continuing antiblack "race riots," black and white liberals founded the National Association for the Advancement of Colored People [NAACP].)

Privately admired by blacks for his fearless excesses, the professional boxer was publicly hated by whites for the same. Displaying an outrageous courage and patriarchal contempt for white supremacy, Jack Johnson mated, married, and abandoned white women. The FBI's campaign against the undefeated fighter eventually led to a white judge charging Johnson with transporting white women (his consorts or wife) across state lines for immoral purposes. Johnson fled into exile, marked an outlaw. Returning to the United States years later, he repatriated as a "criminal." Jack Johnson had become the "dark figure" shading the American body, intercepting rays of light reserved for whites only. Needing to restore itself, to cast off this mocking reflection, white Americans sought and found their first "Great White Hope." They were vanquished, if only in the boxing ring

Yet whites gradually came to embrace the black fighter as a true "American." By the 1930s America's repudiation of the black male fighter gave way to a cultural embrace. Joe Louis bore no resemblance to Jack Johnson and kept his distance from his predecessor. (When Johnson attempted to visit Louis's training camp, he was ejected.)[5] Louis, whose opponents were mostly white, took counsel that Johnson refused to heed: never smile after beating a white opponent; never brag; always, with humility, attribute victories to "luck," not talent, ferocity, or righteous justice. After attending "grooming" or etiquette classes, Louis in fact signed a contract dictating his inoffensive, shadowy behavior.

In 1936, the less racially abrasive Louis would be pitted against Max Schmeling, the German boxer who served in the Luftwaffe. It would be Louis's first public loss. Louis regrouped and redeemed himself in their second encounter in June 1938, again held in New York's Yankee stadium. Then, with African Americans comprising half of the 45,000 in attendance, amid America's increasingly adversarial stance toward Nazi Germany, the announcer introduced the "Brown Bomber" as "The American." That summer Louis became the first great transracial hero for white Americans and the first great cross-gender, cultural hero for twentieth-century black Americans. A few years later, the handsome, victorious Louis (by then a minor "movie star" in Negro films) was featured in recruitment shorts encouraging blacks to enlist in the U.S. segregated armed forces and to join the Allied war effort.

Despite his multiracial appeal and President Harry Truman's 1948 Executive Order desegregating the armed forces, which created the military as a model for integration, Louis's example of humility was repudiated in the 1960s. During the Vietnam war, Cassius Clay metamorphosed as Muhammad Ali to "float like a butterfly and sting like a bee." Unwilling to model for the military state, identified with the Nation of Islam, later forced to relinquish his heavyweight title, he was eventually imprisoned rather than inducted.

But Ali defeated Floyd Patterson, considered by some to be "counterrevolutionary" America's first Negro "Great White Hope"; as the documentary *When We Were Kings* illustrates, Ali would also later depict another African American opponent, Joe Frazier, as a "Great White Hope" and then defeat him in the second "fight of the century."[6] Ali's rhetoric had a limited transracial appeal. (Today, virtually silenced by Parkinson's Disease, Muhammad Ali has become iconized as an American hero.) Mostly, and more significantly, he held a cross-gender appeal for black Americans. Both women and men were thrilled by Muhammad Ali. Denouncing "Uncle Toms," pronouncing himself "the man," Ali also repeatedly, publicly, shamelessly proclaimed himself *pretty*. As "pretty," rather than handsome, he inspired black females and males alike, synthesizing the ethos of an era captured in the incantation: "Black Is Beautiful!" and the social and state police perception: "Black Is Militant."[7]

The broad commercial appeal of black sports heroes today largely precludes any similar adversarial stances against "white power" by "race men and women." Likewise, the transgender appeal dissipates alongside a diminishing political advocacy. The racial formula at work in American culture is fairly simple: For most whites, as long as black fighters do not denounce the entrenched racism of their national culture, society, and state, they qualify as "Americans," albeit validated only because as sports heroes they entertain and/or protect the ("white") nation. For most blacks, as long as African Americans triumph in the sports, commercial culture, or military arenas, they are viewed as a source of collective racial pride and "entertainment" because their victorious battles as African Americans repudiate the myth of white superiority/black inferiority and offer a vicarious thrill. The racial formulas seem rather fixed some ninety

years after the original "racial rude man," Jack Johnson, briefly dominated a sporting world that for decades had Jim Crowed black jockeys
and athletes from the economic profits of commercial sports.

The gender formulas seem less stable around these black cultural
heroes. With the dominance of low-key, nonconfrontational race rhetoric and antiracism among black performers, their transgender cachet
diminishes. The embattled are constantly attracted to fighters. They seek
out other boxers, if only to quietly watch and study their moves.
Therefore, black women and girls routinely watch black male fighters.
How black female spectators perceive(d) the transformation of the
masculinized black warrior into an American commercial fighter has not
been fully explored. Yet what is the significance of male pugilists for black
females today, over half a century after Maya Angelou witnessed and
shared in the euphoria of Joe Louis's victories?

For most Americans, the recognized racialized pugilists or public
fighters remain male. Such cultural warriors mark America's fetish for
racism, spectacle, and hypermasculinity. Behind, beside, or projected
before them, though, are the images of the Others, the racialized *private*
pugilists. The lives of black females reflect the private prizefighter, the
female shadow boxer. Generally appearing in distinct form only after the
male relinquishes the center ring, she rarely garners the attention to
enthrall fans or (male) spectators.

Shadow boxers are fighters who battle as outsiders, at times criminalized as cultural and political outlaws. Sometimes they are defeated by
themselves or the society and state of which they are a part. Sometimes
they are victorious until the next battle. Privately they box with
themselves, their kin, and, sometimes, imaginary opponents. Publicly,
their conflicts engage the state's destructive policies.

We learn from those warring in and for the official military culture.
We also learn from those warring against it. Progressives who see the
entire nation as embattled resist the policing of those racialized as inferior
and those feminized as dependent prey; they also fight against the
dehumanization of those born or carried into poverty and prison.
Attentive Americans have witnessed endless battles. Progressives and
disenfranchised peoples have been boxing for centuries: sparring, duck-
ing, jabbing, always struggling, even when fearful to counter or afraid of

the images they cast. They often find themselves isolated in American society as "opponents" of official bodies.

Defying conventional culture and politics, radical feminism and antiracism have always functioned as heresy. Official political thought has much in common with Western religion. Both tend to project national fears onto rising shadows of dissent and resistance. Both discourage transformation of consciousness that leads to treasonous acts against a corporate or cosmic government. The greatest treason is to usurp "divine" authority—to speak and act in the name of "democracy"—without official or state authorization.[8]

Promoting unorthodox and heretical states of consciousness that further radical politics has always been a suspect state endeavor. On one hand, the state has the power to extinguish a radical movement; on the other hand, it can modify and elevate that movement into the mainstream so that it no longer functions as resistance to official policy. Unofficial narratives, though, continue to be the persistent companions of official texts. Excised and censored as heretical, they still manage to contest and rival institutional views. Unofficial stories rarely cross over into mass appeal, yet they proffer an alternative vision of ourselves and society. They therefore wield a pervasive influence. Revealing their own peculiar power shadowing the official body, competing narratives build comprehensive views as official orthodoxy and unofficial heterodoxy contradict and "complement" each other. Nowhere is this more evident than in the contests surrounding and framing the revolutionary potential of black feminism.

FEMINISM, FETISH, AND ERASURE

For various reasons, the majority of American women do not call themselves "feminists," even those who advocate gender equality and those who are aware that their economic and racial battles for resources are specific to their conditions as women. Part of the aversion toward the label is tied to its restrictive definitions shaped by the interests of white bourgeois women and solipsistic feminism.[9] Given the economic and power ambitions women share with men, it is not surprising that elite portraits of feminism construct a gender equity that is abstracted from racism and classism. Such "equity" liberates only those women already "free" by virtue of their racial and material privileges under capitalism and white supremacy. Gender myopia in feminism mirrors the ideological exceptionalism of antiracist and Marxist abstractions that sever class from race, gender, and sexuality. That affluent white "postfeminists" disavow being handicapped by gender discrimination and that their "nonwhite" counterparts extend this claim to include racial discrimination suggests the bourgeois underpinnings of American social freedom.

TIME magazine's June 1998 cover featured black-and-white head shots of aging white or fair-haired Susan B. Anthony, Betty Freidan, Gloria Steinem, alongside a color photo of youthful TV series cult icon "Ally McBeal."[10] Under the photographs ran the red banner: "IS FEMINISM DEAD?"[11] The cover article by Ginia Bellafante lamented the rise of narcissism and body fetish among contemporary young women, self-proclaimed "postfeminists."[12] Bellafante criticizes the representations of feminism promoted by female hedonistic "Gen-Xers," yet she offers her own depoliticizing images by representing "responsible" feminism as white and bourgeois. Established black feminists or feminists of color (such as Alice Walker, bell hooks, Barbara Smith, Audre Lorde, Cherrie Moraga, Gloria Anzaldua, Chrystos, Paula Gunn Allen) who contributed to women's liberation struggles in the "second wave" go unmentioned in Bellafante's report. This suggests that "Is *White* Feminism Dead?" would have been a more appropriate title for the cover and raises the question: "Why aren't black women considered feminists?" or, more bluntly, bell hooks's bold query: "How can racist women call themselves feminist?"[13]

Had the author researched more, she would have found that hooks's writings convey in a more succinct and holistic fashion her own argument about gender venality. In 1991 hooks wrote:

> Although the contemporary feminist movement was initially motivated by the sincere desire of women to eliminate sexist oppression, it takes place within the framework of a larger, more powerful cultural system that encourages women and men to place the fulfillment of individual aspirations above their desire for collective

change. . . . it is not surprising [then] that feminism has been undermined by the narcissism, greed, and individual opportunism of its leading exponents. A feminist ideology that mouths radical rhetoric about resistance and revolution while actively seeking to establish itself within the capitalist patriarchal system is essentially corrupt. While the contemporary feminist movement has successfully stimulated an awareness of the impact of sexist discrimination on the social status of women in the U.S., it has done little to eliminate sexist oppression.[14]

Bellafante mentions only one black woman—and then as a postfeminist—Rebecca Walker, the daughter of Alice Walker. She describes the former's body-image anthology, *To Be Real*, as "a collection of airy— sometimes even ludicrous—mini-memoirs explaining female experiences."[15] Perhaps Bellafante refers to the younger Walker's anthology only because it includes high-profile white feminists such as Naomi Wolf. Regardless of why this book was chosen, Bellafante contends that its politics reflect the erosion of the militancy and focus of white feminism as found in Simone de Beauvoir's *Second Sex*, Friedan's *Feminist Mystique*, and Kate Millett's *Sexual Politics*.

That Bellafante considers these texts "radical" seems consistent with *TIME*'s erasure of contemporary black feminism and radical white feminism. Despite the racial amnesia, class-driven feminism, and the artificial schism she wedges between black and "nonblack" feminism, Bellafante does make important points about mainstream feminism. Citing her key literary personas, Bellafante argues that these feminists "made big, unambiguous demands of the world [and] sought absolute equal rights and opportunities for women, a constitutional amendment to make it so, a chance to be compensated equally and to share the task of raising a family. But if feminism of the '60s and '70s was steeped in research and obsessed with social change, feminism today is wed to the culture of celebrity and self-obsession." She cites a TIME/CNN poll reporting that education is largely the determining factor in whether a woman identifies as a "feminist" (53 percent of white, college-educated urban women and 50 percent of white women with postgraduate education and no children consider themselves feminists).

Bellafante traces the current denigration of feminism to Camille Paglia's *Sexual Personae*[16] and the "syndrome" it inspired among white, affluent females: Female power lies in female sexuality; such "power," in relation to influential men, transports women beyond "victimhood." In the "syndrome," the article maintains, can be found the banality of the "Spice Girls," the "girl power" of Katie Roiphe's *The Morning After*, and Naomi Wolf's *Promiscuities*.[17] The arguments in these and similar works are based on "feminine" power, which offers little advocacy for the Equal Rights Admendment, full employment, or reproductive rights but many accolades for the "warrior trope" of the seductress. Feminism, when tied to traditional political activism and demands from state authority and institutions for women's liberation, has lost much of its meaning. In such situations, the term is applied indiscriminately. According to Bellafante:

> female singers like Meredith Brooks and Alanis Morissette are installed as icons of woman power (alongside real artist-activists like Tori Amos) simply because they sing about bad moods or boyfriends who have dumped them. In the late '60s, when the label was applied more sparingly, no one thought to call Nancy Sinatra a feminist, and yet if she recorded *These Boots Are Made for Walkin'* in 1998, she'd probably find herself headlining the Lilith Fair.[18]

Bellafante's critique says little about the class nature of postfeminist politics and the ways in which self-advancement and gratification are the measures of success for the materially affluent. Most of the young women she criticizes are graduates of ivy league schools and presumably possess a sense of entitlement and privilege. This is in keeping with the feminist elders—Friedan, Millet—she applauds, who are also beneficiaries of an elite formal education and its attendant privileges. Bellafante blames the shift in emphasis for white, affluent women from activism to sexual displays partly on academe, quoting Barnard College professor Leslie Calman: "Women's studies, a big chunk of it at least, has focused increasingly on the symbols of the body and less on social action and social change."[19] The white "Old Guard" feminists are dismayed by their progeny's depoliticizing, self-obsessive excesses, although supposedly they are only following instruction. Itself preoccupied or obsessed with the young, white female body (enshrined or vilified as seductive siren, from Marilyn Monroe to Monica Lewinsky), mainstream media such as *TIME* fail to consider the activist role of antiracist feminists. Displeasure and fetish over the display of white "girl power" obscure political issues raised by radical white feminists and other progressives.

For instance, for a much smaller readership, during the same month *TIME* marketed "Is Feminism Dead?" *The Nation* published Ellen Willis's "We Need a *Radical* Left."[20] Willis's insightful perspective on liberalism and the "left" expands the range of white feminist concerns reported by Bellafante. Reading Willis as representative of radical white feminism elicits an emphatic "no" to *TIME*'s query: Rather than "dead," feminism and the "left" need to be differentiated.

According to Willis:

> It's not necessary, as many leftists imagine, to round up popular support before anything can de done; on the contrary, the actions of a relatively few troublemakers can lead to popular support. The history of movements is crowded with acts of defiance by individuals and small groups—from the 1937 sit-in of workers in a Flint, Michigan auto plant to Rosa Parks' [1955] refusal to get up . . . —that inspired a wave of similar actions and a broader revolt.

The few embolden the many to break through the malaise of a culture routinized to inequality and injustices. For Willis, the ideas of "militant minorities" can "capture people's imaginations by presenting another possible world." The impulse of institutional elites "wary of the potential threat posed by an organized minority," she writes, "is to make concessions." (It should be noted that elites also have resorted to police repression to maintain power and dominance.) "As a result," Willis maintains, "radical movements that articulate a compelling vision have an impact far beyond their core of committed activists."[21] This impact, however, is not uniformly welcomed among progressives.

Using a metaphor with considerable irony for radicals and revolutionaries, "We Need a *Radical* Left" describes how the "good cop/bad cop routine" is played out in the left's internecine battles:

> [L]iberals dismiss the radicals as impractical sectarian extremists, promote their own "responsible" proposals as an alternative and take the credit for whatever change results. The good news is that this process does bring about significant change. The bad news is that by denying the legitimacy of radicalism it misleads people about how change takes place . . . [and] leaves people unprepared for the inevitable backlash. . . .[22]

Capital, according to Willis, "has no incentive to embrace liberal constraints." Yet feminists have material incentives to embrace the constraints of liberalism.

Dominant forms of feminism that fail to address the rapacious qualities of corporate capital or "predatory capitalism" can be legitimately criticized for ideological limitations that render some feminisms complicit in dehumanizing systems and in mystifying the convergence of corporate wealth and repressive state policies. Neoliberalism or antiradicalism shapes mainstream black feminism's limited critiques of political violence, militarism, monopoly capital, and labor exploitation. In the absence of ideologies and activism for economic justice and human rights, conventional feminisms displace radicalism, reducing radical and revolutionary black feminisms to a shadow's shadow: a poor reflection or appendage of black bourgeois feminism.

FRAMING BLACK FEMINISMS

Constructing a monolithic "black feminism" allows some African Americans to denounce black feminists as "race traitors" who are hostile toward black males. As blacks battle racism as antimale aggression, black women who express disappointment, pain, and outrage over black sexism, heterosexism, and misogyny are routinely chastised.

Prevailing gender and racial bias allow blacks and "nonblacks," males and females, to harbor a general distrust for black feminisms. Seemingly reasonable criticisms may mask bias and a generalizing reductionism. In these instances, black feminisms are framed for alleged crimes as antiblack feminist discourse takes various forms with different political functions. First it constructs and disparages a monolithic black feminism as either a gender or racial recusant. (Ignoring political ideologies constructs an undifferentiated black feminism.) At times this occurs with specious sociological or anthropological arguments, as some critics of black feminisms manipulate historiography to legitimize dismissals of complex political communities and identities.

For instance, some Afrocentric writers argue that sexism and misogyny are a European construction; consequently they dismiss feminism as a "white intervention" to destabilize black male-female relations and African American communities. This position, which can routinely segue into sexism and homophobia, conveniently ignores the intersections between European racial-patriarchal conquest of women and the sexual inequities and abuses of some precolonial African societies. Afrocentric denunciations of black feminism may mirror racist narratives. For example, Eurocentrics have argued that white civilization "rescued" black females from a sexual barbarism that they universalize to all traditional African cultures. Both Afrocentrics and Eurocentrics can foster romantic nostalgia and a false division between antiracist and antisexist politics.

In addition, some disparaging discourse accepts the viability of black feminism only to contain or cauterize it. Distinguishing themselves from those who deny the validity of an experiential and intellectual base for black feminist politics, "advocates" can portray black feminist ideology as limited to the particular experiences of some black women and therefore inapplicable to women or blacks or democratic society as a whole. Such a division diminishes the role of antiracist feminism in democratic politics.

Generalizing accusations maintain that black females are less inclined toward feminism than their white counterparts, attributing that aversion to an alleged emotive nostalgia for "the black community" and strong racial identification with black males. Although there is some validity in this charge, it cannot be generalized. If it is, then it must be assumed that black women, and by extension a feminism that emphasizes antiracism and gender-inclusive community, is not "feminist." Such assumptions crassly simplify black women's lives and struggles in a racist and racialized state. The liberation of the women of an oppressed people—as a group rather than as atomized individuals—is inseparable from, but not reducible to, the liberation of their people or communities of origin and identification.

Collectively, black women's experiences encompass historical, cultural worldviews that privilege ancestors and community. Such experiences grapple with the legacy of a genocidal diaspora in the Americas and centuries of antiblack racism from a motley assortment of ethnic groups, state institutions, and policing agencies. Obviously, gender conservatism and racial defensiveness exist among black females. In a society marred by antiblack racism, a defensive or protective race pride among African Americans can easily be reduced to or made synonymous with black *male* advancement. Doing so leads some black females to valorize black males, even abusive ones. Still, complex gender politics becomes obscured by generalizations of gender regression among black females.

Another dismissal has gained currency among black males and others. In much the same ways as nationalism is portrayed as unidimensional, black feminism is viewed as a handmaiden to Euro-American feminism. As a result, it is argued that black feminism is not "black" enough. In African American antifeminist discourse, charges that black feminisms are surrogates to white feminisms are familiar.

Such arguments usually center on the alleged preoccupation of black feminisms with bourgeois white women. Despite some merit, this criticism also misses the mark. Often, in their service as a corrective to racism, black feminisms function both as the cathartic conscience and domestic worker for racial messes. In their integrationist or assimilationist efforts, they seem overly preoccupied with white, privileged women, who often become the focus of black feminist conversations. But this situation partly mirrors the overpreoccupation of black masculinist discourse with white males and the scant attention it pays to dialogue or criticisms centering on Native, Latino, Asian, or Arab males. The "obsession with white women" is in effect a preoccupation with a bourgeois whiteness that signifies power. Highlighting struggles against antiblack racism and sexism, essentialized black feminism may be accused of focusing on a false division that privileges black/white conflict and consensus over relations with other nonelite ethnic groups.

Ethnic chauvinism and ethnocentrism exist among black women and among women of other ethnicities. Black women may be criticized for emphasizing antiblack racism with the argument that they thereby detract from "multiculturalism" and other women of color. But this criticism is disingenuous if it ignores the fact that antiblack discrimination and violence cut across ethnicity. In racist societies, all racialized people are not created equally unequal. Under white supremacy, dark-skinned, black or Afro-Indians, Latinas, Asians, and Arabs occupy the lowest social strata not only in mainstream America or "white" culture but also in Native, Latino, Asian, and Arab communities. These "black" ethnics face an intensity of racialized abuses, exploitation, and repression that their lighter-skinned counterparts escape or from which they may even benefit. Consider the caste status of the "mulatta" in Latin America and the Caribbean, the "Coloured" in South Africa, and the "mixed race" in the United States vis-à-vis "the black."

The criticism that black feminism diverts attention from black liberation, because of its focus on women, parallels the dismissive that black feminism distracts from women's liberation because of its blackness. Both positions construct barriers that restrict political communities. The walls built by isolationist discourse cause black women who refuse to bind themselves to identities polarized as either "black" or "female" to be accused of gender or racial venality. Their refusal to be bound by one category or another is understandable, given that black feminist formations and politics in the United States, influenced by overlapping cultures and radical struggles, are highly complex.

One antiracist view of black feminism represents it as "endangering" black females by placing them outside of the protective arm of black males and within the destructive reach of whites. (This situation is exemplified by the patriarchal protector tropes in the Tawana Brawley case.) The Million Man March, which provided fertile ground for innumerable debates about black gender politics, offers another vivid illustration of black antiracist counterfeminism. Controversy and conflicts around gender politics in the march created rigid, polarized camps. At the premarch October 1995 public forum, organized by the Institute of African American Studies director Manning Marable at Columbia University, black trade unionist and Committees of Correspondence cofounder Charlene Mitchell was the only woman on the platform. One of the key male speakers was the former New York Nation of Islam minister Conrad Muhammad.

Mitchell was the only panelist to discuss the negative gender politics of the march and the long militant history of black women's leadership in liberation movements. An activist and former Communist Party USA leader in her sixties, Charlene Mitchell had organized for decades in the civil rights, labor, and antiwar movements. Conrad Muhammad, in his thirties, had likely never participated in a mass protest movement. The clash between the two (the other male speakers assumed largely background roles after their initial speeches) was premised then not merely on gender but also on ideology and practice.

During their spontaneous debate, Muhammad responded to Mitchell's feminist critique by attempting to silence or delegitimize her voice. Repeatedly he referred to her as his "mother." Generally this is a sign of respect for an elder, but his use of the term proved condescending and patronizing. It implied that rational analysis existed for him as the young adult male and that for Mitchell, there was only the rocking chair as domestic caretaker. When Mitchell criticized the Nation of Islam–led march as counter to the history and reality of black political leadership as shaped by both women and men, Muhammad's rebuttal used the imagery of racial-sexual violence and the racial protector trope to discredit women's activism in the southern civil rights movement. Interestingly, Mitchell was an adult organizer and Muhammad an infant during that very era.

Recounting the repression of civil rights activists, Muhammad spoke about Birmingham's sheriff "Bull" Conner and the use of cattle prods and water hoses against black demonstrators. Racist violence was pervasive against demonstrators, as was sexual violence. But the Nation of Islam minister's lurid narrative sexualized the violence, describing police dogs jumping up and biting into the "breasts of black women" and white racist cops "thrusting cattle-prods up the vaginas of black women." After the audience was stunned—perhaps not everyone for the reasons he imagined—Muhammad ended his narrative by stating the following: "Well, maybe that's what Sister Charlene might want to happen to black women and girls, but that's not what I want."

The audience was supposed to understand that the only feminist on the platform wished to jeopardize black female physical safety while the counterfeminist wished to protect black females. The African American "need" for the black male protector legitimized patriarchal politics inside and outside the Million Man March. In the auditorium, a number of women cheered Minister Muhammad (some could have been family members) and hissed Ms. Mitchell when she debated him.

In the United States, where the most heinous acts of sexual violence are understood to be marked by "race," the social outrage at sexual violence becomes most virulent once it is racialized. As noted in chapter 3, sexual assaults that cross racial lines raise the specter of racial victimization and redress. There is a certain disingenuousness about this form of moral outrage. Symbols seem to dominate a duplicitous chivalry infused with notions of racial property appended to female sexuality and victimization. Images of male racialized protection and prosecution create a dual fetish. First, there is the desire for the body of the girl-woman to be protected. Second, there is the desire for the agency of the boy-man who is to rescue or avenge her. Given the hero narrative embodied in such constructions, it is not surprising that the "victim" becomes subordinate to the "avenger," a subordination that casts a strong appeal in American culture.

The forum illustrated the pervasive and false notions that militant leadership is a male pursuit and that risk and confrontation with repressive state apparatuses (the police, courts, military) are a male responsibility. The gender composition of the panel also reinforced the perception that intellectual leadership and political discourse are also male endeavors. Critiquing the Million Man March, the panel recycled the masculinist warrior trope; presenting Mitchell, it nevertheless managed to obscure female warrior narratives.

Yet black feminist criticisms about the march were not all able to recover an elusive transgender militancy of past movements. For instance, the African American Agenda 2000, formed largely by black women academics who are part of the Talented Tenth, prepared a critique of the gender politics of the Million Man March. Rather than collectively issue their statement, they elected one woman, Angela Davis—likely because of her iconographic status and press appeal based on her former notoriety as a political outlaw—to read their position paper before national media. Bourgeois, nonradical women in the Agenda 2000 could appear to be to the "left" of the Nation of Islam and march organizers—which included some women, trade unionists, and working-class activists—by appending themselves to a revolutionary icon. In effect, nonradical black feminists capitalized on an *image* tied to past radicalism and contemporary cultural feminism.

When Davis delivered the statement at a national (basically white) press conference just before the march, the "sound bite" approach to news reporting projected the image of a former militant and current prominent black feminist condemning a national endeavor by African American males. (Davis was subsequently vilified in the uncritical cheerleading of nonradical black media for the march.) The extent to which Agenda 2000 attempted to address the concerns raised by the march were erased for the general public. Like the African American Agenda 2000 statement, the Million Man March pledge made important points about black oppression and gender abuse. Both groups raised questions about gender and antiracist radical politics for the twenty-first century. Neither offered a critique of capitalism or "revolutionary" struggle. But each represented itself as a "radical" intervention in American politics.

The Million Man March had a strong appeal to some women precisely because it advocated the "protection of our women." To the extent that African American Agenda 2000 challenged this performance of patriarchal protection, it offered an important service. For it emphasized that the desires of black women and girls for "shelter" and "shadow" in the competent male warrior and provider diverge sharply from black feminist agency.

CONCLUSION

Discomfort with black feminist speech and activism (particularly its most radical expressions) stems from and fosters restricted notions of "feminism" and "antiracism." Social difficulties in accepting and speaking black feminisms on their own terms may stem from a lack of familiarity with language for social and economic justice rooted in race-conscious and radical ideologies. Most often normative feminist and antiracist discussions minimalize the presence of radical black feminism with language that claims to "challenge" but fails to confront the specificity of resistance.

Monolingual feminism or antiracism projects depoliticizing assumptions and abstractions that detract from material conditions of struggle. For instance, mainstream feminism constructs women as a "class" by reductively positing that the most effective challenges to sexism render racial and economic oppression as epiphenomena, despite the fact that there is no historical or contemporary evidence of "abstract womanhood abstractly suffering" and fighting sexism.[23]

Nevertheless, the dominance of these abstractions and the cultural politics they represent promote a homogenized view of women that allows conventional feminism to elide historical black militants as protofeminists. Due to mounting challenges to this erasure, formerly obscure ancestral figures such as Maria Stewart, Ida B. Wells and Ella Baker, and revolutionary icons like Angela Davis and Assata Shakur, are gradually being included in mainstream feminist, antiracist, and political thought. Increasingly, gender inclusive, communal concerns for black male and female life in America, such as those that appear in Toni Morrison's writings, are recognized as *feminist* contributions. Inclusion remains selective, however, for contemporary radical black feminist politics remains contested and largely subordinate in both American culture and elite forms of black feminism.

Language, ideas, and strategies to redress the concerns of black women (and their families and communities) reflect dialects spoken by America's racial "outsiders." Proficiency in the discourses of black feminisms rejects the presumption of a "master" narrative that frames the concerns of all black women. The multiplicity of ideologies reveals varying degrees of political efficacy for social change that are often obscured by the "framing" of feminism that either erases the contributions of black women or depicts a homogenous black feminism as a flawed appendage to either antiracist or feminist struggles.

Resistance has historically challenged and shaped black female conduct across a broad ideological spectrum. Yet it is black women's autonomy from the pervasive dominance of neoliberalism and corporate culture that opens new avenues for political travel. Radical black feminist politics charts unique paths as an alternative to the political malaise. As expressed in *Alice in Wonderland*: Any road will do if you're not going anywhere.

NOTES

DEDICATION

1. Elaine Pagel gives this interpretation of the Nag Hammadi's "Gospel of Thomas," verse 70, in the documentary *From Jesus to Christ*. For an introduction to the Nag Hammadi or Gnostic gospels, see Elaine Pagels, *The Gnostic Gospels* (New York: Random House, 1979).

    Stephen Patterson and Marvin Meyer's translation of verse 70 reads: "Jesus said, 'If you bring forth what is within you, what you have will save you. If you do not have that within you, what you do not have within you [will] kill you.'" See Stephen Patterson and Marvin Meyer, The Gospel of Thomas Homepage, www.epix.net/ ~miser7/thomas.html

PREFACE

1. See "Anthropology of African Americans: From Bones to the Human Genome," James E. Bowman, University of Chicago, and "Anthropological Measurement," Fatimah L. C. Jackson, University of Maryland, papers presented at "In Honor of W. E. B. Du Bois: A Conference on the Study of African American Problems," University of Pennsylvania, February 23-24, 1999.
2. See Ida B. Wells, *Crusade for Justice: The Autobiography of Ida B. Wells*, ed. Alfreda M. Duster (Chicago: University of Chicago Press, 1970); Angela Davis, *Angela Davis: An Autobiography* (New York: Random House, 1974); Assata Shakur, *Assata: An Autobiography* (Westport, CT: Lawrence Hill and Company, 1987).
3. See Joy James, "Symbolic Rage: Prosecutorial Performances and Racialized Representations of Sexual Violence," in *Resisting State Violence: Radicalism, Gender & Race in U.S. Culture* (Minneapolis: University of Minnesota Press, 1996), 133-153.
4. For discussions of black male profeminist activism surrounding the march, see bell hooks, "Marching for Justice: Feminist Interventions," *Black Renaissance Noire*, Vol. 1, No. 2 (Summer/Fall 1997), 32-41.

CHAPTER 1

1. Former Representative Joseph Kennedy (D-MA) introduced HR 611 into the U.S. Congress to close the School of the Americas. For more information on the School of the Americas, see Mary A. Fischer, "Teaching Torture," *GQ* (June 1997); and, David Huey et al., "On the Offensive," *Global Exchange Report* (June 1998). Global Exchange lists Fort Bragg, North Carolina, as the site for the "School of Warfare," which has also fomented anti-indigenous violence in the Americas.

2. The phrase "shadow government" was popularized during the Iran-contra hearings in the 1980s. See *Inside the Shadow Government,* Declaration of Plaintiffs' Counsel filed by the Christic Institute, U.S. District Court, Miami, Florida, March 31, 1988.

3. The history of African American soldiers and warriors in the U.S. is conflictual. During the Civil War, President Abraham Lincoln opposed the use of armed black soldiers. W. E. B. Du Bois's *Black Reconstruction in America: An Essay Toward the History of the Part Which Black Folk Played in the Attempt to Reconstruct Democracy in America, 1860-1880* (New York: Russell and Russell, 1962) states that 200,000 black troops eventually fought in that war, following the model of "General" Harriet Tubman. After the war and Reconstruction, Ida B. Wells and others carried arms to protect themselves as they organized for black freedom and equality. World War I and II saw black organizations (amid protests from black radicals) mobilize to desegregate the armed forces and allow Negro soldiers to serve in combat rather than be restricted to the domestic sector of service units.

   While on U.S. shores, the "Deacons of Defense"—an African American organization committed to armed self-defense against Klan and racist terror emerged during the southern civil rights movement with military strategies that saved the lives of civil rights workers and black community people. During the same period on foreign lands, responding to the perceived incompetence or racism of white officers who seemed to routinely "lose" black infantrymen stationed on front lines in the Vietnam war, African American rebels at point positions allegedly lobbed grenades behind them into the relative safety zones of white officers. Back home, reportedly because of their military training in Nam, Black Panthers such as Geronimo ji Jaga (Elmer Pratt) were spared the martyrdom of Chicago Black Panther Party chair Fred Hampton and Panther leader Mark Clark, who were killed by police in a predawn raid.

   Amid insurrection, military and guerrilla battles, and ideological struggles, literature by black revolutionaries and rebels exerted a transgender appeal for both females and males who saw themselves as colonized people under siege and at war. See Robert Williams, *Negroes with Guns* (New York: Marzani and Munsell, 1962); Amilcar Cabral, *Return to the Source: Selected Speeches of Amilcar Cabral,* ed. Africa Information Service (New York: Monthly Review Press, 1973); Frantz Fanon, *The Wretched of the Earth* (New York: Grove Press, 1963).

4. Americans are both entertained and pacified when violence is used by blacks in boxing spectacles, action films, and on foreign battlefields. However, many conventional Americans become alarmed and incensed when African Americans deploy violence (or merely its imagery) for their own collective, political objectives. In a schizophrenic relationship to violence, America is alternately enamored and terrified by its use.

   In a July 1998 *TIME* magazine special report on gun violence, Richard Lacayo reflected on the magazine's cover story, "The Gun in America," that appeared three decades earlier:

   > It was 1968, just days after the murder of Robert Kennedy, and before him of Martin Luther King Jr., when the exit wound was becoming a standard problem in American politics. . . . But that sequence of killings also produced a briefly effective national revulsion against gun violence. Before the year was out, Congress would pass the Gun Control Act of 1968, a milestone law that banned most interstate sales, licensed most gun dealers and barred felons, minors and the mentally ill from owning guns. . . .

   > Millions in the U.S. believe passionately that their liberty, their safety or both are bound up with the widest possible availability of guns. So 30 years later, guns are still very much with us, murderous little fixtures of the cultural

landscape. We live with them as we live with computers or household appliances, but with more difficult consequences—some of them paid in blood. Among the industrial nations, this cultural predicament is ours alone. Richard Lacayo, "Still Under the Gun," *TIME*, July 6, 1998, 34-35.

5. Kathleen Neal Cleaver, "Back to Africa: The Evolution of the International Section of the Black Panther Party (1966-1972)," in *The Black Panther Party [Reconsidered]*, ed. Charles Jones, (Baltimore: Black Classics Press, 1998), 237. According to Cleaver, soon after a visit from David Hilliard's "emissary," the FBI arrested Geronimo ji Jaga (Elmer Pratt) who was underground in Texas; eventually the Los Angeles Police Department (LAPD) charged him in the shooting of white schoolteacher Caroline Olson. Although Huey Newton barred all Panthers from cooperating with Pratt's defense, Kathleen Neal Cleaver became one of the few Panthers to testify at the trial, stating that he was in northern California at a Black Panther Party meeting during the time of Olson's murder in southern California. Based on the testimony of police informant and perjurer Julio Butler, and the LAPD withholding evidence supporting his innocence, ji Jaga served twenty-seven years in prison before a Judge ruled that he should be released in June 1997 on $25,000 bail, pending a new trial. See Don Terry, "Los Angeles Confronts Bitter Racial Legacy," *New York Times*, July 20, 1997, A1, A10.

   Given his military leadership in the U.S. army and his strategic skills credited for the low Panther casualties following the December 1969 LAPD and SWAT raid on the Los Angeles chapter (days after Chicago police assisted by the FBI executed Fred Hampton and Mark Clark), Pratt's youth seems extraordinary. Kit Kim Holder notes though that the Black Panthers were primarily a youth organization (see Kit Kim Holder, "The History of the Black Panther Party 1966-1972: A Curriculum for Afrikan-American Studies." Ph.D. dissertation, University of Massachusetts-Amherst, 1990).

   For information on the FBI's counterintelligence program, see Ward Churchill and Jim Vander Wall, *Agents of Repression: The FBI's Secret Wars Against the Black Panther Party and the American Indian Movement* (Boston: South End Press, 1990); Churchill and Vander Wall, eds., *COINTELPRO PAPERS* (Boston: South End Press, 1990); and Kenneth O'Reilly, *"Racial Matters": The FBI's Secret File on Black America, 1960-1972* (New York: Free Press, 1989).

6. E. Franklin Frazier, *The Black Bourgeoisie* (Glencoe, IL: Free Press, 1957).

7. Assata Shakur, *Assata: An Autobiography* (Westport, CT: Lawrence Hill & Co., 1987).

8. This work uses the terms "black" and "African American" interchangeably to denote people of African descent living in the United States. "United States" and "America" are commonly referred to as synonymous. The quotation marks around my initial use of "America" recognizes the (imperial) fallacy of equating the United States with the Americas.

   "State" refers to the U.S. government and its attendant apparatuses—educational institutions, media, military, police (in the Gramscian concept of hegemony)— that grant it political legitimacy. To these might be added the "private" sector of corporate wealth that is heavily subsidized by public monies and is deeply invested in shaping domestic and foreign policies. For a discussion of state abuse of power from an antiracist feminist perspective, see Joy James, *Resisting State Violence: Radicalism, Gender and Race in U.S. Culture* (Minneapolis: University of Minnesota Press, 1996).

9. bell hooks, *Yearning: Race, Gender, and Cultural Politics* (Boston: South End Press, 1990), 18.

10. Patricia Hill Collins, *Black Feminist Thought* (Cambridge, MA: Unwin Hyman, 1990).

11. Patricia Hill Collins, *Fighting Words: Black Women & the Search for Justice* (Minneapolis: University of Minnesota Press, 1998), 67.

12. For definitions of "womanist," see Alice Walker, *In Search of Our Mothers' Gardens* (San Diego: Harcourt Brace Jovanovich, 1988), xi.

13. bell hooks, *Feminist Theory: From Margin to Center* (Boston: South End Press, 1984), 24. For the works of womanist theologians, see Katie G. Cannon, *Black Womanist Ethics* (Atlanta: Scholars Press, 1988), Jacquelyn Grant, *White Women's Christ and Black Women's Jesus* (Atlanta: Scholars Press, 1989) and Delores S. Williams, *Sisters in the Wilderness: The Challenge of Womanist God-Talk* (New York: Orbis Books, 1993).

14. bell hooks, "Feminism as a Persistent Critique of History: What's Love Got to Do with It?" in Alan Read, ed., *The Fact of Blackness: Frantz Fanon and Visual Representation* (Seattle: Bay Press, 1996), 81. Quote reprinted in T. Denean Sharpley-Whiting, *Frantz Fanon: Conflicts & Feminism* (Lanham, MD: Rowman and Littlefield, 1997), 88.

15. For anthologies documenting the emergence of black feminism in the late 1960s and early 1970s, see Barbara Smith, ed., *Homegirls: A Black Feminist Anthology* (New York: Kitchen Table: Women of Color Press, 1983); Toni Cade Bambara, ed., *The Black Woman* (New York: New American Library, 1970); and Beverly Guy-Sheftall, ed., *Words of Fire: An Anthology of African American Feminist Thought* (New York: New Press, 1995).

16. My use of the term "antiblack racism" throughout the text is indebted to Lewis Gordon, *Bad Faith and Antiblack Racism* (Atlantic Highlands, NJ: Humanities Press, 1995).

17. For discussions of the marginalization of black women, see Gloria T. Hull, Patricia Bell Scott, and Barbara Smith, eds. *All the Women Are White, All the Blacks Are Men, But Some of Us Are Brave: Black Women's Studies* (Old Westbury, NY: Feminist Press, 1982).

18. For a cogent argument on self-defense amid state repression, see Ward Churchill, *Pacifism as Pathology: Reflections on the Role of Armed Struggle in North America* (Winnipeg, Manitoba Canada: Arbeiter Ring, 1998).

CHAPTER 2

1. See Elihu Rosenblatt, ed. *Criminal Injustice* (Boston: South End Press, 1996); *Can't Jail the Spirit: Political Prisoners in the U.S.* (Chicago: Illinois Committee to End the Marion Lockdown, 1989); Kenneth O'Reilly, *"Racial Matters": The FBI's Secret File on Black America* (New York: Free Press, 1989).

2. Title VII of the 1964 Civil Rights Act defined employment decisions based on race, color, religion, sex, and national origin as unjust; later unjust discrimination was expanded to include age (1967), pregnancy (1978), and disability (1992). In the 1990s, white men make up 33 percent of the U.S. population but comprise 85 percent of tenured professors and law partners; 80 percent of the members of the U.S. House of Representatives; 90 percent of the U.S. Senate; 95 percent of Fortune 500 chief executive officers; and, 100 percent of U.S. presidents. See Alison Jaggar, "Gender, Race and Difference: Individual Consideration vs. Group-Based Affirmative Action in Admission to Higher Education," *Southern Journal of Philosophy,* Vol. 35, suppl., (1997), 21.

3. Troy Duster, "Individual Fairness, Group Preferences, and the California Strategy," *Representations,* Vol. 55 (Summer 1996), 41-58.

4. Ibid., 41. Duster cites John D. Ehrlichman, *Witness to Power: The Nixon Years* (New York: Simon and Schuster, 1982); H. R. Haldeman, *The Haldeman Diaries: Inside the Nixon White House* (New York: G. P. Putnam, 1994); H. R. Haldeman with Joseph DiMona, *The Ends of Power* (New York: Times Books, 1978); and Kenneth O'Reilly, *Nixon's Piano: Presidents and Racial Politics from Washington to Clinton* (New York: Free Press, 1995).

5. Ibid., 41.

6. Duster notes that African Americans, only 7 percent of California's population, are most likely to vote for progressive issues and candidates. This raises the question of political "community" among blacks not merely as an "imaginary" but as a foundation or basis for a political resistance to antidemocratic practices and the resulting backlash from conservatives.

7. Atwater quoted in Thomas Edsall and Mary Edsall, *Chain Reaction* (New York: W. W. Norton, 1991), 221. Following data also from Edsall, *Chain Reaction,* 119-120.

8. Duster, "Individual Fairness, Group Preferences, and the California Strategy."

9. See "A Prominent Scholar's Plan for the Inner Cities Draws Fire," *Chronicle of Higher Education,* Vol. 44, No. 2 (September 5, 1997), A21.

10. See Duster, "Individual Fairness, Group Preferences, and the California Strategy."

11. Currently, a company can enroll in the program if its owner has a personal net worth less than $250,000 and is "socially disadvantaged."

12. Steven Holmes, "U.S. Acts to Open Minority Program to White Bidders," *New York Times,* August 15, 1997, A1.

13. Rochelle Sharpe, "Asian-Americans Gain Sharply in Big Program of Affirmative Action," *Wall Street Journal,* September 9, 1997, 1.

14. Of the 1,000 offers made by the University of Texas law school, only 3 percent went to black/Latino students in 1997, down from 12 percent in 1996.

15. In June 1995 undocumented immigrants rioted at the Esmor Correctional Services Corporation detention center, which attempted to increase its profits by reducing food, repairs and guard salaries. In Texas, the prison population grew from 30,000 to 127,000 in the first half of the 1990s.

16. W. E. B. Du Bois, *Black Reconstruction in America: An Essay Toward the History of the Part Which Black Folk Played in the Attempt to Reconstruct Democracy in America, 1860-1880* (New York: Russell and Russell, 1962).

17. Salim Muwakkil, "My Own Private Alcatraz," *In These Times,* December 23, 1996.

18. Ibid.

19. See Randy Gragg, "A High Security, Low Risk Investment: Private Prisons Make Crime Pay," *Harper's Magazine,* (August 1996), 50-51.

20. Angela Y. Davis, grant proposal for "Critical Resistance" conference, author's papers.

21. American Bar Association, *Death Penalty Report,* 1997.

22. Mumia Abu-Jamal, *Live from Death Row: This is Mumia Abu-Jamal* (New York: Addison-Wesley, 1995).

23. Mumia Abu-Jamal, *Death Blossoms* (Farmington, PA: The Plough Publishing House, 1997).

24. Reginald Stewart, "Women in Prison," *Emerge Magazine* (March 1997), 44-49.

25. Laura Flanders, "Locked-Up Women Locked Out of Coverage," *EXTRA!* May/June 1994.

26. Amnesty International, "'Not Part of My Sentence': Violations of the Human Rights of Women in Custody," March, 1999.

27. Frederick Douglass, "What to the Slave Is the Fourth of July?" in eds., Henry Louis Gates, Jr. and Nellie Y. McKay, *The Norton Anthology of African American Literature* (New York: W. W. Norton, 1997), 379-390.

28. Black Radical Congress Conference Call, author's papers.

29. See Salim Muwakkil, "Black Radicalism: Where Do We Go From Here?" *The Nation,* July 12, 1998, 14-16. Although hampered by a centralized decision-making process, Black Radical Congress (BRC) "principles of unity" sought to foster a broad, united front: "We recognize the diverse historical tendencies in the black radical tradition including revolutionary nationalism, feminism and socialism. . . . Gender and sexuality

can no longer be viewed solely as personal issues but must be a basic part of our analysis, politics and struggles," 15.

30. Combahee River Collective, "The Combahee River Collective Statement," in ed., Barbara Simth, *Home Girls: A Black Feminist Anthology* (New York: Kitchen Table: Women of Color Press, 1983), 273.

31. Sweet Honey in the Rock, "Fannie Lou Hamer," in the album *B'lieve I'll Run On . . . See What the End's Gonna Be* (Redwood Records, December 1977).

32. Amilcar Cabral, *Return to the Source: Selected Speeches of Amilcar Cabral,* ed. Africa Information Service (New York: Monthly Review Press, 1973).

33. Ibid., 76-77.

34. Ibid., 77.

35. K. Kia Buseki Fu-Kiau, *The African Book Without Title* (Cambridge, MA: Fu-Kiau, 1980), 62.

36. See Theologian Bernard Lonergan, *Insight: A Study of Human Understanding* (New York: Longmans 1958, 1978), which discusses an epistemology similar to the African (Afrocentric) ethical paradigm in which knowledge exists for the sake of communal good and individual human liberation (presented as nonoppositional). Experience, reflection, judgment, and action are part of the process by which people (knowingly or unknowingly) learn. Action is indispensable to the learning process: You learn to ride a bicycle or drive a car not from merely reading books about bicycles or cars but from riding or driving. (Actually constructing the vehicles furthers that knowledge.) People know how to live, learn, and teach without oppressive practices by doing activities that confront and diminish them.

37. See K. Kia Bunseki Fu-Kiau, *The African Book Without Title,* 62 and John Mbiti, *Traditional African Religions and Philosophies* (London: Heineman, 1969).

38. Mbiti, *Traditional African Religions and Philosophies.*

39. Fu-Kiau, *The African Book Without Title,* 62-63.

40. See Paula Gunn Allen, *Sacred Hoop: Recovering the Feminine of American Indian Traditions* (Boston: Beacon Press, 1986).

41. Lee Maracle, *Oratory: Coming to Theory* (North Vancouver, BC: Gallerie Women Artists' Monographs), No. 1 (September 1990), 3.

42. See Joy James, "'Discredited Knowledge' in the Nonfiction of Toni Morrison," in *Resisting State Violence: Radicalism, Gender and Race in US Culture* (Minneapolis: University of Minnesota Press, 1996), 171-188.

43. Although she is not conventionally thought of as a "black feminist," Toni Morrison's novels feature strong female protagonists, while her edited anthologies have highlighted the work of Toni Cade Bambara and focus on race, gender, and sex, including the controversial Anita Hill/Clarence Thomas hearings and the O. J. Simpson criminal trial.

44. Toni Morrison, "Rootedness: The Ancestor as Foundation," in ed. Mari Evans, *Black Women Writers* (New York: Doubleday, 1984), 343.

45. The United States dominates international financial institutions such as the World Bank and International Monetary Fund. People in Africa, Latin America, and the Caribbean are poorer in the 1990s than they were in the 1960s, in part because of the policies dictated by these finance institutions. In 1988, UNICEF's State of the World's Children documented that the "Third World" was in debt to the United States and western European financial institutions for over $1 trillion (U.S. currency).

CHAPTER 3

1. Maria W. Stewart, *America's First Black Woman Political Writer: Essays and Speeches,* ed., Marilyn Richardson, (Bloomington: Indiana University Press, 1987).

2. Ibid., 70-71.

3. Miriam Decosta-Willis, ed., *The Memphis Diary of Ida B. Wells* (Boston: Beacon Press, 1997).

4. Ibid., ix

5. For a critical review of black feminist revisionist accounts of Ida B. Wells, see Joy James, "Sexual Politics" in *Transcending the Talented Tenth: Black Leaders and American Intellectuals* (New York: Routledge, 1997), 61-82.

6. Reprinted in Ida B. Wells-Barnett, *Crusade for Justice,* ed. Alfreda Duster (Chicago: University of Chicago Press, 1970).

7. Quoted in Gerder Lerner, *Black Women in White America* (New York: Vintage, 1974), 207.

8. Jack M. Bloom, *Class, Race, and the Civil Rights Movement* (Bloomington: Indiana University Press, 1987).

9. Ibid., 32.

10. African American men had fired on white, unidentified plainclothes detectives, armed with rifles, who were hiding at night in the alley behind the offices of the black-owned business. Wells was the godmother of Thomas and Bettye Moss's infant daughter, Maurine (Wells, *Crusade For Justice,* 47-52).

11. John D'Emilio and Estelle Freedman, *Intimate Matters: A History of Sexuality in America* (New York: Harper & Row, 1988), documents that between 1889 and 1940, at least 3,800 men and women were lynched in the South and the bordering states, with an average of 200 lynchings per year during the 1890s. In his preface to *On Lynchings,* a collection of Wells's three pamphlets—*Southern Horrors: Lynch Law in All Its Phases* (1892); *A Red Record: Lynchings in the U.S., 1892, 1893, 1894* (1895); and *Mob Rule in New Orleans* (1900), August Meier notes that the numbers of African Americans reported lynched averaged over 100 a year during the 1880s and the 1890s, with lynching "peaking" in 1892 when 161 women and men were murdered. Ida B. Wells-Barnett, *On Lynchings: Southern Horrors, A Red Record, Mob Rule in New Orleans* (New York: Arno Press, 1969). Meier refers only to African Americans lynched; D'Emilio includes whites as well. Lynching has become identified with African Americans, yet prior to the Civil War, the majority of lynching victims were white. Similarly, in the early eighteenth century, slavery came to represent the African American condition, although Europeans and Native Americans had been enslaved along with Africans prior to and during that era.

12. Meticulous in her research, Wells used deaths reported in the white press; believing the reports to be an undercount, she nevertheless felt that whites could not argue that their own numbers were exaggerated.

    Wells's citations of reasons given for the lynchings reported in 1892 reveal the source of her outrage: "Rape, 46; murder, 58; rioting, 3; race prejudice, 6; no cause given, 4; incendiarism, 6; robbery, 6; assault and battery, 1; attempted rape, 11; suspected robbery, 4; larceny, 1; self defense, 1; insulting women, 2; desperadoes, 6; fraud, l; attempted murder, 2; no offense stated, boy and girl, 2. . . . In the case of the boy and girl . . . their father, named Hastings, was accused of the murder of a white man; his fourteen-year-old daughter and sixteen-year-old son were hanged and their bodies filled with bullets, then the father was also lynched. This was in November, 1892, at Jonesville, Louisiana" (Wells, *A Red Record,* 20).

13. Wells, *Crusade for Justice,* 65-66.

14. Wells, *A Red Record,* 11.

15. One of Wells's most impressive legacies is her principled journalism to determine and disseminate facts concerning racialized violence, despite the dangers of publicizing the truth. After her 1895 marriage to Ferdinand Barnett, she purchased and became editor of the Chicago-based *African American Conservator,* which her husband had founded.

16. Wells, *Crusade for Justice.* Quote reprinted in Paula Giddings, *When and Where I Enter: The Impact of Black Women on Race in America* (New York: Vintage, 1986), 26. Giddings notes the rising economic influence of the black community; the National Negro Business League reported that at one time, 187,000 African American farmers owned farms in the South, some as large as 1,000 acres. This economic base meant political power during the Reconstruction era, where often in the "Black Belt" blacks outnumbered whites.

17. Quoted in Lerner, *Black Women in White America,* 209.

18. Wells routinely contested antiblack racism in the white press such as that found in the *Memphis Daily Commercial* article of May 17, 1892, entitled "More Rapes, More Lynchings": In response to the article's statement that "The generation of Negroes which have grown up since the war have lost in large measure the traditional and wholesome awe of the white race which kept the Negroes in subjection. . . . There is no longer a restraint upon the brute passion of the Negro," Wells responds: "The thinking public will not easily believe freedom and education more brutalizing than slavery, and the world knows that the crime of rape was unknown during four years of Civil War, when the white women of the South were at the mercy of the race which is all at once charged with being a bestial one." Wells, *A Red Record,* 5.

    Her claim that no rapes of white females by black males were reported during the Civil War is contested by Martha Hodes's "The Sexualization of Reconstruction Politics: White Women and Black Men in the South after the Civil War," in John C. Fout and Maura Shaw Tantillo, eds., *American Sexual Politics: Sex, Gender, and Race Since the Civil War* (Chicago: University of Chicago Press, 1990), 19.

19. Wells, *Crusade for Justice,* 137. This passage appeared in a special correspondence from Liverpool for the *Inter-Ocean,* 9 April 1894, and is in part a response to lynching apologists Women's Christian Temperance Union leader Francis Willard, former *Christian Advocate* editor Oscar P. Fitzgerald, and former Emory University President Atticus Haygood; both men later became bishops. Wells, *Crusade for Justice,* 136.

20. Wells's critique of three rationalizations for terrorism against African Americans in the postbellum South is similar to that of Frederick Douglass. According to Douglass, the:

    > justification for the murder of Negroes was said to be Negro conspiracies, Negro insurrections, Negro schemes to murder all the white people, Negro plots to burn the town. . . . times have changed and the Negro's accusers have found it necessary to change with them. . . . Honest men no longer believe that there is any ground to apprehend Negro supremacy. . . . altered circumstances have made necessary a sterner, stronger, and more effective justification of Southern barbarism, and hence we have. . . . to look into the face of a more shocking and blasting charge. Frederick Douglass, quoted in Wells, *Intimate Matters,* 218.

21. *A Red Record* asserts: "The white man's victory soon became complete by fraud, violence, intimidation and murder. . . . [with] the Negro actually eliminated from all participation in state and national elections, there could be no longer any excuse for killing Negroes to prevent "Negro Domination," 10.

22. Ibid.

23. According to Amnesty International, the General Assembly of the Organization of American States (OAS) discussed a treaty to abolish the death penalty in 1987. That

same year the European Parliament condemned the continuing use of the death penalty in the United States, noting that although an increasing "number of countries are abolishing or no longer applying the death penalty, states in the U.S. are committed to it." In many states, persons under eighteen can be executed; the race of victim and defendant is a factor in death sentencing. Between 1977 and 1986, nearly 90 percent of prisoners executed had been convicted of killing whites, although the number of black victims was approximately equal to that of white victims. See Enid Harlow, David Matas, and Jane Rocamora, eds., *The Machinery of Death: A Shocking Indictment of Capital Punishment in the US* (New York: Amnesty International U.S.A, 1995).

For additional documentation of human rights abuses of the incarcerated, see Elihu Rosenblatt, ed., *Criminal Injustice* (Boston: South End Press, 1996).

24. Threats by the Secret Service to prosecute her for treason failed to stop Wells's educational organizing and protest on behalf of the "martyred" African American soldiers of the 24th Infantry. In 1917, while stationed in Houston, Texas, 100 armed black troops in the 24th Infantry marched on the town to defend themselves against racist assaults. In the aftermath of the confrontation, sixteen whites and four black soldiers died. The U.S. Army hanged nineteen soldiers and court-martialed and imprisoned fifty following the revolt.

25. See Joanne Braxton, *Black Women Writing Autobiography: A Tradition Within Tradition* (Philadelphia: Temple University Press, 1989), 2.

26. Ibid., 138.

27. Wells, *Crusade for Justice,* 72-73.

28. Braxton, *Black Women Writing Autobiography,* 122.

29. Ida B. Wells, *A Red Record,* reprinted in *On Lynchings.*

30. According to Gerda Lerner, "The myth of the black rapist of white women is the twin of the myth of the bad black woman—both designed to apologize for and facilitate the continued exploitation of black men and women. Black women perceived this connection very clearly and were early in the forefront of the fight against lynching. Their approach was to prove the falseness of the accusation, the disproportion between punishment and crime, the absence of equality, and lastly, to point to the different scales of justice meted out to the white and the black rapist. An often neglected aspect of this problem is the judicial indifference to sexual crimes committed by black men upon black women." See Gerda Lerner, "Black Women Attack the Lynching System," in Lerner, *Black Women in White America* (New York: Pantheon Books, 1972), 193-194.

31. If Anita Hill's defense team had used the antebellum imagery of black female sexual victimization against the white male senators interrogating her, Hill might have had a stronger chance of convincing the American public of the veracity of her accusations; perhaps only the black female raped-by-slavemaster narrative could have countered Thomas's black-male-lynching narrative.

32. The Brawley case was "closed" in July 1998 when Steven Pagones was awarded a cash settlement against Brawley (who never attended the trial or had an attorney present), Sharpton, Maddox, and Mason for slander. Pagones, a white former Wappingers Falls assistant district attorney, accused by Brawley's handlers of being her abductor and rapist, had asked for nearly $400 million but was awarded slightly less than $1 million. It was initially thought that the trial, which became known as the "Tawana Brawley Defamation Trial," would last one month; it began in November 1997 and ended in July 1998 with the reading of the verdict. Performance marked the trial throughout. Brawley never testified, neither before the 1988 grand jury that exonerated the accused or the later defamation trial. Appropriating her voice and body to fight their own battles with white men and institutional power, black men offered no evidence of an assault and "shielded" her from testimony that could have clarified the events

surrounding her four day disappearance. As Michael A. Hardy, attorney for Al Sharpton stated, equating Sharpton's actions with Martin Luther King Jr.'s civil rights advocacy (and martyrdom): "We have been here for a greater purpose. . . . Reverend Sharpton's business, if you will, was the business of civil rights" (W. Glaberson, "Sharpton Lawyer Says Brawley Case Is Test of Civil Rights," *New York Times*, July 2, 1998).

33. Alongside community women and men, two white women and I were the only faculty to actively organize with students.

34. Excerpts from this section on Ella Baker first appeared in Joy James, "Ella Baker, 'Black Women's Work' and Activist Intellectuals," *The Black Scholar*, Vol. 24, No. 4, (Fall 1994), 8-15.

35. Joanne Grant, *Fundi: The Story of Ella Baker*, New Day Films, 1981; *Ella Baker: Freedom Bound* (New York: John Wiley and Sons, 1998)

36. See Ella Baker and Marvel Cooke, "The Bronx Slave Markets," *The Crisis: A Record of the Darker Races*, Vol. 42, (November 1935), 330-31, 340.

37. Jacqueline Jones, *Labor of Love, Labor of Sorrow* (New York: Vintage Books, 1986), 161.

38. Ibid., 166.

39. Joanne Grant, *Black Protest: History, Documents and Analyses 1619 to Present* (New York: Ballantine, 1968), 213.

40. Baker and Cooke, "The Bronx Slave Markets," 330.

41. Ibid.

42. Similar trends in the dispensing of federal funds for community programs in the 1960s "war on poverty" are detailed in Richard Cloward and Francis Fox Piven, *Regulating the Poor* (New York: Random House, 1993).

43. Baker and Cooke, "The Bronx Slave Markets," 340.

44. Ibid., 330.

45. Ibid., 340.

46. Ibid., 330.

47. Ibid.

48. Ibid., 340.

49. Ibid.

50. Gloria Hull and Barbara Smith maintain that: "Only a feminist, pro-woman perspective that acknowledges the reality of sexual oppression in the lives of black women, as well as the oppression of race and class, will make black women's studies the transformer of consciousness it needs to be." See Gloria T. Hull, Patricia Bell Scott, and Barbara Smith, eds., *All the Women Are White, All the Blacks Are Men, But Some of Us Are Brave: Black Women's Studies* (Old Westbury, NY: Feminist Press, 1982), xxi. Other black feminists writing on black women's studies include Barbara Christian, Deborah King, and bell hooks.

51. Beth Richie, Loretta Ross, Alice Walker, and bell hooks have written about sexual violence in black women's lives from black men.

52. Judith Rollins, *Between Women: Domestics and Their Employers* (Philadelphia: Temple University Press, 1986), 212-213.

CHAPTER 4

1. Ella Baker, "The Black Woman in the Civil Rights Struggle," quoted in Joanne Grant, *Ella Baker* (New York: Jack Wiley & Sons, 1998), 230. Baker presented this speech in 1969 at the Institute for the Black World in Atlanta, Georgia.

2. Ibid. Harvard historian Evelyn Brooks Higginbotham documents that white Christian philanthropists such as Henry Morehouse and other leaders within the American Baptist Home Missionary Society (ABHMS) in 1896 promoted the concept of the "Talented Tenth" as black elite race leaders. ABHMS funded the emergence of this elite to serve a population facing severe discrimination and persecution following the aborted Reconstruction. ABHMS explicitly created the Talented Tenth with a dual purpose: to function as a model showcase for whites (and blacks) as a living demonstration that black intellectual and moral inferiority were myths and to counter revolutionary and anarchistic tendencies among an increasingly disenfranchised black populace. See Evelyn Brooks Higginbotham, *Righteous Discontent: The Women's Movement in the Black Baptist Church, 1880-1920* (Cambridge, MA: Harvard University Press, 1993).

    In 1903 W. E. B. Du Bois popularized the term in *The Souls of Black Folk* with his essay "The Talented Tenth." A century after white liberal missionaries coined the phrase, the idea of the Talented Tenth is being revitalized by Harvard's black intellectual elites Henry Louis Gates Jr., whose *The Future of the Race* (New York: Knopf, 1996), coauthored with fellow Harvard professor Cornel West, and 1998 PBS/ Frontline documentary *The Two Nations of Black America,* promote the formation of the Talented Tenth.

3. See Higginbotham, *Righteous Discontent.* Today, for U.S.-based revolutionaries and political prisoners to exist as more than a cult of martyrs like the Gnostic Christians, the Talented Tenth, as "buffer zone," would grant the preferential option to the poor, imprisoned, and militant.

4. Combahee River Collective, "The Combahee River Collective Statement," in Barbara Smith, ed., *Home Girls* (New York: Kitchen Table: Women of Color Press, 1983), 273.

5. Earl Conrad, "I Bring You General Tubman," *The Black Scholar,* Vol. 1, No. 3-4 (January-February 1970), 4.

6. Combahee River Collective, "The Combahee River Collective Statement," 279.

7. Ibid., 275-276.

8. Ibid.

9. For an example, see Patricia Hill Collins's discussion of organizing in *Black Feminist Thought* (Cambridge, Mass: Unwin Hyman, 1990).

10. U.S. counterrevolutionary initiatives have been extensive and costly in terms of human rights abuses. See Noam Chomsky, *The Culture of Terrorism* (Boston: South End Press, 1988).

11. bell hooks, "Must We Call All Women 'Sister'?" *Z Magazine* (February 1992), 19-22.

12. At a 1997 New York University forum on black women writers, on a panel shared with Angela Davis, Elaine Brown referred to former Us leader Maulana Karenga as an American "Buthelezi"; Kimberlé Crenshaw makes the same reference to Clarence Thomas in her July 1998 presentation. Karenga's Us was involved in the 1969 shooting at UCLA that killed Black Panthers Alprentice "Bunchy" Carter and John Huggins. Buthelezi is the South African Chief who was a formidable opponent to the African National Congress and the antiracist freedom movement, leading the "Inkata Freedom Fighters" in a murderous alliance with the apartheid police and military.

13. Accounts of the increased powers of state and federal police and the dismantling of welfare and economic support for impoverished peoples during the 1990s regularly appeared in progressive publications such as *The Nation, Emerge* magazine, *The Progressive,* and *Mother Jones.*

14. In *Black Feminist Thought,* Patricia Hill Collins erases black women's associations with radical groups. Citing the literary and political achievements of Angela Davis, Bernice Johnson Reagon, and Ella Baker, she fails to mention the *radical* organizations with which they worked (and for which they are largely known): the Soledad Brothers

Defense Committee, the Communist Party U.S.A, and the Black Panther Party for Davis; and the Student Nonviolent Coordinating Committee for Reagon and Baker.

15. Joan Roelofs, "The Third Sector as a Protective Layer for Capitalism," *Monthly Review,* Vol. 47 (September 1995), 16-17.

16. Teresa L. Ebert, *Ludic Feminism* (Ann Arbor: The University of Michigan Press, 1996), 3.

17. Alice Echols, *Daring to Be Bad: Radical Feminism in America 1967-1975* (Minneapolis: University of Minnesota Press, 1989). Echols's insightful text is somewhat limited by her failure to fully research and analyze the contributions of black feminist radicals such as Frances Beale, a founder of the Student Nonviolent Coordinating Committee's Black Women's Alliance, and Barbara Smith, a founder of The Combahee River Collective.

18. See Echols, *Daring to be Bad,* for documentation of initial funding for *Ms.* In 1998, *Ms.* magazine, with black feminist Marcia Ann Gillespie as Editor in Chief, became completely owned by women.

19. Echols's descriptions of the strife between radical and liberal feminists parallel to some degree the black liberation movement's conflictual relationship between revolutionary nationalism found in the Black Panther Party (which advocated an end to imperialism, capitalism, and racism, and "power to the people," not the police) and the cultural nationalism of Us and its emphasis on an "African" lifestyle. There was overlap between the two "camps"; for instance, the New York chapter of the Black Panther Party synthesized an African (American) aesthetic with critiques of capitalism, government corruption, and police violence.

20. Imprisoned since the mid-1980s (the United States has denied the Italian government's request for extradition or leniency), Sylvia Baraldini has spoken out, from her jail cell in Danbury, Connecticut, on behalf of African American death-row inmate and political prisoner Mumia Abu-Jamal. An internationalist and student radical in the 1960s and 1970s, Baraldini protested the Vietnam war, demonstrated for women's rights, and campaigned against apartheid and colonialism in Africa. Organizing to expose COIN-TELPRO, she was a member of the Committee to Free the Panther 21 (twenty-one defendants who were acquitted of all charges after years of harassment and incarceration in New York). Parole guidelines specify forty to fifty-two months incarceration for the crimes for which Baraldini was convicted; she has served over four times that.

During the 1980s, Susan Rosenberg and Sylvia Baraldini were housed at the Women's High Security Unit at Lexington, Kentucky. The unit was closed in 1988 because of an international human rights campaign that opposed its use of torture against female political prisoners. Both women were subjected to years of isolation in all-white subterranean cells, daily strip-searches, sleep deprivation, sexual abuse, and a complete denial of privacy, including male guards watching them shower.

Syliva Baraldini, Susan Rosenberg, and Marilyn Buck fall within the category of "political prisoner" as defined by Amnesty International, which documents over 100 political prisoners or prisoners of conscience within the United States. Amnesty International has also declared U.S. citizen Lori Berenson a Peruvian political prisoner. The reporter, a former MIT student, went to Peru in 1994 to write about the Peruvian poor and the government's violations of their rights and welfare and was sentenced to life imprisonment by a hooded-military tribunal. Like Berenson, hundreds of Peruvians falsely convicted by Peru's military secret tribunal were never given written notice of the charges or evidence, adequate access to a competent lawyer; or allowed to cross-examine witnesses testifying against them. See Rhoda Berenson's Mother's Day article about her daughter, "A Mother's Story," *Vogue* (May 1997), 310-313.

The U.S. government has condemned Berenson's incarceration. In August 1996 eighty-seven members of the House and twenty members of the Senate sent letters to President Alberto Fujimori noting Peru's violations of international standards and urging its government to grant Berenson "a fair trial." Clinton met with Fujimori in May 1997, formally requesting that Berenson be granted a civilian trial. Despite the rhetoric of diplomacy, U.S. military aid to Peru has continued. Currently there are no indications of a possible new trial for Berenson.

21. See Judi Bari, *Timber Wars* (Monroe, ME: Common Courage Press, 1994). Notorious for its anti-Panther violence, today COINTELPRO largely focuses on white radical peace or environmental activists and members of the Puerto Rican Independence Movement. Currently, the majority of U.S. political arrests stem from antinuclear weapons or anti–School of the Americas demonstrations, while grand juries are used to derail Puerto Rican Independence activism. For evaluations of the political use of grand juries and the policing of the environmental and Puerto Rican Independence movements, see Joy James, ed., *States of Confinement: Policing, Detention & Prisons* (New York: St. Martin's Press, 2000).

22. For more information, see Angela Davis and Bettina Aptheker, eds. *If They Come in the Morning* (New Rochelle, NY: The Third Press, 1971); Angela Davis, *Angela Davis: An Autobiography* (New York: Random House, 1974); and, Joy James, ed., *The Angela Y. Davis Reader* (Oxford: Basil Blackwell, 1998).

23. Echols's summary of this "incident" bears quoting at length: In 1967,

> *Ramparts* magazine revealed that the CIA had subsidized a number of domestic groups including the National Student Association (NSA) and the Independent Research Service (IRS), an organization which Steinem had helped found. The IRS had been established in 1959 to encourage American students to participate in the communist-dominated World Festivals of Youth and Students for Peace and Freedom. Steinem had been the director of the IRS from 1959 through 1960 and had continued to work for the organization through 1962. Redstockings alleged that the CIA established the IRS to organize an anti-communist delegation of Americans to disrupt the festival. They also claimed that Steinem and the IRS had been involved in gathering information on foreign nationals attending the festivals. However, Steinem's own account of the IRS's involvement in the festival differed dramatically from the Redstockings' version. Shortly after the *Ramparts* article appeared, the *New York Times* published an interview with Steinem in which she admitted that she had known about the CIA funding, but claimed that she had never been asked to gather information on Americans or foreigners who participated in the festivals. According to Steinem, the IRS had encouraged Americans to attend the festivals in order to open up the lines of communication between the East and the West. In fact, Steinem maintained that the CIA's involvement was benign, if not enlightened: "Far from being shocked by this involvement I was happy to find some liberals in government in those days who were far-sighted and cared enough to get Americans of all political views to the festival. Echols, *Daring to be Bad,* 265-266.

In 1975, based on the *Ramparts* article, women activists in Redstockings published an exposé, hoping to stay the erosion of radical feminist politics before the more financially endowed cultural or liberal feminist politics represented by *Ms.* and Steinem. Echols's critique of the Redstockings "exposé" notes that throughout the 1950s and 1960s, "liberalism and anti-communism were coterminous" and that "Redstockings presented no evidence to support their insinuation that Steinem and *Ms.* were currently in league with the CIA" (268). Also see Barbara Leon, "Gloria Steinem and the CIA," in Kathie Sarachild, ed., *Redstockings: Feminist Revolution* (New York:

Redstockings, 1975); and "C.I.A. Subsidized Festival Trips," *New York Times,* February 21, 1967, L33.

24. The Communist Party USA had been heavily infiltrated by government agents and decimated by the McCarthy era of the 1950s. At the time of the trial, it could not be termed a "revolutionary" organization nor could the Black Panther Party, although it began as a revolutionary community-based effort to counter police brutality only to be later crippled by infiltration, police violence, and a murderous factionalism (partly instigated by the FBI's COINTELPRO). See Ward Churchill and Jim Vander Wall, *Agents of Repression: The FBI's Secret Wars Against the Black Panther Party and the American Indian Movement* (Boston: South End Press, 1990).

CHAPTER 5

1. "Introduction," John Edgar Wideman, to Mumia Abu-Jamal, *Live from Death Row: This Is Mumia Abu-Jamal,* (Reading, MA: Addison Wesley, 1995).

Mumia Abu-Jamal was convicted in 1982 of the killing of Philadelphia police officer Daniel Faulkner. The controversial nature under which he was tried (perjury by witnesses, police suppression of evidence that would assist the defense, inconsistencies in ballistics reports) has led to international calls for a new trial. Trial inconsistencies and prosecutorial misconduct are raised in the documentary *Mumia Abu-Jamal: The Case for Reasonable Doubt.* Other documentation has noted that Philadelphia is the only city to be investigated by the Justice Department for widespread and rampant police corruption that included coerced testimony and falsification of evidence against defendants.

2. See Wideman, "Introduction," *Live from Death Row.*

The 1974 memoir, *Angela Davis: An Autobiography,* presents the courageous battles of antiracist radicals. It also reinscribes the neoslave narrative. Davis's departure at age fifteen from "Dynamite Hill" in Birmingham, Alabama (so named for Klan bombings of black homes in the previously all-white enclave) for a private high school in Manhattan where she lived with white Quakers; undergraduate study in Massachusetts at Brandeis University and later study abroad in Europe—all mark flight from black-contained sites of segregation and violence into white expansive sites of privilege, education, and stability. Davis subverts the narrative by returning from Europe to continue doctoral studies at the University of California, in order to be near the black liberation movement of the late 1960s. Yet, this subversion is itself subverted decades later by her reconstruction as a "rehabilitated" former political prisoner and current professor in an elite (European-centered) theory program, the History of Consciousness, at the University of California-Santa Cruz. At a March 6-7, 1998, conference entitled "Unfinished Liberation Conference: Power, Caste and Culture" sponsored by the School of Justice Studies at Arizona State University, Davis remarked that she would have written her autobiography differently if she had thought about the consequences of the neoslave narrative. Yet a different narrative would presuppose a different form of radical politics.

Key features of the "rehabilitation process" in order for former prisoners to be mainstreamed is that they appear to conform to the cultural norm. That norm is dynamic rather than static and so has expanded to include traits of the militant antiracism and feminism of the 1960s (for example, encompassing denunciations of racism, homophobia, and sexism and the use of demonstrations and protests for liberal agendas). Unaltered features of the behavioral norm remain employment and a willingness to acknowledge—or at least distance from—the errant past behavior.

3. Toni Morrison, *Song of Solomon* (New York: Random House, 1977).

4. See Harriet Jacobs, *Incidents in the Life of a Slave Girl* (1861) (New York: Oxford University Press, 1988) and Frederick Douglass, *Narrative of the Life of Frederick Douglass* (1845) (New York: Penguin Books, 1982). See Angela Davis's critique of Douglass's limited analysis of the use of incarceration in black oppression, "From the Prison of Slavery to the Slavery of Prison: Frederick Douglass and the convict Prison Lease System," in Joy James, ed., *The Angela Y. Davis Reader* (Oxford: Basil Blackwell, 1998).

5. Malcolm X, *The Autobiography of Malcolm X* (New York: Ballantine, 1965).

6. See George Jackson, *Blood in My Eye* (New York: Random House, 1972) and *Soledad Brother: The Prison Letters of George Jackson* (New York: Random House, 1974).

7. See note 5, page 193, for information on this case. Support for Geronimo ji Jaga (Elmer Pratt) was likely difficult to mobilize, even among progressives given the stigma placed on Black Panthers. For as Bettina Aptheker notes, even the National Committee of the Communist Party USA was initially sharply divided over supporting Angela Davis in 1971 following Jonathan Jackson's attempt to free incarcerated Panthers and Soledad Brothers. See Bettina Aptheker, *The Morning Breaks: The Trial of Angela Davis* (Ithaca, NY: Cornell University Press, 1999), xv-xvi.

8. In the PBS Frontline documentary, *The Two Nations of Black America,* Gates lampoons the Panthers and their confrontations with police surrounding the New Haven 14, in which Ericka Huggins and Bobby Seale were on trial for murder. Eventually both were acquitted; charges had been based on COINTELPRO illegalities. The documentary, which aired during Black History Month, made no mention of COINTELPRO; however, a summary of the FBI's violent campaign against black revolutionaries appears only in the on-line discussion, which most viewers did not see.

9. The film also features the photo of Huey Newton posing in the rattan chair with a carbine. That the "poster" people of the black revolution were young, beautiful, and generally "light skin" (a key marker in their conventional allure) suggests a transgender, sexual appeal of the desirable black American as racial-hybrid.

10. *The Black Panther Party [Reconsidered]'*s "Gender Dynamics" section features auto-biographical and historical essays respectively by former Panther Regina Jennings's "Why I Joined the Party: An Africana Womanist Reflection" and non-Panther scholars: Tracey Matthews, "'No One Ever Asks, What a Man's Role in the Revolution Is': Gender and the Politics of The Black Panther Party, 1966-1971"; and Angela D. LeBlanc-Ernest, "'The Most Qualified Person to Handle the Job': Black Panther Party Women, 1966-1982." Ernest-LeBlanc—director of the Black Panther Party Research Project at Stanford University, which reportedly purchased the Panther papers from Brown, David Hilliard, and Huey Newton's estate for over $1 million—offers an uncritical perspective that promotes Brown's iconic status as *feminist* and *revolutionary.*

11. Brown's long-term affair with a CIA operative and COINTELPRO architect (disclosed in her autobiography, *A Taste of Power: A Black Woman's Story* [New York: Pantheon Books, 1992]) surfaced in the documentary *All Power to the People!* in a male Panther's unsubstantiated allegation that Brown herself was an "agent." This information has been either roundly criticized or generally ignored by black feminists addressing women's roles in this tumultuous organization and era. Like Gloria Steinem, Brown provides complex images of female leadership for radical black feminists to consider and critique.

12. According to Joanne Grant: "By 1974 the Panther Party had little influence, having been greatly weakened by internal splits and by government efforts to suppress it. Many Panthers were killed in gun battles with police, and scores were involved in long legal battles on various charges, including murder. Significantly, the government was unable to obtain convictions in most Panther trials as well as in other political trials of blacks

in the early 70s. Partly this was because more blacks were serving on juries, and partly because jurors seemed to hold the view that many political trials had come about through the activities of agents provocateurs and police spies." See Joanne Grant, *Black Protest: History, Documents and Analyses 1619 to Present* (New York: Ballantine, 1968) 513.

13. Brown's leadership occurred after the "split" and Oakland's expulsion of female leaders Kathleen Cleaver and Ericka Huggins; male leaders Eldridge Cleaver and Geronimo ji Jaga; and the entire New York chapter of the party (which included at one time Assata Shakur). Newton, by then suffering from advanced drug addiction and paranoia, was in exile in Cuba, as Brown ran a centralized, violence-prone elite mainstreaming itself through electoral politics and encouraging Panthers to register to vote as "Democrats."

14. For an analysis, see Angela Y. Davis, "The Making of a Revolutionary," Review of Elaine Brown's *A Taste of Power: A Black Woman's Story,* in *Women's Review of Books* (June 1993).

15. The memoir's depiction of black feminism seems strongly compatible with the cultural feminism of bourgeois white women described by Alice Echols's *Daring to Be Bad* (Minneapolis: University of Minnesota Press, 1989).

16. For instance, Alice Walker's book "blurb" for Brown's memoir reads: "What Elaine Brown writes is so astonishing, at times it is even difficult to believe she survived it. And yet she did, bringing us that amazing light of the black woman's magical resilience, in the gloominess of our bitter despair."

17. That Soviet leaders took opportunities at summit meetings with U.S. President Richard Nixon's cabinet to inquire about Davis during her incarceration and trial, and consequently to rebuke or embarrass the Nixon administration on its human rights abuses toward black Americans, also proved to differentiate her case sharply from Magee's.

18. In a 1993 interview, Geronimo ji Jaga, at that time imprisoned for twenty-three years, made the following observations: "The Black bourgeoisie individualize a lot—they might take an Angela Davis because it is fashionable to get behind Angela Davis to help her get out of prison and then they feel as though they have contributed; but they turned away from Ruchell Magee, who was actually shot and almost killed. So, a few may get behind Geronimo ji-jaga, because he knows Danny Glover or he has been to Vietnam, but they might oppose Sundiata Acoli, who is a very beautiful brother who should be supported a thousand per cent and should be freed. They might get behind Dhoruba bin-Wahad and Mutulu Shakur and ignore Marilyn Buck and Laura Whitehorn. It is a matter of us trying to educate them to the reality, what is happening, so they could broaden their support and base their decisions on principles as opposed to personalities."

    See Heike Kleffner, "The Black Panthers: interviews with Geronimo ji-jaga Pratt and Mumia Abu-Jamal," *Race & Class,* Vol. 35, No. 1 (1993); for additional information on political prisoners cited, see Churchill and Vander Wall, eds., *Can't Jail the Spirit* (Chicago: Editorial El Coqui, 1992).

19. George Jackson's seventeen-year-old brother, Jonathan, had become one of Davis's bodyguards because the activist academic received multiple death threats daily. Campus police provided protection only when she taught classes and met with students; friends and coactivists provided off-campus security, often with guns legally purchased by the twenty-six-year-old assistant professor and kept in her apartment.

    Attempting to publicize state abuses against the Soledad Brothers and dehumanizing prison conditions, and concerned for his brother's welfare, Jonathan Jackson carried guns into a courtroom in Northern California's Marin County. The young Jackson and three prisoners, James McClain, William Christmas, and Ruchell Magee, took as hostages the judge, district attorney, and several members of the jury. After the inmates and the recent high school graduate brought the hostages to a van in the parking lot, San Quentin guards fired on the parked vehicle, killing Judge Haley, Jackson, and prisoners McClain and Christmas, and seriously wounding the district attorney, several jurors, and prisoner Magee who later briefly became Davis's codefendant.

Although she was not in northern California at the time, because the guns were registered in her name, Davis was designated by police as an accomplice. In that era of COINTELPRO and police killings of black revolutionaries, rather than turn herself into the authorities, Davis went underground and for two months was on the FBI's "Ten Most Wanted List." Captured in Manhattan on October 13, 1970, she spent the next sixteen months in jail, mostly in solitary confinement, before being released on bail during her trial. Arraigned in a Marin County court on January 5, 1971 on charges of murder, kidnapping, and conspiracy, she was acquitted the following year.

According to author Ward Churchill, the Black Panther Party was not involved in the hostage taking, partly because when Geronimo ji Jaga heard of the plans, he ordered Panthers not to participate. ji Jaga allegedly feared that a police infiltrator had convinced Jonathan Jackson of the feasibility of a strategy that could lead to—as Huey Newton stated in Jonathan's eulogy—"revolutionary suicide."

20. Quoted in John Kifner, "Eldridge Cleaver, Black Panther Who Became G.O.P. Conservative, Is Dead at 62," *New York Times,* May 2, 1998, B8.

21. In 1991, the Communist Party USA expelled 800 intellectuals and activists, including key black women leaders such as Charlene Mitchell and Angela Davis; however, to date, no comprehensive analysis has been published by former elite members of the CPUSA leadership. Progressive critiques of democratic politics and sexism within organizations are more commonly found concerning the Black Panther Party or the Student Nonviolent Coordinating Committee than the CPUSA.

22. Davis's work with women at the University of California at Santa Cruz has explored the construction of "women of color" as a "race"—which partly explains her broad appeal to progressives seeking a "race"-based politics not limited to African Americans. Of course, the CPUSA also promoted the ideal of multiracial inclusivity.

23. Angela Davis, "Afro Images: Politics, Fashion, and Nostalgia," reprinted in *The Angela Y. Davis Reader,* 271.

24. Ibid., 272.

25. Ibid., 273.

26. *LIFE magazine,* September 11, 1970, Vol. 69, No. 11, 26. The quote stems from a speech Davis made for the Soledad Brothers and is taken from a June 27, 1970, interview with Maeland Productions which was producing a documentary on Davis.

27. The roll call is extensive. According to Amnesty International, there are over one hundred political prisoners in the United States. Black revolutionaries incarcerated through COINTELPRO include Herman Wallace, Albert Wood, Ed Poindexter, Mondo we Langa (David Rice), Mutulu Shakur, and Sundiata Acoli.

28. Joanne Grant refers to Black Panther attorney Charles Garry's assertion that local police working in coordination with the FBI had executed twenty-eight Party members. COINTELPRO extended to the American Indian Movement; and is currently most active against the environmental movement. See Grant, *Black Protest;* Ward Churchill and Jim Vander Wall, *Agents of Repression: The FBI's Secret Wars Against the Black Panther Party and the American Indian Movement* (Boston: South End Press, 1990); and Judi Bari, *Timber Wars* (Monroe, ME: Common Courage Press, 1994).

29. Harriet Beecher Stowe, *Uncle Tom's Cabin* (New York: Bantam Books, 1981).

30. See Alice Walker, "Black Panthers or Black Punks?," *New York Times,* May 5, 1991, A23.

31. Manning Marable's "Along the Color Line" articles appear in scores of progressive publications. The *New York Times* ran an article the following month that was

markedly opposite in tone to Marable's April commentary. See James Dao, "Fugitive in Cuba Still Wounds Trenton: Chesimard Unrepentant at Trooper's '73 Killing; Whitman Is Irate," *New York Times,* May 1, 1998, Bl, B9.

32. Assata Shakur, *Assata: An Autobiography* (Westport, CT: Lawrence Hill and Company, 1987), 242-243.

33. Ibid., 243.

34. On May 2, 1973, a shootout on the New Jersey Turnpike left Zayd Shakur and State Trooper Werner Foerster dead and Assata Shakur and her codefendant Sundiata Acoli wounded. That day, driving a car with Vermont license places on the New Jersey Turnpike, Shakur and her companions, Zayd Malik and Sundiata Acoli, were stopped for a "faulty tail light." According to Shakur, Acoli got out of the car to speak with the troopers. State trooper Harper approached the car, opened the door to question Zayd Shakur and Assata Shakur, then drew his gun and pointed it at the car's occupants, telling them to raise their hands in front of them. Assata Shakur describes what followed:

> I complied and in a split second, there was a sound that came from outside the car, there was a sudden movement, and I was shot once with my arms held up in the air, and then once again from the back. Zayd Malik Shakur was later killed, trooper Werner Foerster was killed, and even though trooper Harper admitted that he shot and killed Zayd Malik Shakur, under the New Jersey felony murder law, I was charged with killing both Zayd Malik Shakur, who was my closest friend and comrade, and charged in the death of trooper Forester. Never in my life have I felt such grief. Zayd had vowed to protect me, and to help me to get to a safe place, and it was clear that he had lost his life, trying to protect both me and Sundiata. Although he was also unarmed, and the gun that killed trooper Foerster was found under Zayd's leg, Sundiata Acoli, who was captured later, was also charged with both deaths.

35. U.S. Representative Maxine Waters, known for her strong antiracist positions, initially with other members of the Congressional Black Caucus voted to support House Resolution 254, passed on September 14, 1998, which called on the Cuban government to extradite Shakur and other U.S. political refugees. Congresswoman Waters retracted her vote, stating that she was not aware that the name listed in the Republican-led resolution, "Joanne Chesimard," was in fact "Assata Shakur" and the Republicans used deceptive practices to pass the bill along with non-controversial legislation such as naming federal buildings. Denouncing the nearly forty-year U.S. embargo on Cuba as a Cold War "relic," Waters wrote the following in a letter to Cuban President Fidel Castro:

> The United States grants political asylum to individuals from all over the world who successfully prove they are fleeing political persecution. Other sovereign nations have the same right, including the sovereign nation of Cuba. . . . .
>
> I respect the right of Assata Shakur to seek political asylum. . . . In a sad and shameful chapter of our history, during the 1960s and 1970s, many civil rights, Black Power and other politically active groups were secretly targeted by the FBI for prosecution based on their political beliefs. The groups and individuals targeted included Rev. Martin Luther King Jr., Cesar Chavez, officials of the American Friends Service Committee, National Council of Churches and other civil rights, religious and peace movement leaders.

Waters adds that "the most vicious and reprehensible acts were taken against" those like Assata Shakur who worked with the Black Liberation Movement. Congress-woman Maxine Waters, correspondence to President Fidel Castro, Habana, Cuba, September 29, 1998.

36. One of the few accounts of the Black Liberation Army that does not rely on mainstream media for its analysis is presented by Assata Shakur's attorney and aunt, Evelyn Williams's *Inadmissible Evidence: The Story of the African American Trial Lawyer Who Defended the Black Liberation Army* (Chicago: Lawrence Hill, 1993). For divergent views on the Black Liberation Army, compare Williams's work and that of former police officer John Castelucci's *The Big Dance: The Untold Story of Kathy Boudin and the Terrorist Family That Committed the Brink's Robbery Murders* (New York: Dodd, Mead & Company, 1986).

37. Jim Fletcher, Tanaquil Jones, and Sylvère Lotringer, *Still Black, Still Strong: Survivors of the War Against Black Revolutionaries* (New York: Semiotext(e), 1993).

38. Assata Shakur, "Prisoner in the United States," in ibid., 206-207.

39. See Evelyn Williams, *Inadmissible Evidence* (Chicago: Lawrence Hill, 1993).

40. In Mumia Abu-Jamal's 1982 trial in Philadelphia, his former membership in the Black Panther Party, which formed in opposition to police abuses, was represented as an indication of his guilt in the killing of a white police officer Daniel Faulkner, as the prosecution portrayed Panthers as violently "antiwhite" and "antipolice."

41. The disparities between juries and defendants continues today, where although the population of New Jersey is predominately white, its prison population is more than 75 percent black and Latino with 80 percent of its incarcerated women, being women of color.

42. "An Open Letter to New Jersey Governor Whitman," author's papers. The writers continue by asking if Whitman's actions are motivated by a desire for "national prominence or to retain" the governorship—Whitman at one time was considered by the Republican National Committee as an ideal candidate for national office yet has won state elections only by slight margins. See Jennifer Preston, "Whitman Praises New Jersey Vote as Major Victory," *New York Times,* November 6, 1997, Al.

43. The media portrayal of victims of the 1973 tragedy that ended in two deaths focused only on whites, prominently featuring images of Foerster's weeping widow. (In similar fashion 20/20 used images of Daniel Faulkner's distraught widow in a January 1999 segment, hosted by Sam Donaldson, that was hostile to advocacy for a new trial for Mumia Abu-Jamal.) No references were made to the slain Zayd Shakur, to Sundiata Acoli, imprisoned for twenty-five years, or to their families. Images are, of course, the dominant factor for creating icons, particularly demonized ones. NBC repeatedly aired a photograph of a black woman with a gun implying that it was Shakur, although the photograph was taken from a highly publicized case where she was accused of bank robbery but later acquitted. (During the trial several witnesses, including the manager of the bank, testified that the woman in that photograph was not Shakur.) Despite NBC's extensive resources for research, it failed to establish the photograph as misidentified; although a subsequent fax and e-mail campaign protested the misinfor-mation, the network continued to identify the woman in the photograph as Shakur.

In the NBC interview, Colonel Carl Williams of the New Jersey State Police (who was fired by Governor Whitman in February 1999 for racial-bias in his statements alleging black and latino proclivity to crime) maintained that Shakur fired a weapon while disputing her statements that she was shot with her arms raised and then shot again in the back. NBC did not convey that State Trooper Harper who testified that he saw Shakur with a weapon later admitted under cross-examination that he had perjured himself in this account. Medical specialists who examined Shakur testified that she was immediately paralyzed after being shot and that both of her arms

were in the air given the trajectory of the bullet(s). In addition, no gun-powder residue was found on her hands. Such testimony supports her account of the confrontation.
44. Shakur's message was sent by the Strategic Pastoral Action (SPAN), Wes Rehberg, with the web site listing: http://www.spanweb.org/.
45. T. Denean Sharpley-Whiting explores the constrictions of postmodernist discourse on progressive and black feminism. See T. Denean Sharpley-Whiting, "Pitfalls, Postmodern Academic Feminist Consciousness, and U.S. Social Crises," in Sharpley-Whiting, *Frantz Fanon: Conflicts & Feminisms* (Lanham, MD: Rowman & Littlefield, 1997).

CHAPTER 6

1. Quentin Tarantino's *Jackie Brown* (1997), which featured former blaxploitation film star Pam Grier, is arguably a sophisticated "black woman's" narrative that emphasizes a politics of survival and ingenuity in a society dominated by white and black men, although Cedric Robinson's critique of the recycling of blaxploitation should be noted. For Hollywood, according to Cedric Robinson, "only Black women possessed the savage, primordial instinct of self-survival to resist sexual degradation and their male predators." See Cedric Robinson, "Blaxploitation and the Misrepresentation of Liberation," *Race & Class,* Vol. 40, No. l (1998), 1-12.
2. Patricia Storace, "Look Away, Dixie Land," *New York Review of Books,* December 19, 1991, 26. Storace also provides a review of *Southern Daughter: The Life of Margaret Mitchell* by Darden Pyron (New York: Oxford University Press, 1991) and *Scarlett: The Sequel to Margaret Mitchell's 'Gone With the Wind'* by Alexandra Ripley (New York: Warner, 1991).
3. See Bob Herbert, "Mr. Lott's 'Big Mistake,'" *New York Times,* January 7, 1999, A31.
4. Donald Bogle satirizes the obsession in *Toms, Coons, Mulattoes, Mammies & Bucks: An Interpretive History of Blacks in American Films* (New York: Continuum, 1989, expanded version; originally 1973), 12.
5. Ibid., 13-14.
6. Ibid., 168.
7. Ibid, 171-172
8. Toni Morrison, *Playing in the Dark: Whiteness and the Literary Imagination* (Cambridge, MA: Harvard University Press, 1992), 66.
9. Paula Giddings, *When and Where I Enter: The Impact of Black Women on Race and Sex in America* (New York: Bantam, 1984).
10. John D'Emilio and Estelle Freedman, *Intimate Matters: A History of Sexuality in America* (New York: Harper & Row, 1988), xvi.
11. Ibid., 87.
12. Michiko Hase notes the commonalities between Pocahontas, the Mexican La Malinche, and the Asian fictional character Madame Butterfly: all served or helped white male colonizers, had sexual relationships with their respective male partners and bore them male children. In various ways, these women (and the Japanese Madame Butterfly) became prototypes of Native, Mexican, and Asian American female stereotypes, inspiring cultural productions. Hase asks: What does the absence of a prototypical African female figure, similar to Pocahontas, La Malinche, and Madame Butterfly, say about colonists' attitudes about Africa and Africans in the Americas and Asia? Michiko Hase, informal dialogue with author.
    Felipe Smith also raises interesting issues about national mythology, black women, and women of color. See Felipe Smith, *American Body Politics: Race, Gender, and Black Literary Renaissance* (Athens, GA: The University of Georgia Press, 1998).
13. Ibid., 105.

14. Ibid., 106-107.
15. Angela Davis, "Rape, Racism and the Capitalist Setting," *The Black Scholar* (April, 1978): 24-30, reprinted in ed. Joy James, *The Angela Y. Davis Reader* (Oxford: Basil Blackwell, 1998).
16. D'Emilio, 297-298.
17. Toni Morrison, *Sula* (New York: Plume, 1973) 103.
18. Ibid, 112-113.
19. Lorraine Hansberry, *To Be Young, Gifted and Black* (New York: Signet, 1969), 98, quoted in Patricia Hill Collins, *Black Feminist Thought* (Cambridge, MA: Unwin Hyman, 1990), 173.
20. See D'Emilio, *Intimate Matters.*
21. Malcom X, *The Autobiography of Malcolm X* (New York: Ballantine, 1965), 117.
22. Tracey A. Gardner, "Racism in Pornography and the Women's Movement," in *Take Back the Night: Women on Pornography,* ed. Laura Lederer (New York: William and Morrow & Co, 1980), 106.
23. D'Emilio, *Intimate Matters,* xvi.
24. Collins, *Black Feminist Thought,* 177.
25. Audre Lorde, *Sister Outsider* (Trumansburg, NY: Crossing Press, 1984).
26. Adam Thonton, Unpublished talk at the University of Massachusetts, Amherst, 1992.
27. See Gardner, "Racism in Pornography and the Women's Movement," 107.
28. Ibid., 107
29. Robert Santiago, "Sex, Lust, and Videotapes," *Essence* (November 1990), Special Men's Issue.
30. Marlon Riggs, "Black Macho Revisited: Reflections of a SNAP! Queen," in Essex Hemphill and Joe Wood, eds., *Brother to Brother: New Writings by Black Gay Men* (Boston: Alyson, 1991), 253.
31. Kobena Mercer and Isaac Julien, "Race, Sexual Politics and Black Masculinity: A Dossier," in Jonathan Rutherford and Rowena Chapman, eds., *Male Order: Unwrapping Masculinity* (London: Lawrence & Wishart, 1988).
32. Ibid.
33. Bogle, *Toms, Coons, Mulattoes, Mammies and Bucks,* 15.
34. bell hooks, "Seduction and Betrayal," *Interrace,* February 1994, 29.
35. Sander Gilman notes that: "Miscegenation was a fear (and a word) from the late nineteenth-century vocabulary of sexuality. It was a fear not merely of interracial sexuality but of its results, the decline of the population. Interracial marriages were seen as exactly parallel to the barrenness of the prostitute; if they produced children at all, these children were weak and doomed" (Sander Gilman, *Difference and Pathology: Stereotypes of Sexuality, Race, and Madness* [Ithaca, NY: Cornell University Press, 1985], 256).
36. Henry Louis Gates, Jr., "The White Negro," *The New Yorker,* May 11, 1998, 62-65.
37. Ibid., 62.
38. See Kimberlé Crenshaw et al., eds., *Critical Race Theory* (New York: The New Press, 1996).
39. Some of the most critical commentary on the film was written by black women. For instance, Jamie Foster Brown notes in the magazine *Sister 2 Sister,* referring to racial portrayals and aborted interracial unions: "People didn't like the fact that he [Beatty] showed Black children with guns, especially since White boys with guns have been shooting up everybody in the real world. And all of us knew that if the White star was in love with a Black Woman (Halle Berry), he would have to die." See Jamie Foster Brown, *Sister 2 Sister,* July 1998, 16. Foster is referring to the June 1998 killings in Jonesboro, Arkansas, in which two eleven- and thirteen-year-old boys fired assault

weapons into their schoolyard, killing a teacher and several classmates and wounding others. In 1999, fifteen died in a high school shooting in Littleton, Colorado.

40. Sorkin quoted in Gates, "The White Negro," 63.

41. Of four reviews published in the *Washington Post,* May 22-23, 1998, only one—in fact the only one written by a woman—raised and critiqued *Bulworth's* representations of gender and sex. See Donna Britt, "Try Again, Warren Beatty, You Missed," *Washington Post,* May 22, 1998, B1.

The promotion for the film became in part promotion for Beatty as a progressive white "race man." A tireless Beatty granted an impressive number of interviews for the film, revealing autobiographical anecdotes that established him as an antiracist white liberal of the old school or precentrist Democrat. At times the messages sent appeared contradictory: for instance, in a summer 1998 "Charlie Rose" television appearance, Beatty claimed to have had a casual friendship with Muhammad Ali in the 1970s, while also expressing an equal admiration for and a social friendship with racial conservative-reactionary Ronald Reagan.

42. Newton, like other members of the elite Oakland leadership, did not consistently, actively work with the rank and file in the Free Breakfast Program or other programs due to the party's organizational structure and disruptive police tactics.

CHAPTER 7

1. A version of this chapter first appeared in Tom Digby, ed., *Men Doing Feminism* (New York: Routledge, 1997).

2. "Footnotes," *Chronicle of Higher Education,* June 12, 1998, A12.

3. See Susan Faludi, *The Backlash Against Feminism* (New York: Doubleday, 1991).

4. All male feminist writers cited here are African American, except Latino/Chicano legal theorist Richard Delgado. His narratives revolve around the persona of a fictional black man, "Rodrigo," whom Delgado identifies as a relative of "Geneva Crenshaw," the black female (super)protagonist of Derrick Bell's "Chronicles."

5. Michael Awkward, *Negotiating Difference: Race, Gender, and the Politics of Positionality* (Chicago: University of Chicago Press, 1995), 52.

6. Ibid., 51, 52.

7. Alice Jardine, "Men in Feminism: Odor di Uomo or Compagnons de Route?" in *Men in Feminism,* eds. Alice Jardine and Paul Smith (New York: Methuen, 1987), 60.

8. Awkward, *Negotiating Difference,* 47.

9. Michele Wallace, "Negative Images: Towards a Black Feminist Cultural Criticism," in Wallace, *Invisibility Blues: from Pop to Theory* (New York: Verso, 1990), 251.

10. Awkward, *Negotiating Difference,* 56.

11. Awkward refers to Sherley Anne Williams's discussion of "womanism" in "Some Implications of Womanist Theory," *Callaloo* Vol. 9 (1986), 304. He does not explore the varied definitions of and ideologies within "black feminism."

12. Awkward, *Negotiating Difference,* 49.

13. Ibid.

14. Hortense J. Spillers, "Mama's Baby, Papa's Maybe: An American Grammar Book," *diacritics* Vol.. 17, No. 2, (Summer 1987), 65-81.

15. Spillers quoted in Awkward: "the black American male embodies the *only* American community of males which has had the specific occasion to learn *who* the female is within itself"; presumably, a number of communities would disagree. *Negotiating Difference,* 52.

16. Awkward, *Negotiating Difference,* 52, 54.

17. Daniel Patrick Moynihan, *The Case for National Action: The Negro Family* (Washington, D.C.: Office of Policy Planning and Research, U.S. Department of Labor, March 1965).

18. Awkward, *Negotiating Difference*, 57.

19. Jean Paul Sartre, *Being and Nothingness* (New York: Citadel Press, 1969). Lewis Gordon, "Effeminacy," in *Bad Faith and Antiblack Racism* (Atlantic Highlands, NJ: Humanities Press, 1995). Gordon counters Eldridge Cleaver's argument in "The Allegory of the Black Eunuchs," in *Soul on Ice* (New York: Delta, 1968), 155-175, where Cleaver maintains that the white male's prototypical role is "effeminate," as "Brain" and "Omnipotent Administrator," while the black male functions as hypermasculine, or "Body" and "Supermasculine Menial."

20. Gordon, "Effeminacy," 124.

21. Ibid

22. Rhona Berenstein, "White Heroines and Hearts of Darkness: Race, Gender and Disguise in 1930s Jungle Films," *Film History*, No. 6 (1994), 314-39, quoted in Cedric Robinson, "Blaxploitation and the Misrepresentation of Liberation," *Race and Class*, Vol. 40, No. 1 (1998), 3-4.

23. Gordon, *Bad Faith and Anitblack Racism*, 125, 126.

24. Ibid., 127.

25. Ibid., 128

26. Ibid.

27. Ibid., 128, 129.

28. Spillers, "Mamma's Baby, Pappa's Maybe," 67.

29. Devon Carbado, "Race, Domestic Abuse, and the O. J. Simpson Case: When All Victims Are Black Men and White Women," author's paper. A revised version of this work appears as "The Construction of O.J. Simpson as Racial Victim," *Harvard Civil Rights–Civil Liberties Law Review*, vol. 32 (1997), 49-103.

30. Ibid.

31. Ibid.

32. Ibid.

33. Awkward, *Negotiating Difference*, 44.

34. Richard Delgado, "Rodrigo's Sixth Chronicle: Intersections, Essences, and the Dilemma of Social Reform," *New York University Law Review*, Vol. 68, No. 639 (June 1993), 639-674, 649.

35. Ibid., 652.

36. Ibid., 669.

37. Ibid., 655.

38. Ibid., 653. Also see, Antonio Gramsci, *The Prison Notebooks, eds. and translators Quintin Hoare and Geoffrey Nowell Smith* (New York: International Publishers, 1971).

39. Delgado's Rodrigo argues the case against interest convergence: Prescriptive discourse set by paradigms rooted in racism and sexism interpret events to conform to the dominant bias.

40. Delgado, "Rodrigo's Sixth Chronicle," 656. As the professor observes: "'Justice first, then peace'—a motto that others have employed in different versions to highlight the incompatibility between an oppressive regime that contains structures of unfairness, and social stability. Such a regime is inherently unstable because of the ever-present possibility of revolt" (Ibid., 672).

CHAPTER 8

1. This phrase is borrowed from T. Denean Sharpley-Whiting.

2. For a discussion of the negative elements of the black male fighter see T. Denean Sharpley-Whiting, "When a Black Woman Cries Rape: Discourses of Unrapeability, Intraracial Sexual Violence, and the *State of Indiana v. Michael Gerard Tyson*," in eds. Sharpley-Whiting and Renee Scott *Spoils of War* (Lanham: Rowan and Littlefield Press, 1997), 45-58.

3. See bell hooks's discussions in the Sut Jhally video, *Cultural Criticism and Transformation*, Media Education Foundation, Northampton, Massachusetts, 1997.

4. Maya Angelou, *I Know Why the Caged Bird Sings* (New York: Bantam, 1970) 136.

5. It is unclear to what degree Jack Johnson's racial-sexual "indiscretions" promote his erasure in white American culture. The *American Heritage Dictionary of the English Language* (Boston: Houghton Mifflin Company, 1976) has citations for heavyweight champions such as the white boxer Jack Dempsey as well as Joe Louis (Joseph Louis Barrow) and Muhammad Ali (Marcellus Cassius Clay), but no listing for Dempsey's peer, and Louis and Ali's predecessor, Jack Johnson.

6. *When We Were Kings*, Polygram Films, 1996. Also see Eldridge Cleaver, "Lazarus Come Forth," in *Soul on Ice*, (New York: Delta, 1968), 84-96. Reading *Soul on Ice* for the first time last summer, I found in Cleaver's prison writings phrases and images—"iconoclast," Frederick Douglass's July 4, 1852 oration, metaphors of boxing and slavery— already used in *Shadowboxing*. As a black prison intellectual, Cleaver brilliantly and problematically dissected American antiblack racism. Known for his misogyny, self-acknowledged "sickness" as a rapist, his unacknowledged sickness as a batterer and homophobe, the late revolutionary-reactionary wrote a scathing, albeit distorted, cultural critique of white supremacy. Significantly, despite his anti-female positions, including his antipathy and violence toward African American women, black women and black feminists read Cleaver: Evelyn Williams's *Inadmissible Evidence: The Story of the African American Trial Lawyer Who Defended the Black Liberation Army* (Chicago: Lawrence Hill, 1993) recounts that while briefly incarcerated in the 1970s on contempt charges levied by a reactionary judge as she served as lead attorney for her niece, Assata Shakur, she read *Soul on Ice* as well as works by Angela Davis.

7. Muhammad Ali and sociologist Harry Edwards (who attempted to organize a black boycott of the 1968 Olympics in Mexico) were the only African American athletes on the U.S. House of Representative's list of radical-revolutionary speakers.

8. Alan Watts makes these points about religion in "The Love of Wisdom," *Philosophy and Society*, Radio Series 4, The Electronic University, San Anselmo, CA.

9. For a discussion of solipsism in white feminism, see Elizabeth Spelman, *Inessential Woman: Problems of Exclusion in Feminist Thought* (Boston: Beacon Press, 1988).

10. The use of black women to introduce some of the most graphic language and lascivious posturing around sex and sexuality has become a recurring feature in film and television, often unexplored by white media critics. The popular TV series *Ally McBeal* offers a "hot" black woman district attorney as roommate and caretaker for the "demure" white corporate lawyer. Working overtime, the black female doubles as both a sassy "new age (black) woman" and comforting mammy. As in television, film representations of black women as crude (for instance, the wife of the black football player in Jerry McGuire) mythologize the (sexual) restraint of white women, as the sexual savage is juxtaposed with the civilized sexual.

11. Ginia Bellafante, "Is Feminism Dead?" *TIME*, June 29, 1998, 54-60. Accompanying Bellafante's piece was "Girl Power" by Nadya Labi on young (post)feminists (60-64). Katha Pollitt, "Dead Again?" *The Nation*, July 13, 1998, 10, critiques Bellafante's article but does not mention race. If mainstream press had bothered to factor race into the equation, readers could have considered how sexual openness does not automatically signify "power" for black females. Historically depicted as sexually aggressive "bad girls," black females were placed at significant risk for sexual abuse. The existential

wealth of whiteness and the material wealth of the bourgeoisie grant female sexual assertion and aggression their cultural "('girl') power."

12. Alice Echols's *Daring to Be Bad: Radical Feminism in America, 1967-1975* (Ann Arbor: University of Michigan Press, 1989) incisively documents that this debate between "old" and "new" white feminists has transpired for decades.

13. bell hooks, *Ain't I a Woman* (Boston: Southend Press, 1981), 195.

14. Ibid., 191.

15. Bellafante, "Is Feminism Dead?" 59. Bellafante writes that Rebecca Walker and others "have inherited the postfeminist tic of offering up autobiography as theory." For Bellafante, Walker "introduces the material by explaining that she first felt guilty about putting together such an introspective, apolitical book. But, Walker says, she resisted the pressure 'to make a book I really wasn't all that desperate to read'" (59).

16. Camille Paglia, *Sexual Personae: Art and Decadence from Nefertiti to Emily Dickinson* (New Haven: Yale University Press, 1990).

17. Katie Roiphe, *The Morning After* (Boston: Little, Brown and Co., 1993); Naomi Wolf, *Promiscuities* (New York: Random House, 1997).

   Bellafante's essay overlooks that white beauty authority Naomi Wolf, along with Harvard University's African American studies chair Henry Louis Gates Jr. and other influential culture-shapers traveled to the White House during Bill Clinton's reelection campaign to strategize on how to rehabilitate Clinton's image as a "friend" of African Americans, the working class, and women. This suggests a more overt political agenda for the "apolitical" women she criticizes. However, the politics may be centrist but not progressive: Clinton has enthusiastically promoted monopoly corporate capital while dismantling support systems for poor people; he is also credited with increasing the police powers of the state and incarceration rates for people of color.

18. Bellafante, "Is Feminism Dead?" 60.

19. Ibid.

20. Ellen Willis, "We Need a *Radical* Left," *The Nation,* June 29, 1998, 18-21.

21. Ibid.

22. Ibid.

23. Angela Davis makes this argument in *Women, Race and Class* (New York: Random House, 1981).

INDEX